THE HISTORY OF LADY JULIA MANDEVILLE

CHAWTON HOUSE LIBRARY SERIES: WOMEN'S NOVELS

Series Editors: Stephen Bending
Stephen Bygrave

TITLES IN THIS SERIES

1 *The Histories of Some of the Penitents in the Magdalen-House*
edited by Jennie Batchelor and Megan Hiatt

2 Stéphanie-Félicité de Genlis, *Adelaide and Theodore, or Letters on Education*
edited by Gillian Dow

3 E. M. Foster, *The Corinna of England*
edited by Sylvia Bordoni

4 Sarah Harriet Burney, *The Romance of Private Life*
edited by Lorna J. Clark

5 Alicia LeFanu, *Strathallan*
edited by Anna M. Fitzer

6 Elizabeth Sophia Tomlins, *The Victim of Fancy*
edited by Daniel Cook

7 Helen Maria Williams, *Julia*
edited by Natasha Duquette

8 Elizabeth Hervey, *The History of Ned Evans*
edited by Helena Kelly

9 Sarah Green, *Romance Readers and Romance Writers*
edited by Christopher Goulding

10 Mrs Costello, *The Soldier's Orphan*
edited by Clare Broome Saunders

11 Sarah Green, *The Private History of the Court of England*
edited by Fiona Price

12 *Translations and Continuations*: *Riccoboni and Brooke, Graffigny and Roberts*
edited by Marijn S. Kaplan

13 Sydney Owenson, *Florence Macarthy: An Irish Tale*
edited by Jenny McAuley

FORTHCOMING TITLES

Ann Gomersall, *The Citizen*
edited by Jennifer Chenkin

Eliza Haywood, *The Rash Resolve and Life's Progress*
edited by Carol Stewart

Mary Brunton, *Self Control*
edited by Anthony Mandal

Isabelle de Montolieu, *Caroline of Lichtfield*
edited by Laura Kirkley

Mrs S. C. Hall, *Sketches of Irish Character*
edited by Marion Durnin

www.pickeringchatto.com/chawtonnovels

Frances Brooke,
The History of Lady Julia Mandeville

EDITED BY

Enit Karafili Steiner

PICKERING & CHATTO
2013

Published by Pickering & Chatto (Publishers) Limited
21 Bloomsbury Way, London WC1A 2TH

2252 Ridge Road, Brookfield, Vermont 05036-9704, USA

www.pickeringchatto.com

All rights reserved.
No part of this publication may be reproduced,
stored in a retrieval system, or transmitted in any form or by any means,
electronic, mechanical, photocopying, recording, or otherwise
without prior permission of the publisher.

© Pickering & Chatto (Publishers) Ltd 2013
© Editorial material Enit Karafili Steiner 2013

To the best of the Publisher's knowledge every effort has been made to contact relevant copyright holders and to clear any relevant copyright issues. Any omissions that come to their attention will be remedied in future editions.

BRITISH LIBRARY CATALOGUING IN PUBLICATION DATA

Brooke, Frances, 1724?–1789.
The history of Lady Julia Mandeville. – New ed. – (Chawton House library series. Women's novels)
1. Epistolary fiction.
I. Title II. Series III. Steiner, Enit Karafili.
823.6-dc23

ISBN-13: 9781848931381
e: 9781848932562

This publication is printed on acid-free paper that conforms to the American National Standard for the Permanence of Paper for Printed Library Materials.

Typeset by Pickering & Chatto (Publishers) Limited
Printed and bound in the United Kingdom by the MPG Books Group

CONTENTS

Acknowledgements	ix
Introduction	xi
Select Bibliography	xxv
Chronology	xxix
The History of Lady Julia Mandeville	1
Editorial Notes	131
Textual Notes	149
Silent Corrections	175
Appendix A: Contemporary Reviews	179
Appendix B: From Frances Brooke's weekly periodical the *Old Maid* (1755–6) and fiction	183

ACKNOWLEDGEMENTS

Any edition of Frances Brooke's work must first acknowledge the fundamental scholarship by Lorraine McMullen, whose *An Odd Attempt in a Woman* (Vancouver: University of British Columbia Press, 1983) broke the silence around an extraordinary woman writer of the eighteenth century. The present edition has also benefited from the extensive biographical and historical information included in Mary Jane Edwards's edition of *The History of Emily Montague* (Oshawa, Ontario: Carleton University Press, 1985) and in Paula Backscheider and Hope Cotton's edition of *The Excursion* (Lexington, KY: University of Kentucky Press, 1997). Indeed, it was on reading Brooke's œuvre through the lens of such informed research that my interest in her first novel, *The History of Lady Julia Mandeville*, was originally sparked. In that regard, special recognition is also due to E. Phillips Poole, whose 1930 edition of this novel gave the work a representative place in Brooke's literary activity.

I am grateful to eighteenth- and nineteenth-century scholars and colleagues who have supported this project and have commented on various parts of this volume: thank you, Allen Reddick, Angela Esterhammer, Petra Schoenenberger and Diane Piccitto. The Advanced Research Colloquium at the University of Zurich also helped test out ideas. Particular thanks to Antoinina Bevan Zlatar for drawing my attention to several Shakespearean resonances in *Julia Mandeville* and to Shane Walshe for expert note checking. Finally, my love and gratitude go to Jürg Steiner for his forbearance and patience, and to Lea and Josh for their incomparable affection.

This volume is dedicated to my parents, Luljeta and Kujtim Karafili, who instilled my love for books.

– ix –

INTRODUCTION

> I early in life discovered, by the meer force of genius; that there were two characters only in which one might take a thousand little innocent freedoms, without being censured by a parcel of impertinent old women, those of a Belle Esprit and a Methodist; and, the latter not being in my style, I chose to set up for the former, in which I have had the happiness to succeed so much beyond my hopes.
>
> Anne Wilmot in *The History of Lady Julia Mandeville* (1763)

Frances Brooke's first novel, *The History of Julia Mandeville*, is largely penned by the *bel esprit* Anne Wilmot, a well-read female character with a captivating command of language and energetic mental powers. Anne Wilmot's preference for the 'innocent freedoms' of the *bel esprit* was undoubtedly shared by the author of *Julia Mandeville*. Living in a time when a professional writing career was 'an odd attempt in a woman', Brooke 'published almost every kind of economically profitable literary type' with notable success.[1] At the end of her life, she was considered to have been 'courted by all the first characters of her time', counting among her friends and supporters Samuel Johnson, Mary Ann Yates, Anna Seward and Fanny Burney.[2] Ever aware of women's delicate social position and the limits they faced, Brooke contributed to their empowerment with representations of femininity that gave women a voice without injuring their reputation. In her fiction, the strongest embodiments of such a profile unite the independence of the unmarried woman or widow with the erudition of the *bel esprit*. This combination first emerges in Brooke's periodical the *Old Maid* (1755–6), published under the pseudonym Mary Singleton, Spinster. Here, as Min Wild observes, a virtuous and experienced spinster takes the liberty to 'use the language and conventions of discourse unfit for Frances Brooke'.[3] Only few years later, a similar female profile crystallizes in *Julia Mandeville*'s widowed *bel esprit*, Anne Wilmot, whose ostensible coquettish whims sit beautifully with extensive knowledge of literature and cultural acumen.

Despite Brooke's being known during her lifetime mostly for *Julia Mandeville*, rather than her other works, this novel attracted little critical commentary in the twentieth century.[4] However, attentive criticism has not failed to recognize the novel's original 'stylistic blending of the modes of sensibility and realism'.[5]

– xi –

In the early twentieth century, the novel's realism was almost eclipsed by A. D. McKillop's categorization of *Julia Mandeville* as a specimen of sentimental fiction *par excellence*. He writes that 'sentimental epistolary novels do not become common immediately after *Clarissa* and *Grandison*, but about the time of the English translation of the *Nouvelle Héloïse*, Mrs Brooke's translation of Mme Riccoboni's *Lettres de Milady Juliette Catesby* (1760) and *Julia Mandeville*'.[6] McKillop's consideration of *Julia Mandeville* as a milestone in the history of the sentimental novel comes with gains and losses. While it makes Brooke's novel central to the genre's development in the eighteenth century, it also restricts it to a particular mode, thus reducing its polyphonic perspective. This perspective reflects the novel's central tensions, which are embodied in a wide spectrum of competing voices. At one end of the spectrum, the tropes of sensibility flourish in the letters of the young couple Henry and Julia. They are the spokespersons of the rhetoric of feeling, created to generate the reader's empathetic response, as they did, for example, in Goethe's *Die Geschwister* (1776), where the female protagonist recognizes herself and her lover in Brooke's 'best, dearest people'.[7] At the other end of the spectrum, Anne Wilmot's biting wit and 'cynical wordliness',[8] reminiscent of Aphra Behn, Delarivière Manley and Eliza Haywood, do not allow the reader to give in wholeheartedly to sentimental identification.[9] Between these poles, the narrative situates the parents of the young couple, Lord Belmont and J. Mandeville, in a position that seeks to reconcile moral benevolence and realistic concerns. From these specific positions, Brooke's characters approach themes that would preoccupy the novel as a genre well into the nineteenth century such as education, marriage, domestic relations, estate management, aesthetics and morality, and not least politics. Brooke's engagement with these themes could have been what compelled Anna Laetitia Barbauld to include *Julia Mandeville* in her fifty-volume *British Novelists* (1810).[10] Besides Charlotte Lennox's *The Female Quixote*, *Julia Mandeville* is the only novel by a woman writer published before 1770 to appear in Barbauld's selection, a choice that indicates this novel's prominence not only in Brooke's oeuvre, but also in the body of the British novel as Barbauld perceived it in 1810.

I.

The distinctiveness of *Julia Mandeville* did not escape the attention of contemporary reviewers. According to the *Monthly Review*, it rose above the 'common production of the novel tribe'.[11] The *Critical Review* claimed that its artistic merits were not only comparable but also superior to the novels of such worthy precursors as Rousseau and Richardson, observing that the novel coupled 'great judgement' with originality of execution, avoiding Rousseau's 'caprice' and Richardson's 'tediousness'. What the reviewer could not endorse was 'the author's

Introduction xiii

introducing politics at all' and the devastating denouement of the story.[12] Indeed, both these points deserve careful consideration.

The politics addressed in the novel mainly pertain to two specific historical events: the negotiations that put an end to the Seven Years War and the murder of Peter III followed by the coronation of his wife, Catherine the Great, in 1762. The reviewer's dissatisfaction betrays a sense of discomfort at the co-existence of domestic and political concerns in a novel written by a woman. What remains unsaid is that in *Julia Mandeville* political references do not stand in isolation but illuminate the characterization and themes of the narrative. Two instances illustrate this claim. The discussions of the peace negotiations add a certain political stance to the domestic profile of the educator. Apart from adhering to a similar educative program, the fathers in the novel, Lord Belmont and J. Mandeville, also agree on the future of Canada. They support the current ministry, talking of the terms of peace as 'an immense addition of empire' and of Canada as being of 'more national consequence to us than all the Sugar-islands on the globe'. Betty Schellenberg demonstrates that this alignment with the government's Tory policy is of a piece with Lord Belmont's and I would add that the same applies to J. Mandeville's insistence on the continuation of the independence of the country gentleman.[13] While this ideal is glorified by the older generation, it becomes both the aspiration and disillusion of the young, represented by Henry Mandeville, who makes the bitter discovery that not all independent country gentlemen deserve respect, nor are all country estates sites of rural prosperity. Thomas Keymer extrapolates Brooke's political allegiances from Lord Belmont's Toryism and the rural paternalism he embodies.[14] The polyphonic nature of the epistolary novel, however, stands in the way of such seamless correspondence between Lord Belmont and Brooke. Moreover, the tragic ending that forces Lord Belmont to reassess critically his role as father and educator also suggests a clear distance between the author and the patriarch. As for Tory politics, they are explicitly mentioned in Anne Wilmot's sassy description of Lady Mary, the aunt who wants to assist Henry Mandeville's social rise: 'I have this morning discovered why Lady Mary is a Tory! She has been flattered by Bolingbroke, and sung by Atterbury; had Addison tuned his lyre to her praise, she had certainly changed parties.' Thus, Anne Wilmot's playfulness (to say the least) additionally deflects the author's alleged endorsement of Lord Belmont and the Tory politics he propagates.

The second inclusion of politics that enhances and even anticipates the themes of the novel is the reference to the succession of Catherine the Great, introduced by J. Mandeville as a 'most extraordinary' event. Faithful to his instructive role, J. Mandeville takes advantage of this occasion to teach his son that 'sudden and violent revolutions are the natural consequences of that instability which must ever attend despotic forms of government'. In contrast to despotism, he hails 'Happy Britain! where the laws are equally the guard of prince and people, where liberty and prerogative go hand in hand, and mutually support each other.' The news from Russia is deployed to establish a direct correlation between stability and forms of government. But if the Belmont estate is celebrated as the healthy product of British constitution – cultivated by the responsible and benevolent hands of the independent country gentleman – the catastrophe of *Julia Mandeville* emerges as a 'sudden and violent revolution' that sheds doubts over Belmont's own use of power and influence. Consequently, the political pronouncements need to be considered in light of the novel's dénouement.

In the words of the *Monthly Review*, Brooke's 'heart-rending, tragic' ending was 'scarce to be supported by a Reader of any feeling'. Although Richardson's influence could not be overlooked, she had departed from her master by writing a novel 'less tedious, because less laboured, than those of the celebrated Richardson' and a catastrophe almost too extreme even for a novel in Richardson's style.[15] So much did the tragic reversal of events affect contemporary readers that its genesis gave rise to contradictory reports. The *British Magazine and Review* wrote with striking emphasis that Brooke's initial ending never involved such a devastating tragedy: 'amiable diffidence ... led our ingenious author, at the insistence of a particular friend, to forego her original design in the management of the catastrophe, against her own more enlightened judgment!'[16] Contradicting this assumption, another reviewer suggested that 'it has been often, however, wished that the catastrophe had been less melancholy; and of the propriety of this opinion the authoress herself is said to have been satisfied, but did not chuse to make the alteration.'[17] In fact, *Julia Mandeville* went through nine editions in Brooke's lifetime without experiencing any plot alteration, and its tragic ending did not prevent its author from writing the sequel *The History of Charles Mandeville* (1790).

Twentieth-century critics read the tragic denouement as the completion of the Shakespearean formula of the 'star-crossed lovers', a recasting of this theme within the mould of the novel of sensibility that crowded the eighteenth-century book market.[18] Indeed, there are numerous references to Shakespeare's plays, predominantly in Anne Wilmot's letters, whose eye discerns the pull of attraction between the lovers and predicts in the midst of the idyllic scenes of the first volume the destructive role of the hero: 'This cruel Harry will be the death of us all.' However, Brooke's greatest indebtedness to Shakespeare is her skill at capturing the psychology of a mind in love and pain; the lovers' total codependence on finding happiness in nothing but each other; the contradictory expectations that make the heart a battleground; the oscillations between hope and despair, fulfilment and self-annihilation, ecstatic delight and excessive grief. Such perception and skill to put inner workings of the psyche into words is evinced in one of the few letters written by the heroine:

Introduction xv

> How inconsistent is a heart in love! I entreated Mr. Mandeville not to write to me, and am chagrined at his too exact obedience: I think, if he loved as I do, he could not so easily obey me. He writes to Lady Anne; and, though by my desire, I am ashamed of my weakness; – but I wish he wrote less often: there is an air of gaiety in his letters which offends me.

The narrative abounds in psychological insights, so that it is surprising that the reviewer of *Julia Mandeville*'s first modern edition laments the novel's lacking verisimilitude in its representations of men and women who are 'drawn to comply with a psychological convention'.[19] Unless 'psychological convention' refers to the reiteration of a universal vision of love and suffering, the comment seems unjustified.

While *Julia Mandeville* shares *Romeo and Juliet*'s interest in intergenerational relationships and the *peripetia* due to the ill-fated delay of a letter, it also pursues other themes. Although entangled in a conflict of interests, parent–child relations are not strained by the emotional coldness, violent tirades and the family feud of the play. On the contrary, an atmosphere of mutual respect and love pervades parent–child relations, which serves only to exacerbate the pang of untimely death and thwarted happiness. The tragedy is relentless because the factors leading to it are not self-evident. Instead, they haunt the reader, prompting her to revisit the story in order to uncover the latent tensions under the veil of idyllic and sentimental tropes.

II.

The central conflict at the heart of *Julia Mandeville* rests on concerns of status and wealth. Henry and Julia want to be free to marry the person of their choice in spite of monetary constraints, whereas their parents want them to bestow themselves on someone of equal worth and wealth. Concealment creeps into the innocence and purity of Belmont when Henry, compelled by inferior fortune, decides to hide his passion for Julia, the heiress of Belmont, until he increases his income and becomes a financially eligible suitor. He puts his hopes in a friend who has lavishly promised assistance, but lets him down bitterly. This disappointment makes him realize that, in this society, excellence of character rarely meets its reward as it did in Lord Belmont's case. In Lord Belmont, his daughter and his estate, Henry sees not only the beauty of reciprocal love and care, but also an opportunity to escape falsity and secret intentions. But Belmont has its share of untold schemes, too. Benevolent as these schemes claim to be by making Henry the heir of Belmont and Julia's future husband, they also lead to tragedy. Brooke constructs Henry's death scene in such a way that accentuates the hero's exasperation with hidden agendas. When a gravely wounded Henry experiences a moment of self-criticism for having initiated a duel based upon rumours and

for having failed to trust Lord Belmont's liberality, the narrative, after flirting
with tragedy, could return to the cheerful tone of the first volume and fulfil the
prospect of felicity for which it has kept us hoping. However, this possibility is
shattered by the disclosure of a deep, long-standing secret: the union between
Henry and Julia is neither a decision of a few days nor the result of liberality, but
Lord Belmont and J. Mandeville's most cherished and carefully planned scheme.
As Anne Wilmot's account unambiguously suggests, it is this revelation that, far
from energizing Henry, leads to irreparable despair: 'the agitation of his mind
caused his wounds to bleed afresh; successive faintings were the consequence,
in one of which he expired'. From this moment, peace and innocence disappear
from Belmont, never to return, and the reader is left with the poignant question:
why did love and respect not suffice to prevent a tragedy of this magnitude?

The most obvious and least satisfactory reason is the delay of Lord Belmont's
letter that invites Henry to return to the estate where he is to become both
Belmont's successor and Julia's husband. More productive explanations can be
achieved by attempting to interpret the emphasis that the narrative lays on the
fathers' roles, their beliefs, intentions and interactions with their children. Rel-
egating the tragic outcome to a cruel twist of fate entails losing the complexity of
a story that devotes careful attention to parents whose own voices and calculations do not release them from moral responsibility. This explains why instead
of ending the novel upon the deaths of Henry and Julia, Brooke has the reader
keep the company of the grief-stricken parents and friends during the fortnight
following the catastrophe. During this time, the characters reflect upon their
roles in the events and envisage a future with a conscience burdened by the guilty
realization that their own dealings played into the hands of fate.

Lord Belmont, the patriarch in *Julia Mandeville*, seems to carry the heaviest
burden. In his last letter, the penultimate of the novel, he writes:

> By an over-solicitude to continue my family and name, and secure the happiness of
> my child, I have defeated my own purpose, and fatally destroyed both. Humbled in
> the dust, I confess the hand of Heaven: the pride of birth, the grandeur of my house,
> had too great a share in my resolves!

Concerns of property prompted by pride appear to be at the root of the tragedy. In this respect, the novel supports Rousseau's view that civilization's most
fatal development was the invention of property, which resulted in the divi-
sions between masters and servants, as well as rulers and subjects. Private
property made social equality impossible and transformed the instinct for self-
preservation (*amour de soi*) into active egotism (*amour proper*), the latter being
identifiable in the novel with the 'over-solicitude' to continue the 'grandeur' of
lineage. Rousseau articulated his distrust toward private property in *Emile, or
On Education* (1762), where Emile's tutor compiles an educational programme

Introduction xvii

that should teach his pupil to avoid and overcome the allurements of property. *Emile* was published only a year before *Julia Mandeville* and was discussed by almost every influential periodical. As an avid reader and successful translator of the French *roman*, Brooke could not have missed *Emile*'s notoriety.[20] Some of the concerns of Emile's tutor resonate in the letters by J. Mandeville, who has gone to great expense to educate his son 'with an independence to which I would have him sacrifice every other consideration'. This independence should render young Henry immune to the 'poison most fatal to youth, the intoxicating cup of prosperity'.

Rousseau encourages his readers to judge for themselves how the rules illustrated by his narrative 'could be put into practice'.[21] Not only does Brooke take this advice to heart but she does so with more realism: first, instead of having Henry raised in strict isolation like *Emile*, Brooke probes Rousseau's educational scenario within the bounds of civil society; second, the hypothetical relationship between the tutor Jean-Jacques and the orphan Emile (we never know how as an infant Emile comes under Jean-Jacques's care) finds a more verisimilar enactment in the father–son relationship between J. Mandeville and Henry. However, the tutor in Brooke's novel shares Jean-Jacques's conviction that proper education will secure the moral probity and happiness of the child. As a subsequent step, Brooke's tutor adopts a core principle in Rousseau's didactic programme, namely a principle of obscurity that seeks to conceal from the child his own obedience as well as another's dominion: 'Let him not know what obedience is', writes Jean-Jacques, 'when he acts nor what dominion is when someone acts for him.'[22] *Julia Mandeville* suggests that this principle lies disturbingly close to the instrumentalization of the young portrayed by Lord Belmont and J. Mandeville's secret agreement 'on an intermarriage between our children' to 'keep up the splendour of our name'. It comes as a shock even to the most perceptive character of the novel, Anne Wilmot, that the fathers have dexterously orchestrated the rise of feeling and the final union of their children. By falling in love, the young couple have unwittingly obeyed their fathers' wishes and fulfilled their longstanding schemes. The fathers have managed to cultivate similar taste and principles in their offspring, keeping Julia isolated in the innocence of the country, and ensuring that Henry does not place his affections elsewhere. Indeed, the latter succeeds thanks to J. Mandeville's most cunning, if not immoral, scheme: in order to control his son's affections and keep at bay unwanted temptation, he secretly arranges for an Italian Countess to seduce Henry into becoming her *cavalier servente*. While J. Mandeville prides himself upon his ingenious plan, Brooke sets up this story as a prelude to Henry's accumulated frustration and love-induced madness.

The novel then seems to concur with Rousseau on the feasibility of moulding human beings, but, at the same time, it questions the ambiguous role of the

xviii   *The History of Lady Julia Mandeville*

educator, who combines non-coercive presence with invisible and unremitting tutelage. In *Emile*, Rousseau proposed this as the most natural way of socialization when he urged parents to 'Let him [the child] always believe he is the master, and let it always be you who are. There is no subjection as perfect as that which keeps the appearance of freedom.'[23] A quasi-omniscient (and therefore quasi-divine) responsibility lies on the shoulder of Rousseau's preceptor, who should direct his didactic scenario in such a way that the wished-for desires are called forth in the child: 'he ought to want only what you want him to do. He ought not to make a step without you having foreseen it.'[24] The narrative of *Julia Mandeville* approaches these precepts sceptically: not only does it refuse to endorse unquestioned reliance on paternal foresight and control, but it also disrupts the paradisiacal tone that accompanies the descriptions of domestic life through the appalling ending. As in *Romeo and Juliet*, in this novel, too, time works against the lovers. But here, the misunderstanding that costs the lovers' lives arises from their being instrumentalized by their educators. Hence, *Julia Mandeville*, while recognizing the influence of education, suggests well-pondered reservations about some of the core principles upon which rests Rousseauan socialization.[25]

III.

It is not accidental that the events unfold in the countryside, the place of 'renewal' in Rousseau's *Emile* that in the second volume of *Julia Mandeville* transforms from idyllic bliss into gothic horror. Brooke's descriptions of the countryside complement her reflections on paternal guidance with representations of patriarchal power over the estate. Here, the estate becomes an arena of aesthetic, educational and political significance. The grounds of Belmont, the beautiful mountain reminiscent of Shakespeare's heights of Belmont from which Portia sees Venice and its world of vendetta, rise as the uncontested model of responsible estate management and innocent pleasures. Investment in landscape design makes Belmont a place of cultural heritage, as it is brought into connection with the great names of English architecture and gardening. We are told that

> The house, which is the work of Inigo Jones, is magnificent to the utmost degree; it stands on the summit of a slowly rising hill, facing the South; and, beyond a spacious court, has in front an avenue of the tallest trees, which lets in the prospect of a fruitful valley, bounded at a distance by a mountain, down the sides of which rushes a foaming cascade which spreads into a thousand meandering streams in the vale below.

This description may have been inspired by Wilton House at Wiltshire, remodelled in 1630 by Jones in the Palladian style. It could also be a conflation of Wilton House and Stowe House, where Jones is honoured among the 'British Worthies'. Stowe became the object of William Gilpin's first discussion of landscape and architecture in his *A Dialogue upon the Gardens of the Right Hon-*

Introduction   xix

ourable the Lord Viscount Cobham, at Stow in Buckinghamshire (1748). There
are several moments in the novel that hint at Gilpin's *Dialogue*: Lord Belmont
takes his party to his favourite retreat, which he calls 'the hermitage', possibly
modelled upon the Hermitage at Stowe described in Gilpin's *Dialogue*; during
the pre-nuptial festivities, Lord Belmont decides to commemorate the wedding
day by building 'a temple of love and Friendship at a little villa', possibly a reference to the Temple of Friendship built in 1739 at Stowe; and, lastly, upon Julia's
death, Lord Belmont announces that he will erect an obelisk to pay homage to
his daughter's memory, a monument that finds its fictional referent in the golden
statues dedicated to Romeo and Juliet by their parents, but could also have been
inspired by General James Wolfe's obelisk built in Stowe in 1759. One can con-
fidently say that Brooke was knowledgeable about the contemporary vogue for
landscape edifices. For example, she registers fascination with Eastern art and
culture by referring to a Chinese House that decorates the lawn of Lord T—,
the friend who disappoints Henry's hopes. Stowe is known to have held the first
Chinese House in 1738, which by the fictional time of *Julia Mandeville*, that is,
1762, had been removed to another property.[26] By placing the Chinese House
in Lord T—'s gardens, Brooke may be hinting that she knew that it was not at
Stowe at the time. More importantly, placing the Chinese House in the garden of
a shallow character like Lord T— would align Brooke with Gilpin, who showed
no appreciation for Chinese art: 'Their Ingenuity lies chiefly in the knick-knack
Way', as one of the interlocutors in the *Dialogue* puts it.[27]

The salient aspect of Brooke's interest in gardens and landscaping resides in
the fact that she regards pictorial consciousness as concomitant with ideology
and anticipates both late eighteenth-century writers and estate improvers. *Julia
Mandeville* portrays the estate as an emblematic site of moral and social heritage, connecting its management with the social and political system for which
it stands:

> Here Lord Belmont enjoys the most unmixed and lively of all human pleasures,
> that of making others happy. His estate conveys the strongest idea of the patriarchal
> government; he seems a beneficent father surrounded by his children, over whom
> reverence, gratitude, and love, give him an absolute authority, which he never exerts
> but for their good: Every eye shines with transport at his sight; parents point him out
> to their children; the first accents of prattling infancy are taught to lisp his honoured
> name; and age, supported by his bounteous hand, pours out the fervent prayer to
> heaven for its benefactor.

Brooke's most prominent predecessors were Fielding's Allworthy, Richardson's
Sir Charles Grandison and Riccoboni's Lord Danby in *Letters from Juliet Lady
Catesby*, which Brooke had translated. In particular, the description of Grandison Hall as a place of fruitfulness and abundance supports the rightful and
responsible administration of the novel's eponymous hero. The close association

of Lord Belmont with divine authority brings to mind Richardson's Sir Charles whose 'symbolic position as the lord of Grandison Hall' raises him to the status of 'a providence surrogate'.[28] However, Brooke complicates the image of a god-like landlord with that of a quasi-divine educator. Lord Belmont's care as a landlord has brought prosperity to Belmont, but his imperfect foresight, that indispensable ability in Rousseau's educational system, provokes a catastrophe at a domestic and political level: first, it fails to ensure his daughter's felicity, and, second, it destroys the possibility of providing Belmont with the heir that paternal care had gone to great lengths to shape. By inextricably linking estate management and 'rural paternalism' with domestic matters, the narrative ends on a note of double disenchantment. In this light, it initially offers a gratifying view of patriarchy only to retrieve it when disaster strikes, thus magnifying the failure of the patriarch.

It can be argued therefore that *Julia Mandeville* both popularized and complicated the cult of virtuous sensibility by muddling the correlation between virtue and reward, intention and outcome. Brooke's distaste for novels that capitalized on Richardson's tragic treatment of the question in *Clarissa* rings through in her disparaging opinion of Frances Sheridan's *The Memoirs of Miss Sidney Bidulph* (1761), in which, 'a good woman is made to suffer every thing dreadful as the consequences of the Virtuous actions; a moral, in my mind very unfit for young people to learn virtue from.'[29] While recognizing the appeal of persecuted virtue, or in Anne Wilmot's words, 'the pleasure we take in tragedy', Brooke chooses a path that abandons the overt domestic cruelty of *Pamela, Clarissa* or *Miss Sidney Bidulph* for an investigation of the subtle abuses lurking beneath, and even enabled by, the power of sentimental discourse. The necessity for introspection felt by the characters in the aftermath of tragedy hints at Brooke's awareness that she had opted for a narrative with no straightforward answers: Lord Belmont's regretted pride, Henry's repining at his own impetuousness and Anne Wilmot's self-accusations testify to the multiplicity of interpretations. But perhaps the most surprising and thought-provoking criticism comes from the heroine, whose dying words offer an instance of epiphany that may not wholly justify the end, but nonetheless bequeath a moral insight to the reader: 'I have been to blame', Julia says on her deathbed, 'not in loving the most perfect of human beings; but in concealing that love, and distrusting the indulgence of the best of parents.' In what seems a sentimental act of goodness gone too far, the heroine identifies secrecy and concealment as the source of a failed relationship between parents and children, proposing instead transparency as the *sine qua non* of education and domestic relations.

Introduction xxi

A New Edition

Julia Mandeville was published by Robert Dodsley, whom Brooke called the 'Porter of the Temple of Fame', where 'there is no getting in without his Assistance.' Brooke's impressive connections must have helped catch Dodsley's attention, with Johnson in particular possibly having been instrumental, since there are several references to him in her letters. For instance, she draws on Johnson's expertise when writing that emerging authors at the beginning of their career are at the mercy of booksellers: 'Believe me for Johnson says so an Author's first two or three Works must be in a Manner given away to get a name.'[30] Dodsley published *Julia Mandeville* on 20 June 1763, about a month before Frances Brooke's departure for Quebec, where her husband had been assigned a position as chaplain of the garrison. It appeared in two duodecimo volumes, the most current format for novels in the long eighteenth century, and was being sold for 6*s.*[31]

During Brooke's lifetime, *Julia Mandeville* (1763) went through nine editions, the latest appearing in 1788, only a few months before the author's death. While modern editions of Brooke's *The History of Emily Montague* (1769) and *The Excursion* (1777) were published in 1985 and 1997, respectively, the latest edition of *Julia Mandeville* dates as far back as eighty-two years ago with *Lady Julia Mandeville, by Frances Brooke*, ed. E. Phillips Poole (London: Scholartis Press, 1930). The 1930 edition offers an introduction containing a biographical sketch of Frances Brooke's life, short descriptions of her works, and a section on *Julia Mandeville*. However, it lacks textual variants and explanatory notes. Certain aspects are also in need of update, if not correction: for instance, Poole reprints the 1773 edition of the novel, explaining in the prefatory note that this was the last edition published in Brooke's lifetime. As a matter of fact, two further editions followed in 1782 and 1788, before Brooke passed away on 23 January 1789. Moreover, Poole was unable to track down the first edition, which is accessible to us today. For this reason, he assumes that *Julia Mandeville* was published in 1760, and that it was such a success that by 1763, before her departure for Quebec, it had made her 'a literary lion of a minor order'.[32] If she had indeed risen to some literary fame (which at this time was rather modest since the reviewer of the *Monthly Review* calls her 'the ingenious unknown writer'),[33] then it must have been for her earlier works, especially the translation of Riccoboni's *Lettres de Milady Juliette Catesby à Milady Henriette*, whose third edition coincides with the first edition of *Julia Mandeville*.

A few days before leaving for Quebec, Brooke received 100 guineas from Dodsley for her first novel and the translation.[34] She embarked for England in the autumn of 1764 and returned to Quebec in 1765. During her stay in England in 1765, she must have known that Dodsley was preparing new editions of *Julia Mandeville*. However, there are no signs that she assisted with the revisions. As

xxii   *The History of Lady Julia Mandeville*

Poole rightly notes, there are no substantial changes between the editions. Mostly, the editions differ in decisions of punctuation, which may or may not have been authorized by Brooke. This present edition appears as part of the Pickering and Chatto Chawton House Novels Series and accordingly uses the second edition (1763) held by Chawton House Library as its copy text. As the textual variants show, the second edition is closest to the first in decisions of punctuation that are more thoroughly revised in the 'New Edition' of 1763. Both the aim and newness of the present edition consists of its tracing the changes that the novel underwent during Frances Brooke's lifetime and in situating the novel within the history of ideas that shaped its plot, tone and ideological significance. For this reason, it provides an overview of the reception of *Julia Mandeville*, by way of assembling excerpts of contemporary reviews (see Appendix A), as well as passages relevant to issues raised in *Julia Mandeville* from her other novels, her translation of Riccoboni's novel and her periodical the *Old Maid* (see Appendix B).

Notes

1. F. Brooke, *The Old Maid, By Mary Singleton, Spinster* (London: A. Millar, 1764), p. 1. See also Frances Brooke, *The Excursion*, ed. P. Backscheider and H. D. Cotton (Lexington, KY: University of Kentucky Press, 1997), p. 9.

2. *Historical Magazine; or, Classical Library of Remarkable Events, Memoirs, and Anecdotes* (London: D. Brewman, 1789), 4 vols, vol. 1, p. 190.

3. M. Wild, '"Prodigious Wisdom": Civic Humanism in Frances Brooke's *Old Maid*', *Women's Writing*, 5:3 (1998), pp. 421–35, on p. 422.

4. By 1783, when she published the libretto of *Rosina* (a tremendously successful pastoral story that went through six editions in the first year), Brooke was advertised as the 'author of Julia Mandeville'. As late as 1793, Mary Hays refers to her as the 'author of Julia Mandeville'. See M. Hays, *Letters and Essays, Moral and Miscellaneous* (London: T. Knott, 1793), p. 55.

5. L. McMullen, *An Odd Attempt in a Woman: The Literary Life of Frances Brooke* (Vancouver: University of British Columbia Press, 1983), p. 66. Backscheider and Cotton, *The Excursion*, p. xix.

6. A. D. McKillop, '*The English Women Novelists and their Connection with the Feminist Movement* (1688–1797). By Joyce M. Horner; *Lady Julia Mandeville*. By Frances Brooke, E. Phillips Poole', *Modern Language Notes*, 46:8 (1931), pp. 554–5, on p. 555.

7. J. W. von Goethe, *Die Geschwister* (Leipzig: G. J. Göschen, 1787), p. 40, my translation. A year after its first appearance, *Julia Mandeville* went through its fourth edition in England and was also translated into French and German. *Die Geschichte der Julia Mandeville, von dem Uebersetzer der Briefe der Lady Catesby.* Aus dem Englischen (Leipzig: Junius, 1764); *Histoire de Julie Mandeville, ou lettres traduites de l'anglois sur la troisième édition*, traduit par M. A. Bouchaud (Paris: Duchesne, 1764). The novel was reviewed in *La Gazette littéraire de l'Europe*, 1 (30 May 1764) by Voltaire and also by *L'Année Littéraire*. See *La Gazette Littéraire de l'Europe* (Paris: Imprimerie de la Gazette de France, 1764), pp. 331–4; E. Fréron (ed.), *L'Année Littéraire* (Amsterdam: C. J. Panckoucke, 1764), vol.5, pp. 172–202.

8. J. Richetti, *The English Novel in History 1700–1780* (New York: Routledge, 1999), p. 29.

Introduction

xxiii

9. In *The Feminead, or Female Genius* (1757), a tribute to women writers of his day, John Duncombe draws a clear line between the scandalous Behn, Manley, and Susanna Centlivre and respectable women writers like Frances Brooke. See J. Duncombe, *The Feminead, or Female Genius* (London: R. and J. Dodsley, 1757).

10. For an analysis of this collection see C. L. Johnson, '"Let Me Make the Novels of a Country": Barbauld's "The British Novelists"', *A Forum on Fiction*, 34:2 (2001), pp. 163–79, on p. 166.

11. *Monthly Review; or, Literary Journal* (London: R. Griffiths, 1763), pp. 159–60.

12. *Critical Review*, July–December (London: A. Hamilton, 1763), pp.41–45, on p. 45.

13. B. A. Schellenberg, *The Professionalization of Women Writers in Eighteenth-Century Britain* (Cambridge: Cambridge University Press, 2005), p. 60.

14. T. Keymer, 'Sentimental Fiction: Ethics, Social Critique and Philanthropy', in J.Ricchetti (ed.), *The Cambridge History of English Literature, 1660–1780* (Cambridge: Cambridge University Press, 2005), pp. 572–601, on p. 592.

15. *Monthly Review; or, Literary Journal* (London: R. Griffiths, 1763), pp. 159–60.

16. 'Mrs. Brooke', *British Magazine and Review*, 2 (February 1783), 102.

17. *Aberdeen Magazine, Literary Chronicle, and Review* (Aberdeen: J. Chalmers, 1789), p. 170.

18. M. J. Edwards, Introduction in Frances Brooke, *The History of Emily Montague* (Oshawa: Carleton University Press, 1985), p. xx.

19. E. C. B., 'Lady Julia Mandeville by Frances Brooke, E. Phillips Poole', *Review of English Studies*, 7:28 (1931), pp. 484–5, on p. 484.

20. The English translation also included Sophia in the title. See *Emilius and Sophia: or A New System of Education. Translated from French of J. J. Rousseau. Citizen of Geneva. By the translator of Eloisa* (London: R. Griffiths, T. Beckett, 1762). In 1760, Brooke published the translation of Marie Jeanne Riccoboni's *Lettres de Milady Juliette Catesby à Milady Henriette*. Riccoboni enjoyed great popularity in France and England and was held by Adam Smith in his *Theory of Moral Sentiments*, together with Racine, Voltaire, Richardson and Marivaux, as 'the poets and romance writers, who best paint the delicacies and refinements of love and friendship, and of all other private domestic affections'. See A. Smith, *Theory of Moral Sentiments* (London: Henry G. Bohn, 1853), p. 201.

21. J.-J. Rousseau, *Emile or On Education*, ed. and trans. A. Bloom (New York: Basic Books, 1979), p. 51.

22. Rousseau, *Emile*, p. 85.

23. Ibid., p. 120.

24. Ibid., *Emile*, p. 120.

25. Rousseau critically revisited his educational plan in the sequel *Émile et Sophie, ou les Solitaires*, published posthumously in 1780, where the tutor Jean-Jacques experiences the breakdown of his pupil and of his own precepts.

26. R. Batchelor, 'Concealing Bounds: Imagining the British Nation through China', in F. A. Nussbaum (ed.), *The Global Eighteenth Century* (Baltimore, MD: Johns Hopkins, 2003), pp. 79–92, p. 90.

27. W. Gilpin, *A Dialogue upon the Gardens of the Right Honourable the Lord Viscount Cobham, at Stow in Buckinghamshire* (London: J. and J. Rivington, 1748), p. 28.

28. L. A. Chaber, '"Sufficient to the Day": Anxiety in *Sir Charles Grandison*', *Eighteenth-Century Fiction*, 1:4 (1989), pp. 281–304, on p. 287.

29. Letter to Richard Gifford, Saturday, n. d., Harvard Houghton Manuscript, 1310, letter 3.

30. Letter to Richard Gifford, December 4, n. d., conjectured 1756. Harvard Houghton Manuscript, 1310, letter 17.
31. *A Catalogue of Valuable Books, in Different Languages and Faculties: to be Sold by Way of Sale, at the Shop of W. Gordon, Bookseller in the Parliament Close* (Edinburgh, 1765), p. 29. Its third edition, also published in 1763, was listed for 5s. See: C. William, *A Catalogue of Valuable and Elegant Books, Being several Libraries, lately Purchased, Many of them on Royal paper, and Bound in Russia Leather* (London, 1768), p. 88.
32. *Lady Julia Mandeville, by Frances Brooke*, ed. E. Phillips Poole (London: Scholartis Press, 1930), p. 15.
33. *Monthly Review; or, Literary Journal* (London: R. Griffiths, 1763), pp. 159–60.
34. I. Reed, 'Memoranda from Mr. Dodsley's Papers,' Yale University Library, Osborn Collection, p. 25.

SELECT BIBLIOGRAPHY

Consulted Editions

Brooke, F., *The History of Lady Julia Mandeville* (London: R. and J. Dodsley, 1763).

Brooke, F., *The History of Lady Julia Mandeville*, 2nd edn (London: R. and J. Dodsley, 1763).

Brooke, F., *The History of Lady Julia Mandeville*, new edn (London: R. Dodsley, 1763).

Brooke, F., *The History of Lady Julia Mandeville*, 3rd edn (London: R. and J. Dodsley, 1764).

Brooke, F., *The History of Lady Julia Mandeville*, 4th edn (London: J. Dodsley, 1765).

Brooke, F., *The History of Lady Julia Mandeville*, 5th edn (London: J. Dodsley, 1769).

Brooke, F., *The History of Lady Julia Mandeville*, 6th edn (London: J. Dodsley, 1773).

Brooke, F., *The History of Lady Julia Mandeville*, 7th edn (London: J. Dodsley, 1782).

Brooke, F., *The History of Lady Julia Mandeville*, new edn (London: J. Dodsley, 1788).

Lady Julia Mandeville, by Frances Brooke, ed. E. Phillips Poole (London: Scholartis, 1930).

Pre-Twentieth-Century Sources

Aberdeen Magazine, Literary Chronicle, and Review (Aberdeen: J. Chalmers, 1789), p. 170.

Barbauld, A. L., *The British Novelists*, 50 vols (London: Rivington, 1810), vol. 27.

Brooke, B., 'Authentic Memoirs of Mrs Yates', *Gentleman's Magazine*, 58 (July 1787), pp. 585–9.

Brooke, F., *The Old Maid, By Mary Singleton, Spinster* (1755–6; rev. edn, London: A. Millar, 1764).

Cooper, M. S., *The Exemplary Mother; or, Letters between Mrs. Villars and her Family* (London: 1769).

Critical Review, or, Annals of Literature (London: A. Hamilton, 1763), vol. 16, pp. 41–5.

Duncombe, J., *The Feminead, or Female Genius* (London: R. and J. Dodsley, 1757).

Hays, M., *Letters and Essays, Moral and Miscellaneous* (London: T. Knott, 1793), p. 55.

Historical Magazine; or, Classical Library of Remarkable Events, Memoirs, and Anecdotes, 4 vols (London: D. Brewman, 1789), vol. 1, p. 190.

xxvi — *The History of Lady Julia Mandeville*

Fréron, E. (ed.), *L'Année Littéraire* (Amsterdam: C. J. Panckoucke, 1764), vol. 5, pp. 172–202.

La Gazette Littéraire de l'Europe (Paris: Imprimerie de la Gazette de France, 1764) pp. 331–4.

London Magazine; or Gentleman's Monthly Intelligencer (London: R. Baldwin, 1763), vol. 32, pp. 374–436.

Monthly Review; or, Literary Journal (London: R. Griffiths, 1763), vol. 29, pp. 159–60.

Reeve, C., *The Progress of Romance, Through Times, Countries and Manners* (Colchester: W. Keymer 1785).

Twentieth and Twenty-First Century Sources

Benedict, B. M., 'The Margins of Sentiment: Nature, Letter, and Law in Frances Brooke's Epistolary Novels', *ARIEL: A Review of International English Literature*, 23:3 (July 1992), pp. 7–25.

Blain, V., P. Clements and I. Grundy, 'Brooke, Frances', in *The Feminist Companion to Literature in English* (New Haven, CT and London: Yale University Press, 1990), pp. 142–43.

Boyd, D. E., and M. Kvande (eds), *Everyday Revolutions: Eighteenth-Century Women Transforming Public and Private* (Newark, DE: Delaware University, 2008).

Conway, A., 'The Professionalization of Women Writers in Eighteenth-Century Britain', *Scriblerian and the Kit-Cats*, 41.1 (2008), pp. 57–8.

D. Saar and M. A. Schofield (eds), *Eighteenth-Century Anglo-American Women Novelists: A Reference Guide* (New York: Macmillan, 1996), pp. 18–43.

Doody, M. A., 'George Eliot and the Eighteenth-Century Novel', *Nineteenth-Century Fiction*, 35 (December 1980), pp. 260–91.

E. C. B., 'Lady Julia Mandeville by Frances Brooke, E. Phillips Poole', *The Review of English Studies*, 7.28 (1931), pp. 484–5.

Edwards, M. J., 'Frances Brooke's *The History of Emily Montague*: A Biographical Context', *English Studies in Canada*, 7.2 (Summer 1981), pp. 171–82.

F. Nussbaum and P. B. Anderson (eds), *An Annotated Bibliography of Twentieth-Century Critical Studies of Women and Literature, 1660–1800* (New York and London: Garland Publishing, 1977), p. 110.

Foster, J. R., *History of the Pre-Romantic Novel in England* (New York: Modern Language Association, 1949).

McKillop, A. D., '*The English Women Novelists and their Connection with the Feminist Movement (1688–1797).* By Joyce Horner; *Lady Julia Mandeville.* By Frances Brooke, E. Phillips Poole', *Modern Language Notes*, 46:8 (1931), pp. 554–5.

McMullen, L., 'Double Image: Frances Brooke's Women Characters', *World Literature Written in English*, 21:2 (Summer 1982), pp. 356–63.

McMullen, L., *An Odd Attempt in a Woman: The Literary Life of Frances Brooke* (Vancouver: University of British Columbia Press, 1983).

Messenger, A., *His and Hers: Essays in Restoration and Eighteenth-Century Literature* (Lexington, KY: University Press of Kentucky, 1986).

New, W. H., 'Frances Brooke's Chequered Gardens', *Canadian Literature*, 52 (1972), pp. 24–38.

Perkins, P., 'Introduction: "Excellent Women, and not too Blue": Women Writers in Late Eighteenth- and Early Nineteenth-Century Edinburgh', *Scottish Cultural Review of Language and Literature*, 15 (2010), pp. 13–53.

Singer, G. F., *The Epistolary Novel: Its Origins, Development, Decline and Residuary Development* (New York: Russell & Russell, 1933).

Spencer, J., *The Rise of the Woman Novelist: From Aphra Behn to Jane Austen* (Oxford: Basil Blackwell, 1986).

Teague, F., 'Frances Brooke's Imagined Epistles', *Studies on Voltaire and the Eighteenth Century*, 304 (1992), pp. 711–12.

Tierney, J. E. (ed.), *The Correspondence of Robert Dodsley 1733–1764* (Cambridge: Cambridge University Press, 1988).

Todd, J., *The Sign of Angellica: Women, Writing, and Fiction 1660–1800* (London: Virago; New York: Columbia University Press, 1989).

Utter, R. P., and G. B. Needham, *Pamela's Daughters* (New York: Macmillan, 1936).

Wild, M., '"Prodigious Wisdom": Civic Humanism in Frances Brooke's *Old Maid*', *Women's Writing*, 5:3 (1998), pp. 421–35.

FRANCES BROOKE: A BRIEF CHRONOLOGY

1724 Frances Brooke (née Moore), eldest daughter of Mary Knowles and Thomas Moore, curate of Claypole, is baptized on 24 January in the parish of Claypole.

1725 Frances's sister, Catherine Moore, is born.

1726 Her father is appointed rector of Carlton Scroop, Lincolnshire.

1727 Frances's sister, Sarah Moore, is born. Frances's father dies and the family moves to Peterborough to live with Sarah Knowles, Mary Moore's mother.

1736 Mary Moore dies. The three sisters move in with Sarah Knowles Steevens, wife of Roger Steevens, rector of Tydd St Mary, Lincolnshire. Catherine Moore dies at the age of eleven.

1748 Frances moves to London, while Sarah goes to live with her mother's brother, Richard Knowles, curate of Thistleton, Lincolnshire.

1755 On 15 November, Frances publishes the first issue of the *Old Maid*, a weekly periodical that appeared under the pseudonym Mary Singleton.

1756 Frances marries the Reverend John Brooke.
After David Garrick's rejection of *Virginia*, Frances publishes it with Andrew Millar as *Virginia: A Tragedy with Odes, Pastorals, and Translations*.

1757 Frances's husband is appointed chaplain to the British army. The Brookes' son, John Moore Brooke, is born on 10 June.

1758 John Brooke serves as chaplain at Ford Louisbourg, Nova Scotia, Canada.

1760 Frances publishes her translation from French of Marie Jeanne Riccoboni's novel *Letters from Juliet, Lady Catesby, to her Friend, Lady Henrietta Campley*. There are two editions within the year. John Brooke arrives in Quebec and is unofficially appointed chaplain to Quebec garrison.

1763 The third edition of *Letters from Juliet, Lady Catesby, to her Friend, Lady Henrietta Campley* is published, followed by Frances Brooke's first novel, *The History of Lady Julia Mandeville*.

1763 Brooke arrives in Quebec with her son and sister.

1764	Brooke returns to London on her husband's behalf to present a petition from the Protestant residents of Quebec to the Reverend Dr Burton, Secretary of the Society for the Propagation of the Gospel in Foreign Parts.
1765	Brooke returns to Quebec, while her sister leaves for England.
1768	The Brookes return to London.
1769	James Dodsley publishes Brooke's *The History of Emily Montague*.
1770	Brooke publishes her translation from French of Nicolas Framery's *Memoirs of the Marquis de St Forlaix*.
1771	Her translation of Claude Millot's *Elements of the History of England* appears.
1773	Richard and Mary Anne Yates and James Brooke, Frances's brother-in-law, purchase the King's Theatre at Haymarket. Frances Brooke co-manages the theatre with her friend, the actress Mary Ann Yates. The theatre opens on 29 November under the new name the Opera House.
1777	Brooke's third novel *The Excursion* is published by Thomas Cadell.
1778	James Brooke sells his entire interests in the Opera House to Richard Brinsley Sheridan and Thomas Harris.
1779	Brooke starts working on a biography of Samuel Johnson.
1781	On 31 January, Brooke's tragedy *The Siege of Sinope* is performed at Covent Garden. Thomas Cadell publishes *The Siege*.
1782	Brooke writes the libretto of *Rosina*; the comic opera is performed at Covent Garden on 31 December.
1783	Cadell publishes *Rosina*.
1785	The second edition of *The Excursion* appears.
1785	Frances Brooke leaves London to be near her son in Sleaford, Lincolnshire.
1788	Brooke's *Marian*, a comic opera, is performed at Covent Garden.
1789	John Brooke dies at Colney, Norfolk on 21 January; Frances Brooke dies in Sleaford on 23 January.
1790	*The History of Charles Mandeville*, the sequel to Brooke's *Julia Mandeville*, is published posthumously by Thomas Cadell.

NOTE ON THE TEXT

Until Brooke's death in January 1789, the following editions of *The History of Julia Mandeville* were printed by R. Dodsley and J. Dodsley: first edition on 20 June 1763; the second edition on 15 September 1763; a 'New Edition' on 21 December 1763;[1] the third edition in 1764; the fourth edition in 1765; the fifth edition in 1769; the sixth edition in 1773; the seventh edition in 1782; a 'New Edition' in 1788. Editions of the novel also appeared in Dublin, but, to my knowledge they were not authorized by Brooke and therefore have not been consulted.

The 'New Edition' from 1763 introduces different punctuation and capitalization, which are for the most part adopted by the editions from 1769, 1773, 1782 and 1788. The new punctuation predominantly consists of the replacements of commas with semicolons and of periods with exclamation marks. The capitalization of words such as 'Lady', 'Lord', 'Heaven', 'Prince', 'Sovereign' and 'Friendship', is inconsistent in all editions. Variant punctuation and spelling from one edition to the other has been noted, while following exactly the punctuation and spelling of the copy text. Typographical errors have been noted in the Silent Corrections. The 'New Edition' from 1763 abandons the capitalization of foreign words, italicizing them instead. However, only the editions from 1769, 1773, 1782 and 1788 follow this decision. Remaining faithful to the second edition in 1763, the present edition preserves the capitalization of foreign words and provides a translation in the explanatory notes. It has been a conscious decision to keep editorial intrusions to a minimum.

The textual notes indicate variant wording and punctuation. The closing bracket separates the wording of the second edition from that of other editions. Semi-colons separate one edition from the other. The following abbreviations are used to distinguish the three editions that appeared in 1763:

> First edition in 1763: 1763a
> Second edition in 1763: 1763b
> New Edition in 1763: 1763c

Notes

1. J. E. Tierney (ed.), *The Correspondence of Robert Dodsley, 1733–1764* (Cambridge: Cambridge University Press, 1988), p. 481.

– xxxi –

THE

HISTORY

OF

Lady Julia Mandeville.

In TWO VOLUMES

By the TRANSLATOR of

LADY CATESBY'S LETTERS

THE SECOND EDITION

VOL I.

LONDON:

Printed for R. and J. Dodsley in Pall-Mall.
MDCCIXIII.

VOLUME I

To George Mordaunt, Esq;

Belmont-House, July 3, 1762.

I AM indeed, my dear George, the most happy of human beings; happy in the paternal regard of the best of parents, the sincere esteem of my worthy relations, lord and lady Belmont; and the friendship, the tender friendship of their/ lovely daughter, the amiable lady Julia.[1] An encrease[a] of fortune, which you are kind enough to wish me, might perhaps add something to my felicity, but is far from being necessary to constitute it, nor did it ever excite in my bosom an anxious wish. My father, though he educated me to become[2] the most splendid situation, yet instructed me to be satisfied with my own moderate one; he taught me that independence[3] was all a generous mind required; and that virtue, adorned by that liberal education his unsparing bounty lavished on me, would command through life that heart-felt esteem from the worthy of every rank, which the most exorbitant wealth alone could never procure its possessors. Other parents hoard up riches for their children; mine with a more noble, more enlightened solicitude, expended his in storing my mind with generous sentiments and useful knowledge, to which/ his unbounded goodness added every outward accomplishment that could give grace to virtue, and set her charms in the fairest light.

Shall I then murmur because I was not born to affluence? No, believe me, I would not be the son of any other than this most excellent of men, to inherit all the stores which avarice and ambition sigh for.[b] I am prouder of a father to whose discerning wisdom, and generous expanded heart, I am so obliged, than I should be of one whom I was to succeed in all the titles and possessions in the power of fortune to bestow. From him I receive, and learn properly to value, the most real of all treasures, independence and content.

What a divine morning! how lovely is the face of nature! The[c] blue serene of Italy, with the lively verdure of England.[4d]/ But behold a more charming object than nature herself! the sweet, the young, the blooming lady Julia, who is this instant stepping into her post chaise with lady Anne Wilmot. How unspeak-

– 3 –

4 *The History of Lady Julia Mandeville*

ably lovely! she[a] looks up to the window, she smiles; I understand that smile, she permits me to have the honour of following her:[5] I'll order my horses, and whilst they are getting ready, endeavour[b] to describe this most angelic of woman kind.[c]

Lady Julia then, who wants[6] only three months of nineteen, is exactly what a poet or painter would wish to copy who intended to personify the idea of female softness.[7] Her[d] whole form is delicate and feminine to the utmost degree: her complexion is fair, enlivened by the bloom of youth, and often diversified by blushes more beautiful than those of the morning: her features are regular, her mouth and teeth particularly/ lovely; her hair light brown; her eyes blue, full of softness, and strongly expressive of the exquisite sensibility[8] of her soul. Her countenance, the beauteous abode of the loves and the smiles, has a mixture of sweetness and spirit, which gives life and expression to her charms.

As her mind has been adorned, not warped, by education, it is just what her appearance promises;[e] artless, gentle, timid, soft, sincere, compassionate; awake to all the finer impressions[9] of tenderness,[10] and melting with pity for every human woe.

But my horses are in the court, and even this subject cannot detain me a moment longer. Adieu!

H. MANDEVILLE./

To GEORGE MORDAUNT, Esq;

YOUR raillery,[11] my dear Mordaunt, gives me pain;[f] that I have the tenderest attachment to lady Julia is certain; but it is an attachment which has not the least resemblance to love. I should be the most ungrateful of mankind to make so ill a return to the friendship lord Belmont honours me with, and the most selfish to entertain a wish so much to lady Julia's disadvantage. My birth, it must be confessed, is not unworthy even her, since the same blood fills our veins, my father being descended from the eldest brother of the first earl of Belmont, great grandfather of the present: but it would ill become a man whose whole expectations are limited to the inheritance of 700l.[g] a year[12] (long[h] very long, may it be before the greatest of all misfortunes makes even/ that little mine)[i] to aspire to the heiress of twice as many thousands.[13]

What I feel for this most charming of women is the tenderness of a relation,[14] mixed with that soft and lively esteem which it is impossible to refuse to the finest understanding and noblest mind in the world, lodged in a form almost celestial.[15]

Love, for I have tasted its poisoned cup,[16] is all tumult, disorder, madness; but my friendship for lady Julia, warm and animated as it is, is calm, tranquil, gentle; productive of a thousand innocent pleasures, but a stranger to every kind

Volume I   5

of inquietude: it does not even disturb my rest, a certain consequence of love, even in its earliest approaches.

Having thus vindicated myself from all suspicion of a passion, which in the present/ situation of my fortune I should think almost a criminal one, I proceed to obey you in giving you the portraits of my noble friends, though, I assure you, my sketches will be very imperfect ones.

Lord Belmont, who lives eight months of the year at this charming seat, with all the magnificence and hospitality of our ancient English nobility, is about sixty years old; his person is tall, well made, graceful; his air commanding, and full of dignity: he has strong sense, with a competent share of learning, and a just and delicate taste for the fine arts; especially musick,[a] which he studied[b] in Italy, under the best masters that region of harmony afforded. His politeness is equally the result of a natural desire of obliging, and an early and extensive acquaintance with the great world./

A liberality which scarce his ample possessions can bound, a paternal care of all placed by Providence under his protection, a glowing zeal for the liberty, prosperity, and honour of his country, the noblest spirit of independence, with the most animated attachment and firmest loyalty to his accomplished sovereign,[17] are traits too strongly marked to escape the most careless observer; but those only who are admitted to his nearest intimacy are judges of his domestic[c] virtues, or see in full light the tender, the polite, attentive husband, the fond indulgent parent, the warm unwearied friend.

If there is a shade in this picture, it is a prejudice, perhaps rather too strong, in favour of birth, and a slowness to expect very exalted virtues in any man who cannot trace his ancestors as far back, at least, as the conquest.[18]/

Lady Belmont, who is about six years younger than her lord, with all the strength of reason and steadiness of mind generally confined to the best of our sex, has all the winning softness becoming the most amiable of her own; gentle, affable, social, polite, she joins the graces of a court to the simplicity of a cottage;[19] and by an inexpressible safe and sweetness in her address, makes all who approach her happy: impartial[d] in her politeness, at her genial board no invidious distinctions take place, no cold regards damp the heart of an inferior: by[e] a peculiar delicacy of good breeding, and engaging attention to every individual, she banishes reserve, and diffuses a spirit of convivial joy around her: encouraged[f] by her notice the timid lose their diffidence in her presence, and often surprized exert talents of pleasing they were before themselves unconscious of possessing./

The best,[g] and most beloved of wives, of mothers, of mistresses, her domestic[h] character is most lovely; indeed all her virtues are rendered doubly charming, by a certain grace, a delicate finishing, which it is much easier to feel than to describe.

The œconomy of her house, which she does not disdain herself to direct, is magnificent without profusion, and regular without constraint:[a] The effects of her cares appear, the cause is unobserved; all wears the smiling easy air of chance, though conducted with the most admirable order.[20]

Her form is perfectly elegant; and her countenance, without having ever been beautiful, has a benignity in it more engaging than beauty itself./

Lady Anne Wilmot, my father, and myself, make up the present party at Belmont. Lady Anne, who without regularity of features has that animation which is the soul of beauty, is the widow of a very rich country gentleman; if it be just to prostitute the name of gentleman to beings of his order, only because they have estates of which they are unworthy, and are descended from ancestors whom they dishonour;[b] who, when riding post through Europe, happened to see her with her father at Turin; and as she was the handsomest English woman[c] there, and the whim of being marryed[d] just then seized him, asked her of Lord –, who could not refuse his daughter to a jointure of 3000*l.*[e] a year. She returned soon to England with her husband, where during four years she enjoyed the happiness of listening to the interesting histories of the chace, and entertaining the – shire hunt at dinner: her/ slumbers broke by the noise of hounds in a morning, and the riotous mirth of less rational animals at night. Fortune however at length took pity on her sufferings, and the good 'squire[f] overheating himself at a fox chace,[21g] of which a fever was the consequence, left her young and rich, at full liberty to return to the chearful haunts of men, with no very high ideas of matrimonial felicity, and an abhorrence of a country life, which nothing but her friendship for Lady Belmont could have one moment suspended.

A great flow of animal spirits, and a French education,[22] have made her a Coquet[h], though intended by nature for a much superior character. She is elegant in her dress, equipage, and manner of living, and rather profuse in her expences. I had first the honour of knowing her last winter at Paris, from whence she has been returned/ about six weeks, three of which she has passed at Belmont.

Nothing can be more easy or agreeable than the manner of living here; it is perfectly domestic,[i] yet so diversified with amusements as to exclude that satiety from which the best and purest of sublunary enjoyments are not secure, if continued in too uniform a course: We read, we walk, we ride, we converse;[j] we play, we dance, we sing; join the company, or indulge in pensive solitude and meditation, just as fancy leads; liberty, restrained alone by virtue and politeness, is the law, and inclination the sovereign guide, at this mansion of true hospitality. Free from all the shackles of idle ceremony, the whole business of Lord Belmont's guests, and the highest satisfaction they can give their noble host, is to be happy, and to consult their own taste entirely in their manner of being so./

Reading, musick,[k] riding, and conversation are Lord Belmont's favourite[l] pleasures, but none that are innocent are excluded; balls, plays, concerts, cards,

Volume I 7

bowls, billiards, and parties of pleasure round the neighbouring country, relieve each other; and whilst their variety prevents any of them from satiating, all conspire to give a double poignancy to the sweeter joys of domestic[a] life, the calm and tender hours which this charming family devote to the endearing conversation of each other, and of those friends particularly honoured[b] with their esteem.

The house, which is the work of Inigo Jones,[23] is magnificent to the utmost degree; it stands on the summit of a slowly rising[c] hill,[d] facing the South; and, beyond a spacious court, has in front an avenue of the tallest trees,[24] which lets in the prospect of a fruitful valley, bounded at a distance/ by a mountain, down the sides of which rushes a foaming cascade[e] which spreads into a thousand meandering streams in the vale below.

The gardens and park, which are behind the house, are romantic[f] beyond the wantonness of imagination; and the whole adjoining country diversifyed[g] with hills, valleys, woods, rivers, plains, and every charm of lovely unadorned nature.

Here Lord Belmont enjoys the most unmixed and lively of all human pleasures, that of making others happy. His estate conveys the strongest idea of the patriarchal government;[25] he seems a beneficent father surrounded by his children, over whom reverence, gratitude, and love, give him an absolute authority, which he never exerts but for their good: Every[h] eye shines with transport at his sight; parents point him/ out to their children; the first accents of prattling infancy are taught to lisp his honoured name; and age, supported by his bounteous hand, pours out the fervent prayer to heaven for its benefactor.

To a life like this, and to an ardent love of independence, Lord Belmont sacrifices all the anxious and corroding cares of avarice and ambition; and finds his account in health, freedom, chearfulness, and 'that sweet peace which goodness bosoms ever.'[26] Adieu! I am going with Lord Belmont and my father to Acton-Grange,[27] and shall not return till Thursday.

H. MANDEVILLE.[i]

To GEORGE MORDAUNT, Esq;

FRIDAY.

WE returned yesterday about six in the evening, and the moment we alighted, my Lord leading us into the/ garden, an unexpected scene opened on my view, which recalled the idea of the fabulous pleasures of the golden age,[28] and could not but be infinitely pleasing to every mind uncorrupted by the false glare of tinsel pomp, and awake to the genuine charms of simplicity and nature.

On a spacious lawn, bounded on every side by a profusion of the most odoriferous flowering shrubs, a joyous band of villagers were assembled: the young men drest in green, youth, health, and pleasure in their air, led up their artless charmers in straw hats adorned with the spoils of Flora,[29] to the rustic[j] sound of

8   *The History of Lady Julia Mandeville*

the tabor and pipe:[a] Round the lawn, at equal intervals, were raised temporary arbors of branches of trees, in which refreshments were prepared for the dancers: and between the arbors, seats of moss for their parents, shaded from the sun by green awnings on poles, round/ which were twined wreaths of flowers, breathing the sweets of the spring. The surprize, the gaiety of the scene, the flow of general joy, the sight of so many happy people, the countenances of the enraptured parents, who seemed to live over again the sprightly season of youth in their children, with the benevolent pleasure in the looks of the noble bestowers of the feast, filled my eyes with tears, and my swelling heart with a sensation of pure yet lively transport, to which the joys of courtly balls are mean.[30]

The ladies, who were sitting in conversation with some of the oldest of the villagers, rose at our approach, and my Lord giving Lady Anne Wilmot's hand to my father, and honoring me with Lady Julia's, we mixed in the rustic ball. The loveliest of women had an elegant simplicity in her air and habit which became the scene,/ and gave her a thousand new charms: she was drest in a straw-coloured lustring[31b] night gown,[c] the lightest gauze linen, a hat with purple ribbons, and a sprig of glowing purple amaranthus[32] in her bosom:[d] I know not how to convey an idea of the particular style of beauty in which she then appeared. – Youth, health, sprightliness and innocence, all struck the imagination at once. – Paint[e] to yourself the exquisite proportion, the playful air, and easy movement of a Venus[33], with the vivid bloom of an Hebe;[34] – however[f] high you raise your ideas, they will fall infinitely short of the divine original.

The approach of night putting an end to the rural assembly, the villagers retired to the hall, where they continued dancing, and our happy partie[g] passed the rest of the evening in that sweet and lively conversation, which is never to be found but amongst/ those of the first sense and politeness, united by that perfect confidence which makes the most trifling subjects interesting; none[h] of us thought of separating, or imagined it midnight, when my father opening a window, the rising sun broke in upon us, and convinced us on what swift and downy pinions[35] the hours of happiness flit away. Adieu!

H. MANDEVILLE.[i]

To GEORGE MORDAUNT, Esq;

BELMONT.

NO, my friend, I have not always been this hero: too sensible to the power of beauty, I have felt the keenest pangs of unsuccessful love: but I deserved to suffer; my passion was in the highest degree criminal,[36] and I blush,[37] though at this distance of time, to lay open my heart/ even to the indulgent eyes of partial friendship.

Volume I

When your father's death called you back to England, you may remember I continued my journey to Rome:[38] where a letter from my father introduced me into the family of count Melespini, a nobleman of great wealth and uncommon accomplishments. As[a] my father, who has always been of opinion that nothing purifies the heart, refines the taste, or polishes the manners, like the conversation of an amiable, well-educated,[b] virtuous woman, had particularly entreated for me the honour of the countess's friendship, whom he had known almost a child, and to whom he had taught the English language; I was admitted to the distinction of partaking in all her amusements, and attending her every where in the quality of Cecisbeo.[39] To the arts of/ the libertine, however fair, my heart had always been steeled; but the countess joined the most piercing wit, the most winning politeness, the most engaging sensibility, the most exquisite delicacy, to a form perfectly lovely. You will not therefore wonder that the warmth and inexperience of youth, hourly exposed in so dangerous a situation, was unable to resist such variety of attractions. Charmed with the flattering preference she seemed to give me, my vanity fed by the notice of so accomplished a creature, forgetting those sentiments of honour which ought never to be one moment suspended, I became passionately in love with this charming woman: for some months I struggled with my love; till, on her observing that my health seemed impaired,[40] and I had lost my usual vivacity, I took courage to confess the cause, though in terms which sufficiently spoke my despair of touching a heart which I feared was too sensible to virtue/ for my happiness: I implored her pity, and protested I had no hope of inspiring a tenderer sentiment.[c] Whilst I was speaking, which was in broken interrupted sentences, the countess looked at me with the strongest sorrow and compassion painted in her eyes; she was for some moments silent, and seemed lost in thought; but at last, with an air of dignified sweetness, 'My dear Enrico,'[41] said she, 'shall I own to you that I have for some time feared this confession? I ought perhaps to resent this declaration, which from another I could never have forgiven: but as I know and esteem the goodness of your heart, as I respect your father infinitely, and love you with the innocent tenderness of a sister, I will only entreat you to reflect how injurious this passion is to the count, who has the tenderest esteem for you, and would sacrifice almost his life for your happiness: be assured of my/ eternal friendship, unless[d] you forfeit it by persisting in a pursuit equally destructive to your own probity and my honor; receive the tenderest assurances of it,' continued she, giving me her hand to kiss, 'but believe at the same time, that the count deserves and possesses all my love, I had almost said, my adoration. The fondest affection united us, and time, instead of lessening, every hour increases our mutual passion. Reserve your heart, my good Enrico, for some amiable lady of your own nation, and believe that love has no true pleasures but when it keeps within the bounds of honour.'

10 *The History of Lady Julia Mandeville*

It is impossible, my dear Mordaunt, to express to you the shame this discourse filled me with: her gentle, her affectionate reproofs, the generous concern she showed[a] for my error, the mild dignity of her aspect, plunged me into inexpressible confusion, and shew'd[b] my fault in its[c]/ blackest colours,[d] at the same time that her behaviour, by increasing my esteem, added to the excess of my passion. I attempted to answer her; but it was impossible; awed, abashed, humbled before her, I had not courage even to meet her eyes: like the fallen angel in Milton, I felt

> – 'How awful goodness is, and saw
> Virtue in her own shape how lovely.'[42]

The countess saw, and pitied,[e] my[f] confusion, and generously relieved me from it by changing the subject: she talked of my father, of his merit, his tenderness for me, and expectations of my conduct; which she was sure I should never disappoint.[g] Without hinting at what had past,[h] she with the most exquisite delicacy gave me to understand it would be best I should leave Rome, by saying she knew how ardently my father wished for my return,/ and that it would be the height of cruelty longer to deprive him of the pleasure of seeing a son so worthy of his affection:[i] 'The count and myself,' pursued she, 'cannot lose you without inexpressible regret, but you will alleviate it by letting us hear often of your welfare. When[j] you are united to a lady worthy of you, my dear Enrico, we may perhaps make you a visit in England: in the mean time be assured you have not two friends who love you with a sincerer affection.'

At this moment the count entered, who, seeing my eyes filled with tears of love, despair, and admiration, with the tenderest anxiety enquired the cause. 'I shall tell you news which will afflict you, my lord,' said the countess:[k] 'Signor Enrico[43] comes to bid us farewel; he is commanded by his father to return to England; tomorrow is the last day of his stay in/ Rome: he promises to write to us, and to preserve an eternal remembrance of our friendship, for which he is obliged only to his own merit: his tender heart, full of the most laudable, the most engaging sensibility, melts at the idea of a separation which will not be less painful to us.'

The count, after expressing the most obliging concern at the thought of losing me, and the warmest gratitude for these supposed marks of my friendship, insisted on my spending the rest of the day with them. I consented, but begged first to return to my lodgings on pretence of giving some necessary orders, but in reality to give vent to my full heart, torn with a thousand contrary emotions, amongst which, I am shocked to own, hatred to the generous count was not the weakest. I threw myself on the ground in an agony of despair; I wept, I called heaven to witness the purity of my love; I accused the countess/ of cruelty in thus forcing me from Rome:[l] I rose up, I begun a letter to her, in which I vowed an eternal silence and respect, but begged she would allow me still the innocent

Volume I 11

pleasure of beholding her; swore I could not live without seeing her, and that the day of my leaving Rome would be that of my death. – But why do I thus tear open wounds which are but just healed? let it suffice that a moment's reflexion convinced me of my madness, and showed the charming countess in the light of a guardian angel snatching me from the edge of a precipice.[44] My reason in some degree returning, I drest myself with the most studious care, and returned to the Melespini palace, where I found the abbate Camilli, a near relation of the family, whose presence saved me the confusion of being the third with my injured friends, and whose lively conversation soon dissipated the air of constraint I felt on/ entering the room, and even dispelled part of my melancholy.[45]

The count, whose own probity and virtue set him far above suspecting mine, pressed me, with all the earnestness of a friendship I so little merited, to defer my journey a week: on which I raised my downcast eyes[46] to madam Melespini; for such influence had this lovely woman over my heart, did not dare to consent till certain of her permission; and reading approbation in a smile of condescending sweetness, I consented with a transport which only those who have loved like me can conceive: my chearfulness returning, and some of the most amiable people in Rome coming in, we past the evening in the utmost gaiety. At taking leave I was engaged to the same company in different parties of amusement for the whole time I had to stay, and had the joy of being every day with the countess; though I never/ found an opportunity of speaking to her without witnesses, till[a] the evening before I left Rome, when going to her house an hour sooner than I was expected, I found her alone in her closet.[47] When I approached her, my voice faltered, I trembled,[b] I wanted power to address her; and this moment, sought with such care, wished with such ardor, was the most painful of my life. Shame alone prevented my retiring; my eyes were involuntarily turned towards the door at which I entered, in a vain hope of that interruption I had before dreaded as the greatest misfortune; and even the presence of my happy envied rival would at that moment have been most welcome.

The Countess seemed little less disconcerted than myself; however recovering herself sooner, 'Signor Enrico,' said she, 'your discretion charms me; it is absolutely necessary you should leave Rome;/ it has already cost me an artifice unworthy of my character to conceal from the Count a secret which would have wounded his nice honor, and destroyed his friendship for you. After this adored husband, be assured[c] you stand first of all your sex in my esteem: the sensibility of your heart, though at present so unhappily misplaced, encreases[d] my good opinion of you: may[e] you, my dear Enrico, meet with an English Lady worthy of your tenderness, and be as happy in marriage as the friends you leave behind. Accept,' pursued she, rising and going to a cabinet, 'these miniatures[48] of the Count and myself, which I give you by his command; and when you look on them believe they represent two faithful friends, whose esteem for you neither time nor absence can lessen.'

I took the pictures eagerly, and kissed that of the Countess with a passion I could/ not restrain, of which however she took not the least notice. I thanked her, with a confused air, for so valuable a present; and intreated her to pity a friendship too tender for my peace, but as respectful and as pure as she herself could wish it.

The abbate Camilli here joined us, and once more saved me a scene too interesting for the present situation of my heart. The[a] Count entered the room soon after, and our conversation turned on the other cities of Italy, which I intended visiting; to most of which he gave me letters of recommendation[49] to the noblest families, wrote[b] in terms so polite and affectionate as stabbed me to the heart with a sense of my own ingratitude. He did me the honor to accept my picture, which I had not the courage to offer the Countess. After protracting till morning a parting so exquisitely painful, I tore myself from all I loved, and bathing with tears[50] her hand which I pressed/ eagerly to my lips, threw myself into my chaise, and, without going to bed, took the road to Naples. But how difficult was this conquest! How often was I tempted to return to Rome, and throw myself at the countess's feet, without considering the consequences of so wild an action! You, my dearest Mordaunt, whose discerning spirit knows all the windings, the strange inconsistences of the human heart, will pity rather than blame your friend, when he owns there were moments in which he formed the infamous resolution of carrying her off by force.[51]

But when the mill of passion a little dispersed, I began to entertain more worthy sentiments; I determined to drive this lovely woman from my heart, and conquer an inclination, which the Count's generous unsuspecting friendship would have made criminal even in the eyes of the most abandoned libertine;[52] rather owing this resolution/ however to an absolute despair of success than either to reason or a sense of honor, my cure was a work of time. I was so weak during some months as to confine my visits to the families where the Count's letters introduced me, that I might indulge my passion by hearing the lovely Countess continually mentioned.

Convinced at length of the folly of thus feeding so hopeless a flame,[53] I resolved to avoid every place where I had a chance of hearing that adored name:[c] I left Italy for France, where I hoped a life of dissipation would drive her for ever from my remembrance. I even profaned my passion for her by meeting the advances of a Coquette,[54] but disgust succeeded my conquest, and I found it was from time alone I must hope a cure.[d] I[e] had been near a year at Paris, when, in April last, I received a letter from my father, who pressed my return, and appointed me to meet him immediately at the Hague,/ from whence we returned together; and after a few days stay in London, came down to Belmont,

Volume I 13

where the charms of Lady Julia's conversation, and the esteem she honors me with, entirely compleated my cure, which time, absence,[a] and the Count's tender and affectionate letters, had very far advanced. There is a sweetness in her friendship, my dear Mordaunt, to which love itself must yield the palm;[55] the delicacy, yet vivacity of her sentiments, the soft sensibility of her heart, which without fear listens to vows of eternal amity and esteem.[b] – O Mordaunt, I must not, I do not hope for, I do not indeed wish for, her love; but can it be possible there is a man on earth to whom heaven destines such a blessing?[c]

H. MANDEVILLE.[d]/

To Col.[56] BELLVILLE.

TUESDAY, Belmont.

OH! you have no notion what a reformation:[e] Who but Lady Anne Wilmot at chapel every Sunday?[f] grave, devout, attentive;[g] scarce stealing a look at the prettiest fellow in the world, who sits close by me! Yes, you are undone, Bellville; Harry Mandeville, the young, the gay, the lovely Harry Mandeville, in the full bloom of conquering three and twenty, with all the fire and sprightliness of youth, the exquisite symmetry and easy grace of an Antinous;[57] a countenance open,[h] manly, animated; his hair the brightest chesnut; his complexion brown, flushed with the rose of health; his eyes dark, penetrating, and full of fire, but when he addresses our sex softened into a sweetness which is almost irresistible; his nose inclining to the aquiline;[58] his lips full and red, and his teeth of the most pearly whiteness./

> There, read and die with envy:
> 'You with envy, I with love.'[59]

Fond of me too, but afraid to declare his passion; respectful – awed by the commanding dignity of my manner – poor dear creature,[i] I think I must unbend a little, hide half the rays of my divinity, to encourage so timid a worshiper.

Some flattering tawdry[60] coxcomb,[61] I suppose; some fool with a tolerable outside.[62j]

No, you never was more mistaken, Bellville: his charms I assure you are not all external. His understanding is of the most exalted kind, and has been improved by a very extraordinary education, in projecting which his father has employed much time and thought, and half ruined himself by carrying it into execution. Above all the Col. has cultivated in his son an ardent love of independence, not quite so well/ suited to his fortune; and a generous, perhaps a romantic, contempt of riches, which most parents if they had found would have eradicated with the utmost care. His heart is warm, noble, liberal, benevolent: sincere, and violent in his friendships, he is not less so, though extremely placable,[63] in his

14   *The History of Lady Julia Mandeville*

enmities; scorning disguise, and laying his faults as well as his virtues open to every eye: rash, romantic, imprudent; haughty to the assuming sons of wealth, but to those below him,

> 'Gentle
> As Zephyr blowing underneath the violet:'[64]

But whither am I running? and where was I when this divine creature seduced me from my right path? Oh, I remember, at chapel: it must be acknowledged my digressions are a little Pindaric.[65a] True, as I was saying, I go constantly to chapel./ 'Tis strange, but this lady Belmont has the most unaccountable way in the world of making it one's choice to do whatever she has an inclination one should, without seeming to desire it. One sees so clearly that all she does is right, religion sits so easy upon her, her style of goodness is so becoming, and graceful, that it seems want of taste and elegance not to endeavour[b] to resemble her. Then my Lord too loves to worship in the beauty of holiness; he makes the fine arts subservient to the noblest purpose,[66] and spends as much on serving his Creator as some people of his rank do on a kennel of hounds.[67] We have every external incitement to devotion; exquisite paintings, an admirable organ, fine voices, and the most animated reader of prayers in the universe.

Col. Mandeville, whom I should be extreamly[c] in love with if his son was not five and twenty years younger,[68] leaves us tomorrow/ morning, to join his regiment, the – shire militia: he served in the late war[69] with honour, but meeting with some ill usage from a minister on account of a vote in parliament, he resigned his commission, and gave up his whole time to the education of my lovely Harry, whose tenderness and merit are a full reward for all his generous attention. Adieu!

A. WILMOT.

To Col. BELLVILLE.

Belmont, THURSDAY.

IL divino Enrico[70] is a little in the Penseroso.[71] Poor Harry! I am charmed with his sensibility, he has scarce been himself since he parted with his father yesterday. He apologizes for his chagrin, but says no man on earth has such obligations to a parent. Entre nous,[72] I fancy I know some few sons who would be of a different way of thinking: the Col.[d]/ has literally governed his conduct by the old adage[73] that, 'Learning is better than house and land;' for as his son's learning advanced, his houses and lands melted away, or at least would have done, had it not been for his mother's fortune, every shilling of which, with half the profits of his estate, he expended on Harry's education, who certainly wants only ten thousand pounds a year to be the most charming young fellow in the universe.

Volume I   15

Well he must e'en[74] make the most of his perfections, and endeavour[a] to marry a fortune, on which subject I have a kind of a glimpse of a design, and fancy my friend Harry has not quite so great a contempt of money as I imagined.

You must know then, (a pretty phrase that,[b] but to proceed) you must know, that we accompanied Col. Mandeville fifteen miles, and after dining together at an inn, he took the road to his regiment,/ and we were returning pensive and silent to Belmont, when my Lord, to remove the tender melancholy[c] we had all caught from Harry, proposed a visit at Mr. Westbrook's, a plump, rich, civil, cit,[75] whose house we must of necessity pass. As my lord despises wealth, and Mr. Westbrook's genealogy in the third generation loses itself in a livery stable,[76d] he has always avoided an intimacy; which the other has as studiously sought; but as it is not in his nature to treat any body with ill-breeding, he has suffered their visits, though he has been slow in returning them; and has sometimes invited the daughter to a ball.

The lady wife, who is a woman of great erudition, and is at present intirely lost to the world, all her faculties being on the rack composing a treatise against the immortality of the soul, sent down an apology; and we were entertained by Mademoiselle la Fille,[77] who is little, lean, brown,[78] with small pert black eyes, quickened/ by a large quantity of abominable bad rouge: she talks incessantly, has a great deal of city vivacity, and a prodigious passion for people of a certain rank,[e] a phrase of which she is peculiarly fond. Her mother being above the little vulgar cares of a family, or so unimportant a task as the education of an only child,[79] she was early entrusted[f] to a French chamber-maid, who, having left her own country on account of a Faux Pas[80] which had visible consequences, was appointed to instill the principles of virtue and politeness into the flexible mind of this illustrious heiress of the house of Westbrook, under the title of governess. My information of this morning further says, that, by the cares of this accomplished person, she acquired a competent, though incorrect, knowledge of the French language; with cunning, dissimulation, assurance, and a taste for gallantry; to which if you add a servile passion for quality, and an oppressive insolence to all, however worthy, who want/ that wealth which she owes to her father's skill in Change alley,[81g] you will have an idea of the bride I intend for Harry Mandeville. Methinks,[82] I hear you exclaim; 'Heavens! what a conjunction'! 'Tis mighty well, but people must live, and there is 80,000*l*.[h] attached to this animal, and if the girl likes him, I don't see what he can do better, with birth, and a habit of profuse expence, which he has so little to support. She sung, for the creature sings, a tender Italian air,[83] which she addressed to Harry in a manner and with a look, that convinces me her stile is l'amorose,[84] and that Harry is the present object. After the song I surprised him talking low to her, and pressing her hand, whilst we were all admiring an India cabinet;[85] and on seeing he was observed, he left her with an air of conscious guilt which convinces me he intends to follow the

16   *The History of Lady Julia Mandeville*

pursuit, and is at the same time ashamed of his purpose. Poor fellow! I pity him; but marriage is his/ only card. I'll put the matter forward, and make my lord invite her to the next ball. Don't you think I am a generous creature, to sacrifice the man I love to his own good? When shall I see one of your selfish sex so disinterested? no,[a] you men have absolutely no idea of sentiment.

Adio![86] A. Wilmot.[b]

To George Mordaunt, Esq;

IT is the custom here for every body to spend their mornings as they please, which does not however hinder our sometimes making parties all together[c] when our inclinations happen all to take the same turn. My lord this morning proposed an airing to the ladies, and that we should, instead of returning to dinner, stop at the first neat farm house[d] where we could hope for decent accommodations. Love of variety made the proposal agreeable to us all; and a servant being ordered/ before to make some little provision, we stopped, after the pleasantest airing imaginable, at the entrance of a wood, where, leaving our equipages to be sent to the neighbouring village, we walked up a winding path to a rustic building, embosomed in the grove, the architecture of which was in the most elegant stile of simplicity: the trees round this lovely retreat were covered with wood bines[e] and jessamines, from which a gale of perfume met our approach: the gentlest breath of Zephyr just moved the leaves, the birds sung in the branches, a spring of the clearest water broke from the rising ground on the left, and murmuring along a transparent pebbly bottom, seemed to lose itself in a thicket of roses: no rude sound disturbed the sweet harmony of nature; all breathed the soul of innocence and tranquillity, but a tranquillity raised above itself. My heart danced with pleasure, and the lovely lady Julia happening to be next/ me, I kissed her hand with an involuntary fervor, which called up into her cheeks a blush 'celestial rosy red.'[87] When we entered the house, we were struck with the propriety, the beauty, the simplicity of all around us; the apartments were few, but – airy and commodious; the furniture plain, but new and in the most beautiful taste; no ornaments but vases of flowers, no attendants but country girls, blooming as the morn, and drest with a neatness inexpressible.

After an elegant cold dinner, and a desert of cream and the best fruits in season, we walked into the wood with which the house was surrounded, the romantic variety of which it is impossible to describe; all was nature, but nature in her most pleasing form. We[f] wandered over the sweetly varied[g] scene, resting at intervals in arbours[h] of intermingled roses and jessamines, till we reached a beautiful mossy grotto,/ wildly lovely, whose entrance was almost hid by the vines which flaunted over its top. Here we found tea and coffee prepared as if by invisible hands. Lady[i] Anne exclaimed that all was enchantment; and Lord

Volume I 17

Belmont's eyes sparkled with that lively joy, which a benevolent mind feels in communicating happiness to others.

Lady Julia alone seemed not to taste the pleasures of the day: Her[a] charming eyes had a melancholy languor I never saw in them before: she was reserved, silent, absent; and would not have escaped Lady Anne's raillery, had not the latter been too much taken up with the lovely scene to attend to any thing but joy.

As friendship has a thousand groundless fears, I tremble lest I should have been so unhappy as to offend her:[b] I remember she seemed displeased with my kissing her/ hand, and scarce spoke to me the whole day: I will beg of Lady Anne to ask the cause, for I cannot support the apprehension of having offended her.

It was with difficulty Lord Belmont forced us at night from this enchanting retirement, which he calls his hermitage[88], and which is the scene of his most pleasing hours. To Lady Anne and me it had a charm it did not want, the powerful charm of novelty: it is about four miles from Belmont house, not far distant from the extremities of the park. To this place I am told[c] Lord Belmont often retires, with his amiable family, and those[d] particularly happy in his esteem, to avoid the hurry of company, and give himself up entirely to the uninterrupted sweets of domestic enjoyment. Sure no man but Lord Belmont knows how to live!

H. MANDEVILLE.[e]/

To Col. BELLVILLE.

LORD,[f] these prudes – no, don't let me injure her – these people of high sentiment, are so tremblingly alive all o'er[89][g] – there is poor Harry in terrible disgrace with Lady Julia for only kissing her hand, and amidst so bewitching a scene too, that I am really surprized at his moderation;[h] all breathed the soul of pleasure; – rosy bowers and mossy pillows, cooing doves and whispering Zephyrs[90] – I think my Lord has a strange confidence in his daughter's insensibility to trust her in these seducing groves, and with so divine a fellow in company[i] – But as I was saying, she takes the affair quite seriously, and makes it an offence of the blackest die[j] – Well, I thank my stars, I am not one of these sensitive plants; he might have kissed my hand twenty times[k] without my being more alarmed/ than if a fly had settled there; nay a thousand to one whether I had even been conscious of it at all.

I have laughed her out of her resentment, for it is really absurd; the poor fellow was absolutely miserable about it, and begged my intercession, as if it had been a matter of the highest importance. When I saw her begin to be ashamed of the thing, Really my dear, says I, I am glad you are convinced how ridiculous your anger was for illnatured people might have put strange constructions. – I know but one way of accounting rationally – if I was Harry I should be extremely flattered – one would almost suppose[l] – This answered; – I carryed[m] my point, and

18   *The History of Lady Julia Mandeville*

transferred the pretty thing's anger to me; it blushed with indignation, drew up, and, if mamma had not happened to enter the room at that instant, an agreeable scene of altercation would probably have ensued: she took that opportunity/ of retiring to her apartment, and we saw no more of her till dinner, when she was gracious to Harry, and exceedingly stately to me.

O mon Dieu! I had almost forgot: we are to have a little concert this evening and see, my dear Lord appears to summon me. Adio! Caro![91]

A. WILMOT.[a]

To HENRY MANDEVILLE, Esq;

YES, my dear son, you do me justice: I am never so happy as when I know you are so. I perfectly agree with you as to the charms of Lord Belmont's hermitage, and admire that genuine taste for elegant nature which gives such a spirited variety to the life of the wisest and most amiable of men.

But does it not, my dear Harry, give you at the same time a very contemptible/ idea of the power of greatness to make its possessors happy, to see it thus flying as it were from itself, and seeking pleasure not in the fruition, but in the temporary suspension, of those supposed advantages it has above other conditions of life? Believe me, it is not in the costly dome, but in the rural cott, that the impartial Lord of all has fixed the chearful seat of happiness. Health, peace, content, and soft domestic tenderness,[92] the only real sweets of life, driven from the gilded palace, smile on the humble roof of virtuous industry.

The poor complain not of the tediousness of life: their daily toil makes short the flying hours, and every moment of rest from labour [b]is to them a moment of enjoyment. Not so the great: surrounded from earliest youth by pleasures which court their acceptance, their taste palled by habit, and the too great facility of satiating every wish, lassitude and disgust creep/ on their languid hours; and, wanting the doubtful gale of hope to keep the mind in gentle agitation, it sinks into a dead calm more destructive to every enjoyment than the rudest storm of adversity. The haughty dutchess[c], oppressed with tasteless pomp, and sinking under the weight of her own importance, is much less to be envyed[d] than 'the milk-maid singing blithe,'[93] who is in her eyes the object only of pity and contempt.

Your acquaintance with the great world, my dear Harry, has shown you the splendid misery of superior life: you have seen those most wretched to whom heaven has granted the amplest external means of happiness. Miserable slaves to pride, the most corroding of human passions, strangers to social pleasure, incapable of love or friendship, living to others not to themselves, ever in pursuit of the shadow of happiness, whilst the substance glides past/ them unobserved, they drag on an insipid joyless being: unloved and unconnected, scorning the tender ties which give life all its sweetness, they sink unwept and unlamented to the grave. They know not the conversation of a friend, that conversation which 'brightens the eyes:'[94] their pride, an invasion on the natural rights of mankind, meets with perpetual mortification; and their rage for dissipation, like the burning thirst of a fever, is at once boundless and unquenchable.

Yet, tho'[a] Happiness[b] loves the vale,[95] it would be unjust to confine her to those humble scenes; nor is her presence, as our times afford a shining and amiable example, unattainable to royalty[c] itself; the wise and good, whate'er their rank, led by the hand of simple unerring nature, are seldom known to miss their way to her delightful abode./

You have seen Lord Belmont (blest with wisdom to chuse, and fortune to pursue his choice, convinced that wealth and titles, the portion of few, are not only foreign to, but often inconsistent with, true happiness) seek the lovely goddess, not in the pride of show, the pomp of courts, or the madness of dissipation; but in the calm of retirement, in the bosom of friendship, in the sweets of dear domestic life, in the tender pleasing duties of husband and of father, in the practice of beneficence, and every gentler virtue. Others may be like him convinced, but few like him have spirit and resolution to burst the magic fetters of example and fashion, and nobly dare to be happy.

What pleasure does it give me to find you in so just a way of thinking in regard to fortune! Yes, my dear Harry, all that in reality deserves the name of good, so far as it centers in ourselves, is within/ the reach, not only of our moderate income, but of once much below it. Great wealth is only desirable for the power it gives us of making others happy, and when one sees how very few make this only laudable use of extreme affluence, one acquiesces chearfully in the will of heaven[d], satisfied with not having the temptation of misapplying those gifts of the supreme being[e], for which we shall undoubtedly be accountable.

Nothing can, as you observe, be more worthy a reasonable creature than Lord Belmont's plan of life: he has enlarged his own circle of happiness, by taking into it that of all mankind, and particularly of all around him: his bounty glides unobserved, like the deep silent stream, nor is it by relieving so much as by preventing want, that his generous spirit acts: it is his glory and his pleasure/ that he must go beyond the limits of his own estate to find objects of real distress.

He encourages industry, and keeps up the soul of chearfulness amongst his tenants, by maintaining as much as possible the natural equality of mankind on his estate:[f] His farms are not large, but moderately rented; all are at ease, and can provide happily for their families, none rise to exorbitant wealth. The very cottagers are strangers to all that even approaches want: when the busier seasons of the year are past, he gives them employment in his woods or gardens; and finds double beauties in every improvement there, when he reflects that from thence

20 *The History of Lady Julia Mandeville*

'Health to himself and to his infants bread,
The labourer[a] bears.'[96] –

Plenty, the child of industry, smiles on their humble abodes, and if any unforeseen/ misfortune nips the blossoms of their prosperity, his bounty, descending silent and refreshing as the dews of heaven[b], renews their blooming state, and restores joy to their happy dwellings.

To say all in one word, the maxims by which he governs all the actions of his life are manly, benevolent, enlarged, liberal; and his generous passion for the good of others is rewarded by his Creator[c], whose approbation is his first point of view, with as much happiness to himself as this sublunary state is capable of. Adieu!

Your affectionate   J. MANDEVILLE.[d]

To Col. BELLVILLE.

YES, I am indeed fond of your Italiano; it is the language of Love and the Muses: has a certain softness and all that; – and by no means difficult to understand – at least it is tolerable easy to understand as much of it as I do, as much/ as enables one to be conceited, and give one's self airs amongst those who are totally ignorant: when this happens, I look astonished at the Gothic[97] creatures. – 'Heavens! my dear Madam, not know Italian? how I pity your savage ignorance! not know Italian! La Lingua D'Amore?[98] Oh! Mirtillo! Mirtillo! Anima mia!'[99] – The dear creatures stare, and hate one so cordially, it is really charming. – And if one now and then unluckily blunders upon somebody who is more in the secret than one's self, a downcast look, and Ho vergogna Signora[100],[e] saves all, and does credit at once to one's learning and one's modesty. Flattered too by so plain a confession of their superiority, they give you credit for whatever degree of knowledge you desire, and go away so satisfied – and exclaim in all companies, 'upon[f] my word, Lady Anne Wilmot is absolutely an exquisite mistress of Italian, only a little too diffident.'/

I am just come from playing at ball in the garden, Lord Belmont of the party: this sweet old man! I am half in love with him, though I have no kind of hopes, for he told me yesterday, that, lovely as I was, Lady Belmont was in his eyes a thousand times more so. How amiable is age like his! so condescending to the pleasures of the young! so charmed to see them happy! he[g] gains infinitely in point of love by this easy goodness, and as to respect, his virtues cannot fail to command it.

Oh! à propos to age, my Lord says he is sure I shall be a most agreeable old woman, and I am almost of his opinion. Adieu! creature! I can no more.

By the way, do you know that Harry's Cittadina[h] has taken a prodigious Penchant[101] for me, and vows no woman on earth has so much wit, or spirit, or

Volume I   21

politesse,[102] as Lady Anne Wilmot.[a] Something like a glimmering/ of taste this: I protest I begin to think the girl not quite so intolerable.

Je suis votre,[103]

To the Earl of BELMONT.

My Lord,

AN unforeseen inevitable misfortune having happened to me, for which a too careless œconomy had left me totally unprovided, I find it necessary to sell my estate and quit the country.

I could find a ready purchaser in Mr. Westbrook, who, with the merciless rapacity of an exchange-broker, watches like a harpy[104] the decline of every gentleman's fortune in this neighbourhood, in order to seize on his possessions: but the tender affection I bear my tenants, makes me solicitous to consult their good as much as possible in the sale, since my hard fate/ will not allow me longer to contribute to it myself: I will not here say more than that I cannot provide more effectually for their happiness than by selling to your lordship.

I am, my[b] Lord,
Your Lordship's most
Obedient[c] and devoted Servant,
JAMES BARKER.

To JAMES BARKER, Esq;

SIR,

I Am extremely concerned any accident should have happened which makes it possible I should lose from my neighbourhood a gentleman of family, of so very worthy a character, and one I so greatly esteem: but I hope means may be found to prevent what would be so extremely/ regretted by all who have the pleasure of knowing you.

As I have always regarded the independent country gentlemen[105] as the strength and glory of this kingdom, and the best supports of our excellent constitution, no increase of power or property to myself shall ever tempt me to lessen the number of them, where it can possibly be avoided. If you have resolution to enter on so exact a system of œconomy as will enable you to repay[d] any sum you may want in seven years, whatever that sum is, I shall be most happy in advancing it and will take it back in the manner most easy to you. I think I could trace out a plan by which you might retrench considerably in a manner scarce perceptible. I will to-morrow morning call upon you when I am riding out, when we will talk further on this subject; be assured, none of the greedy Leviathans[106] of our days can feel half the/ pleasure in compleating a purchase that I shall do in declining this, if I can be so happy as to keep you amongst us. Your accepting this without

22 *The History of Lady Julia Mandeville*

hesitation, will be a proof of your esteem which I can never forget, as it will shew you think too highly of me to fear my making an ill use hereafter of having had the happiness of doing for you what, if we were to change present situations, I know you would rejoice in doing for me. I have a fund which I call the bank of friendship[a], on which it is my rule to take no interest, which you may command to its utmost extent.

I am, dear[b] Sir,

Your affectionate friend,
and obedient servant,
BELMONT./

To Col. BELLVILLE.

THURSDAY.

WE have been dining Al fresco[107] in a rustic temple in a wood near the house: romanesque,[108] simple; the pillars trunks of ancient oaks, the roof the bark of trees, the pavement pebbles, the seats moss; the wild melody of nature our musick; the distant sound of the cascade just breaks on the ear, which, joined by the chant[c] of the birds, the cooing of the doves, the lowing of the herds, and the gently breathing[d] western[e] breeze, forms a concert most divinely harmonious.

Really this place would be charming if it was a little more replete with human beings; but to me the finest landscape is a dreary wild, unless adorned by a few groups of figures. – There are 'squires indeed –/ well absolutely[f] your 'squires are an agreeable race of people, refined, sentimental,[109] formed for the Belle passion; tho'[g] it must be owned the 'squires[h] about Belmont are rational animals compared to those my Caro Sposo[110] used to associate with: my Lord has exceedingly humanized them, and their wives and daughters are decent creatures: which really amazed me at first, for you know, Bellville, there is in general no standing the country misses.

Your letter is just brought me: all you say of levees[111] and drawing rooms, is thrown away.

'Talk not to me of courts, for I disdain
All courts when he is by: far be the noise
Of kings and courts from us, whose gentle souls
Our kinder stars have steered[i] another way.'[112]/

Yes, the rural taste prevails; my plan of life is fixed; to sit under a hill and keep sheep with Harry Mandeville.

O mon Dieu! what do I see coming down the avenue? Is it in woman to resist that equipage? Papier machée – highly gilded – loves and doves – six long tailed[j] grey Arabians – by[k] all the gentle powers of love and gallantry, Fondville himself[l] – the dear enchanting creature –[m] nay then – poor Harry – all is over with him

Volume I 23

– I discard him this moment, and take Fondville for my Cecisbeo – fresh from Paris – just imported – O[a] all ye gods!

FRIDAY Morning.
I left you somewhat abruptly, and am returned to fill up my epistle with the adventures of yesterday./

The great gates being thrown open, and the chariot drawn up to the steps, my charming Fondville, drest in a suit of light-coloured[b] silk embroidered with silver, a hat with a black feather under his arm, and a large bouquet of artificial flowers in his button-hole, all Arabia breathing from his well-scented[c] handkerchief, descended, like Adonis from the carr of Venus,[113] and, full of the idea of his own irresistibility, advanced towards the saloon – he advanced not with the doubtful air of a bashful lover intimidated by a thousand tender fears, but in a minuet[114] step, humming an opera tune, and casting a side glance at every looking glass in his way. The first compliments being over, the amiable creature seated himself by me, and begun the following conversation:

Well, but my dear lady Anne, this is so surprizing – your ladyship[d] in Campagna?[115] I thought Wilmot had given you a surfeit of the poet's Elyzium[116] – horrid retirement[e]/ – how do you contrive to kill time? – tho'[f] Harry Mandeville indeed – a widow of spirit may find some amusement there.[g]

Why really, Fondville, a pretty fellow does prodigiously soften the horrors of solitude.[h]

O, nothing so well.[i]

And Harry has his attractions.[j]

Attractions! ah! L'Amore![117] the fairest eyes of Rome –[k]

But pray, my dear lord, how did the court bear my absence?[l]

In despair: the very Zephyrs[118] about Versailles have learnt to sigh, la belle Angloise.[119m] /

And Miremont?[n]

Inconsolable: staid away from two operas.[o]

Is it possible? the dear constant creature! how his sufferings touch me – but here is company.[p]

Any body one knows?[q]

I rather think not.[r]

What the good company of the Environs,[120] the Arriere ban,[121] the Posse Comitatus?[122s]

Even so: my lord 'brings down the natives upon us,'[123] but, to do the creatures justice, one shall seldom see tamer savages.[t]

Here the door opening, Fondville rose with us all, and leaning against the wainscoat[u],/ in an attitude of easy indifference, half bowing, without deigning to turn his eyes on those who entered the room, continued playing my fan,[124]

24 The History of Lady Julia Mandeville

and talking to me in a half whisper,[125] till all were seated; when my dear lady Belmont, leading the conversation, contrived to make it general, till, tea being over, my lord proposed a walk in the gardens; where having trifled away an hour very pleasantly, we found music ready in the saloon at our return, and danced till midnight.

Lord Viscount Fondville (he would not have you omit Viscount for the world)[a] left us this morning: my lord is extremely polite and attentive to him, on the supposition of his being my lover; otherwise he must expect no supernumerary[126] civilities at Belmont; for, as it is natural to value most those advantages one possesses ones self,[b] my lord, whose nobility is but of the third generation, but whose ancestry loses/ itself in the clouds, pays much greater respect to a long line of illustrious ancestors than to the most lofty titles; and I am sorry to say my dear Fondville's pedigree will not stand the test; he owes his fortune and rank to the iniquity of his father, who was deep in the infamous secret of the South Sea bubble.[127]

'Tis however a good-natured, inoffensive, lively, showy animal, and does not flatter disagreeably. He owns Belmont not absolutely shocking, and thinks lady Julia rather tolerable, if she was so happy as to have a little of my spirit and enjouement. [128c] Adio![d]

A. WILMOT.

O Ciel! what a memory! this is not post day. You may possibly gain a line or two by this strange forgetfulness of mine./

SATURDAY.

Nothing new, but that La Signora Westbrook, who visited here yesterday, either was, or pretended to be, taken ill before her coach came, and Harry, by her own desire, attended her home in lady Julia's post chaise.[129] He came back with so grave an air, that I fancy she had been making absolute, plain, down-right love to him: her ridiculous fondness begins to be rather perceptible to every body: really[e] these city girls are so rapid in their amours,[130] they won't give a man time to breathe.

Once more, Adieu[f]!/

To GEORGE MORDAUNT, Esq;

June 13th.[g]

I Have just received a letter which makes me the most unhappy of mankind: 'tis from a lady whose fortune is greatly above my most sanguine hopes, and whose merit and tenderness deserve that heart which I feel it is not in my power to give her. The general complacency of my behaviour to the lovely sex, and my having been accidentally her partner at two or three balls, has deceived her into an

Volume I 25

opinion that she is beloved by me; and she imagines she is only returning a passion, which her superiority of fortune has prevented my declaring. How much is she to be pitied! my heart knows too well the pangs of disappointed love not to feel most tenderly for the sufferings of another, without the additional motive to compassion of being the undesigned/[131] cause of those sufferings, the severest of which human nature is capable. I am embarrassed to the greatest degree, not what resolution to take, that required not a moment's deliberation, but how to soften the stroke, and in what manner, without wounding her delicacy, to decline an offer, which she has not the least doubt of my accepting with all the eager transport of timid love, surprised by unexpected success.

I have wrote[a] to her, and think I shall send this answer; I enclose[b] you a copy of it: her letter is already destroyed: her name I conceal.[c] The honor of a lady is too sacred to be trusted, even to the faithful breast of a friend./

To Miss [d]–

NO words, madam, can express the warmth of my gratitude[132] for your generous intentions in my favor, tho'[e] my ideas of probity will not allow me to take advantage of them.

To rob a gentleman, by whom I have been treated with the utmost hospitality, not only of his whole fortune, but of, what is infinitely more valuable, a beloved and amiable daughter, is an action so utterly inconsistent with those sentiments of honor which I have always cultivated, as even your perfections cannot tempt me to be guilty of. I must therefore, however unwillingly, absolutely decline the happiness you have had the goodness to permit/ me to hope for, and beg leave to subscribe myself,

Madam,
with the utmost gratitude
and most lively esteem,
your most obliged and
devoted servant,
H. Mandeville.

I ought perhaps to be more explicit in my refusal of her, but I cannot bring myself to shock her sensibility, by an appearance of total indifference. Surely this is sufficiently clear, and as much as can be said by a man sensible of, and grateful for, so infinite an obligation.

You will smile when I own, that, in the midst of my concern for this lady, I feel a secret, and, I fear, an ungenerous, pleasure, in sacrificing her to lady Julia's friendship, tho'[f] the latter will never be sensible of the sacrifice./

Yes, my friend, every idea of an establishment in the world, however remote or however advantageous, dies away before the joy of being esteemed by her, and

26 *The History of Lady Julia Mandeville*

at liberty to cultivate that esteem; determined[a] against marriage, I have no wish, no hope, but that of being for ever unconnected, for ever blest in her conversation, for ever allowed, uninterrupted, unrestrained by nearer ties, to hear that enchanting voice, to swear on that snowy hand eternal amity, to listen to the unreserved sentiments of the most beautiful mind in the creation, uttered with the melody of angels. Had I worlds, I would give them to inspire her with the same wishes!

H. MANDEVILLE.[b]/

To Col. BELLVILLE.

WEDNESDAY Night.

I Can't conceive, Bellville, what it is that makes me so much the men's taste: I really think I am not handsome – not so very handsome – not so handsome as lady Julia, – yet I don't know how it is – I am persecuted to death amongst you – the misfortune to please every body – 'tis amazing – no regularity of features – fine eyes indeed – a vivid bloom – a seducing smile – an elegant form – an air of the world – and something extremely well in the Toute ensemble[133] – a kind of an agreeable manner – easy, spirited, Degagée[134] – and for the understanding – I flatter myself malice itself cannot deny me the beauties of the mind. You might justly say to me, what the queen of Sweden[135] said to Mademoiselle le Fevre,[136] 'with such an understanding,/ are not you ashamed to be handsome?'[137]

THURSDAY Morning.

Absolutely deserted. Lord and Lady Belmont are gone to town this morning on sudden and unexpected business: poor Harry's situation would have been pitiable, had not my lord, considering how impossible it was for him to be well with us both à Trio,[138] sent to Fondville to spend a week here in their absence, which they hope will not be much longer. Harry, who is viceroy, with absolute power, has only one commission, to amuse lady Julia and me, and not let us pass a languid hour till their return.

O Dio![139] Fondville's Arabians![140] the dear creature looks up – he bows – 'That bow might from the bidding of the gods command me' –/[141]

Don't you love quotations! I am immensely fond of them: a certain proof of erudition: and, in my sentiments, to be a woman of literature is to be –– In short, my dear Bellville, I early in life discovered, by the meer[142] force of genius; that there were two characters only in which one might take a thousand little innocent freedoms, without being censured by a parcel of impertinent old women,[c] those of a Belle Esprit[143] and a Methodist;[144] and, the latter not being in my style, I chose to set up for the former, in which I have had the happiness to succeed so much beyond my hopes, that the first question now asked amongst polite peo-

Volume I 27

ple, when a new piece comes out, is, 'What does lady Anne Wilmot say of it?' A scornful smile from me would damn the best play that ever was wrote[a]; as a look of approbation, for I am naturally merciful, has saved many a dull[b] one. In short, if you should happen to write an insipid poem, which is extremely/ probable, send it to me, and my Fiat[145] shall crown you with immortality.

Oh! heavens! à propos, do you know that Bell Martin, in the wane of her charms, and past the meridian of her reputation, is absolutely married[c] to sir Charles Canterell? Astonishing! till I condescend to give the clue. She praised his bad verses. A thousand things appear strange in human life, which, if one had the real key, are only natural effects of a hidden cause. 'My dear sir Charles, says Bell, that divine sapphic[146] of yours – those melting sounds – I have endeavoured[d] to set it – But[e] Orpheus[147] or Amphion[148] alone – I would sing it – yet fear to trust my own heart – such extatic numbers – who that has a soul' – She sung half a stanza, and, overcome by the magic force of verse, leaning on his breast, as if absorbed in speechless transport, 'she fainted, sunk, and dyed away'.[149] Find me the poet upon earth who could have/ withstood this. He married her the next morning.

Oh! Ciel![150] I forgot the Caro[151] Fondville. I am really inhuman. Adieu!

'Je suis votre amie tres fidelle'.[152]

I can absolutely afford no more at present.

To Henry Mandeville, Esq;

London, June 20th.[f]

YOU can have no idea, my dear Mr. Mandeville, how weary I am of being these few days only in town: that any one, who is happy enough to have a house, a cottage, in the country, should continue here at this season, is to me inconceivable: but that gentlemen of large property, that noblemen, should imprison themselves in this smoking furnace, when the whole land is a blooming garden, a wilderness of sweets; when pleasure courts/ them in her fairest form; nay, when the sordid god of modern days, when Interest joins his potent voice; when power, the best power, that of doing good, solicits their presence, can only be accounted for, by supposing them under the dominion of fascination, spell-caught by some malicious demon, an enemy to human happiness.

I cannot resist addressing them in a stanza or two of a poem, which deserves to be written in letters of gold:

'Mean time, by pleasure's sophistry allur'd,
From the bright sun and living breeze ye stray:
And, deep in London's gloomy haunts immur'd,
Brood o'er your fortune's, freedom's health's decay,
O, blind of choice, and to yourselves untrue!/

28   *The History of Lady Julia Mandeville*

The young grove shoots, their bloom the fields renew,
The mansion asks its lord, the swains their friend;
While he doth riot's orgies haply share,
Or tempt the gamester's dark destroying snare,
Or at some courtly shrine with slavish incense bend.
And yet full oft your anxious tongues complain
That careless tumult prompts the rustic throng;
That the rude village inmates now disdain
Those homely ties which rul'd their fathers long:
Alas! your fathers did by other arts
Draw those kind ties around their simple hearts,
And led in other paths their ductile will:/
By succours, faithful counsel, courteous chear,
Won them the ancient manners to revere,
To prize their country's peace, and heaven's due rites fulfil.[153]

Can a nobleman of spirit prefer the rude insults of a licentious London rabble, the refuse of every land, to the warm and faithful attachment of a brave, a generous, a free, and loyal yeomanry in the country.[a] Does not interest, as well as virtue and humanity, prompt them, by living on their estates, to imitate the heavens, which return the moisture they draw from the earth, in grateful dews and flowers?

When I first came to Belmont, having been some years abroad, I found my tenants poor and dejected, scarce able to gain a hard penurious living. The neighbouring gentlemen spending two thirds of/ the year in London, and the town, which was the market for my estate, filled only with people in trade, who could scarce live by each other:[b] I struck at the root of this evil, and, by living almost altogether in the country myself, brought the whole neighbourhood to do the same:[c] I promoted every kind of diversion, which soon filled my town with gentlemen's families, which raised the markets, and of consequence the value of my estate: my tenants grew rich at the same rents which before they were unable to pay; population increased,[d] my villages were full of inhabitants, and all around me was gay and flourishing.[e] So simple, my dear Mr. Mandeville, are the maxims of true policy: but it must be so; that machine which has the fewest wheels is certainly most[f] easy to keep in order.

Have you had my old men to dine? at sixty I admit them to my table, where they are always once a fortnight my guests./ I love to converse with those, 'whom age and long experience render wise';[154] and, in my idea of things, it is time to slacken the reins of pride, and to wave all sublunary distinctions, when they are so near being at an end between us. Besides I know, by my own feelings, that age wants the comforts of life: a plentiful table, generous wines, chearful[155] converse, and the notice of those they have been accustomed to revere, renews in some degree the fire of youth, gives a spring to declining nature, and perhaps prolongs as well as enlivens[a] the evening of their days. Nor is it a small addition to my satisfaction, to see the respect paid them by the young of their own rank, from the observation of their being thus distinguished by me: as an old man, I have a kind of interest in making age an object of reverence; but, were I ever so young, I would continue a custom, which appears to me not less just than humane./

Adieu! my esteemed, my amiable friend! how I envy you your larks and nightingales!

Your faithful BELMONT.

To Col. BELLVILLE.

THURSDAY.

POSITIVELY, Bellville, I can answer for nothing: these sylvan[156] scenes are so very bewitching, the vernal grove, and balmy Zephyr,[157] are so favourable to a lover's prayer, that, if Fondville was any thing but a pretty man about town,[b] my situation would be extremely critical.

This wicked Harry too has certainly some evil design; he forms nothing but enchanting rural parties, either à quarrée,[158] or with others of the young and gay: not a maiden aunt has appeared at Belmont since his reign commenced. He suffers no ideas to enter our imaginations but those/ of youth, beauty, love, and the seducing pleasures of the golden age. We dance on the green, dine at the Hermitage,[c] and wander in the woods by moonlight, listening to the song of the nightingale, or the sweeter notes of that little syren[159] lady Julia, whose impassioned sounds would soften the marble heart of a virgin of eighty-five.

I really tremble for my fair friend; young, artless, full of sensibility, exposed hourly to the charms of the prettiest fellow upon earth, with a manner so soft, so tender, so much in her own romantic way –

A rap at my door – Fondville is sent for away – company at his house – sets out immediately – I must bid the dear creature adieu –

I am returned: pity me, Bellville.[d]/

'The streams, the groves, the rocks remain,
But Damon still I seek in vain.'[160]

Yes, the dear man is gone; Harry is retired to write letters, and Lady Julia and I are going to take a walk, Tete à Tete,[161] in the wood. Jesu Maria! a female Tete à Tete! – I shall never go through the operation – if we were en confidence[162] indeed, it might be bearable: but the little innocent fool has not even a secret.

Adio!

Your's[e] A. WILMOT.[f]/

To George Mordaunt, Esq;

O[a] Mordaunt! I am indeed undone: I was too confident of my own strength: I depended on the power of gratitude and honor over my heart, but find them too weak to defend me against such inexpressible loveliness:[b] I could have resisted her beauty only, but the mind which irradiates those speaking eyes – the melting music of those gentle accents, 'soft as the fleeces of descending snows,'[163] the delicacy, yet lively tenderness of her sentiments – that angel innocence – that winning sweetness – the absence of her parents, and lady Anne's coquetry with lord Fondville, have given me opportunities of conversing with her, which have for ever destroyed my peace – I must tear myself from her – I will leave Belmont the moment my lord returns – I am for ever lost – doomed to wretchedness – but/ I will be wretched alone – I tremble lest my eyes should have discovered – lest pity should involve her in my misery.

Great heavens! was I not sufficiently unhappy? to stab me to the heart, I have just received the following letter from lord Belmont.[c]

To[d] Henry Mandeville, Esq;

June 22d.

THE present member of parliament for – being in a state of health which renders his life extremely uncertain, it would be very agreeable to me if my dear Mr. Mandeville would think of offering himself a candidate to succeed him. I will however be so plain as to tell him, he will have no assistance from me except my wishes, and has nothing to trust to but his merits and the name of Mandeville;/ it being a point both of conscience and honor with me, never to intermeddle in elections. The preservation of our happy constitution depends on the perfect independence of each part of which it is composed on the other two:[164] and the moment, heaven grant that moment to be far distant![e] when the house of lords can make a house of commons, liberty and prerogative will cease to be more than names, and both prince and people become slaves.[f165]

I therefore always, tho'[g] the whole town is mine, leave the people to their free and uninfluenced choice: never interfering farther than to insist on their keeping themselves as unbiassed[h] as I leave them. I would not only withdraw my favor from, but prosecute, the man who was base enough to take a bribe, tho'[i] he who offered it was my nearest friend./

By this means I have the pleasure also of keeping myself free, and at liberty to confer favors where I please; so that I secure my own independence by not invading that of others.

This conduct, I cannot help thinking, if general, would preserve the ballance[j] of our glorious constitution; a ballance of much greater consequence to Britons than the ballance of power in Europe, tho'[k] so much less the object of their attention. In this we resemble those persons, who, whilst they are busied in regulating the domestic concerns of their neighbours,[a] suffer their own to be ruined.

But to return from this unintended digression: You will perhaps object to what I have proposed, that during your father's life you are not qualified for a seat in parliament.[b] I have obviated this objection. Lady Mary, the only sister of my father,/ has an ample fortune in her own power to dispose of: some part of it was originally her own, but much the larger part was left her by her lover, Sir Charles Barton, who was killed in queen[c] Anne's wars,[166] the very morning before he was to have set out for England to complete his marriage. Being the last of his family, he had made a will, in which he left his estate to lady Mary,[167] with a request, that, if she did not marry, she would leave it to one of the name of Mandeville. As she loves merit, and has the happiness and honor of our house warmly at heart, I have easily prevailed on her to settle 500l.[d] a year on you at the present, and to leave you a good part of the rest at her death. Her design hitherto, I will not conceal from you, has been to leave her fortune to my daughter, of whom she is infinitely fond; but Julia has enough, and by leaving it to you, she more exactly fulfils the will of Sir Charles, who, tho'[e] he has not expressly made the/ distinction, certainly meant it to a male of the Mandeville name. The estate is about 2000l.[f] a year; her own fortune of 14000l.[g] I shall not oppose her leaving to my daughter.

I know too well the generous sentiments of your heart to doubt that, in procuring this settlement, I give to my country a firm and unshaken patriot, at once above dependence on the most virtuous court, and the mean vanity of opposing the just measures of his prince[h], from a too eager desire of popularity: not that I would have you insensible to praise, or the esteem of your country; but seek it only by deserving it, and tho'[i] it be in part the reward, let it not be the motive of your actions: let your own approbation be your first view, and that of others only your second.

You may observe, my dear Mr. Mandeville, I only caution you against being led/ away by youthful vanity to oppose the just measures of your prince:[j] I should wrong the integrity of your heart, if I supposed you capable of distressing the hands of government for mercenary or ambitious purposes: a virtuous senator will regard, not men, but measures, and will concur with his bitterest enemies in every salutary and honest purpose; or rather, in a public light, he will have no enemies, but the enemies of his country.

It is with caution I give even these general hints; far be it from me to attempt to influence your judgment: let your opinion be ever free and your own; or, where your inexperience may want information, seek it from the best, and most enlighten'd[k] of mankind, your excellent father, who has long sat with honor in the same house.

Let me now, my amiable friend, thank you for your obliging attention, not only/ to the ladies, of whom I could not doubt your care, but of my tenants, one of whom writes me word, that, coming to enquire when I should return, with a look of anxiety which shew'd[a] my return was of consequence to him, you took him aside, and, enquiring his business, found he wanted, from an accident which had involved him in a temporary distress, to borrow 100*l.*[b] for which you gave him a draught on your banker, with a goodness and sweetness of manner, which doubled the obligation; making only one condition, which the overflowing of his gratitude has made him unable to keep, that it should be a secret to all the world.

Can Lady Mary do too much for a man who thus shews himself worthy the name of Mandeville, the characteristick[c] of which has ever been the warmest benevolence?/

Another would, perhaps, insist on returning the money to you, but I will not rob you of the pleasure of making an honest man happy: you will however observe, that it is this once only I indulge you; and that you are the only person from whom I have ever suffered my family, for such I esteem all placed by Providence under my protection, to receive an obligation: 'tis a favor I have refused even to your father.

Do not answer this: I shall possibly be with you before a letter could reach me.

Adieu. Your affectionate BELMONT.[d]

Can I, after this letter, my dear Mordaunt, entertain a wish for lady Julia, without the blackest ingratitude? no, tho' I will not accept his generous offer, I can never forget he has made it. I will leave Belmont – I will forget her – what[e] have I said? forget her? I must first lose all sense of my own being./

Am I born to know every species of misery? I have this moment received a second letter from the lady I once mention'd[f] to you, filled with the softest and most affecting expressions of disinterested tenderness: indiscreet from excess of affection, she adjures me to meet her one moment in the rustic temple, where she is waiting for me; her[g] messenger is gone, and, as I will not hazard exposing her by sending my servant, I have no choice left but to go: Heaven knows how unwillingly! should we be seen, what an appearance would such a meeting have! I left Lady Julia to write letters, and on that account excus'd[h] myself from attending her: yet can I leave her whom love alone has made imprudent, to the consequence of her indiscretion, and the wild sallies of a mind torn by disappointment and despair! I will go: but how shall I behold her! how tell her pity is all I can return to so generous a passion? These trials are too great for a heart like mine,/ tender, sympathetic, compassionate; and softened by the sense of it's[i] own sufferings: I shall expire with regret and confusion at her sight. Farewell.

H. MANDEVILLE.[j]

Volume I 33

To Col. BELLVILLE.

OUR party last night did not turn out so much in the still-life way as I expected – unfortunate that I am – two rivals at once – la Bellissima[168] Julia has most certainly a penchant for Harry – 'tis absurd, for the thing is impossible. In the first place I am rather afraid he has a kind of attachment to this creature, and in the second, I know Lord Belmont's sentiments on this head, and, that with all his generosity, no man breathing has a greater aversion to unequal marriages:[169] the difference is so immense in every thing but birth and merit, that there remains not a shadow of hope for her. But these people of high/ heroics are above attending to such trifling things as possibilities – I hope I am mistaken, but the symptoms are strong upon her, as you shall judge.

I left you last night, to accompany Lady Julia to the wood we are both so fond of: the evening was lovely beyond description, and we were engaged in a very lively conversation; when, as we approached the temple, we saw Harry, who had just left us on pretence of writing letters, come out of it with the detestable Westbrook leaning familiarly on his arm, her pert eyes softened into languishment, and fixed eagerly on his: the forward creature started at seeing us, and attempted to fly, which Harry prevented, and, withdrawing his arm from hers, as if mechanically, advanc'd[a] slowly towards us, with a look so confus'd[b], a mien so disorder'd[c], so different from that easy air which gives ten thousand graces to the finest form in the world, as convinced me/ that this meeting was not accidental. Lady Julia stop'd[d] the moment she saw them; a deep blush overspread her face, she fixed her eyes on the ground, and waited their approach silent and unmov'd as a statue. Not so the cit:[e] the creature's assurance, and the ease with which she recovered herself and addressed Lady Julia, excited equally my astonishment and indignation. She told her she came to wait on her Ladyship, and the fineness of the evening had tempted her to leave her coach at the entrance of the wood: that as she walked thro'[f] she happen'd[g] to meet Mr. Mandeville, quite by chance she assured her Ladyship; as he would testify. Harry disdain'd[h] to confirm her falshood[i] even by an assenting look: his silence, the coldness of his manner, with the air of dignity and spirit Lady Julia assumed, almost disconcerted her; we walk'd[j] silently to the house, where the girl only stay'd[k] till her coach was order'd round, and then left us; her eyes/ ask'd[l] Harry's attendance, but he chose not to understand their language.

This evening was the only unpleasant one I ever past[m] at Belmont: a reserve unknown before in that seat of sincere friendship, took place of the sweet confidence which used to reign there, and to which it owes its most striking charms. We[n] retired earlier than usual, and Lady Julia, instead of spending half an hour in my apartment, as usual, took leave of me at the door and passed on to her own.

34   *The History of Lady Julia Mandeville*

I am extremely alarmed for her – it would have been natural to have talked[a] over so extraordinary an adventure with me, if not too nearly interested – There was a constraint in her behaviour to Harry all the evening – an assumed[b] coldness – his assiduity seem'd[c] to displease her – she sighed often – nay once, when my eyes met hers, I observed a tear ready to start – she may/ call this friendship if she pleases, but these very tender, these apprehensive, these jealous friendships, between amiable young people of different sexes, are exceedingly suspicious.

It is an hour later than her usual time of appearing, and I hear nothing of her: I am determined not to indulge this tender melancholy, and have sent up to let her know I attend her in the saloon,[170] for I often breakfast in my own apartment, it being the way here for every body to do whatever they like. –

Indeed! a letter from Lady Julia! – a vindication? – nay then – 'guilty upon my honor.' – Why imagine I suspect her? – O! Conscience! Conscience![d]

Her extreme fear of my supposing her in love with Harry, is a convincing proof that she is, tho' such is her amiable sincerity,/ that I am sure she has deceived herself before she would attempt to deceive me; but the latter is not so easy; sitters by see all the game.

She tells me, she cannot see me till she has vindicated herself from a suspicion which the weakness of her behaviour yesterday may have caused: That she is not sure she has resolution to mention the subject when present; therefore takes this way to assure me, that, tender and lively as her friendship for Mr. Mandeville is, it is only friendship; a friendship which his merit has hitherto justified, and which has been the innocent pleasure of her life. That born with too keen sensibilities (poor thing! I pity her sensibilities) the ill treatment of her friends wounds her to the soul. That[e] zeal for his honor and the integrity of his character, which she thinks injured by the mysterious air of last night's/ adventure, her shock at a clandestine and dissembled appointment so inconsistent with that openness which she had always admired in him, as well as with the respect due to her, now so particularly in her father's absence under his protection, had occasioned that concern which she fears may make her appear to me more weak than she is.[f]

In short, she takes a great deal of pains to lead herself into an error; and struggles in those toils which she will find great difficulty in breaking.

Harry's valet has just told my woman his master was in bed but two hours last night: that he walked about his room till three, and rose again at five, and went out on horseback, without a servant. The poor fellow is frighted[171] to death about him, for he is idolized by his servants,/ and this man has been with him from his child–hood.[g] But adieu! I hear Lady Julia upon the stairs: I must meet her in the saloon.

Eleven o'clock.

Poor soul! I never saw any thing like her confusion when we met: she blushed, she trembled, and sunk half motionless into her chair:[a] I made the tea, without taking the least notice of her inability to do it; and by my easy chit chat[b] manner soon brought her to be a little composed: though her eye was often turned towards the door, though she started at every sound, yet she never asked the cause of Harry's absence, which must however surprize her, as he always breakfasts below.

Foreseeing we should be a very awkward party to day a Trio,[c] I sent early in the morning to ask three or four very agreeable/ girls about two miles off, to come and ramble all day with us in the woods: happily for poor Lady Julia, they came in before we had done breakfast, and I left them to go and look at some shellwork,[172] whilst I came up to finish my letter.

Harry is come back, and has sent to speak with me: I am really a person of great consequence at present. I am in a very ill humor[d] with him; he may well be ashamed to appear, however the worst of criminals deserves to be heard. I will admit him: he is at the door. Adio.[e]

A. Wilmot.[f]/

To George Mordaunt, Esq;

Wednesday, Five in the Morning.

GREAT heaven! what a night have I past! all other fears give way before that of displeasing her. Yes, let me be wretched, but let her not suppose me unworthy: let her not see me in the light of a man who barters the sentiments of his soul for sordid views of avarice or ambition, and, using means proportioned to the baseness of his end, forges a falsehood to excuse his attendance on her, seduces an heiress to give him clandestine assignations, and in a place guarded, doubly guarded at this time, by the sacred and inviolable laws of hospitality, from such unworthy purposes.

I will clear my conduct, though at the hazard of exposing her whose love for me/ deserves a different treatment: let her be the victim of that indiscretion by which she has ruined me – and can I be thus base? – Can I betray the believing unsuspecting heart? – My[g] mind is distracted – but why do I say betray? I know Lady Anne's greatness of mind, and for Lady Julia – yes, the secret will be as safe with them as in my own bosom.

Shall I own all my folly? I cannot, though she shall never know my passion for herself, support one moment the idea of Lady Julia's imagining I love another.

I will go to Lady Anne, as soon as she is up, and beg her to convince her lovely friend my meeting this Lady was accidental: I will not, if I can avoid it, say more./

36 *The History of Lady Julia Mandeville*

I cannot see her before this explanation. I will ride out, and breakfast with some friend: I would not return till they are gone back to their apartments, that I may see Lady Anne alone.

Twelve o'clock.

Lady Anne has probed me to the quick: I have trusted her without reserve as to this affair, I have begged her to vindicate me to Lady Julia, who is walking in the garden with some ladies of the neighborhood:[a] we are going to follow them, I am to take the ladies aside, whilst Lady Anne pleads my cause: she calls me. Farewell.

Twelve at Night.

She forgives me, and I am most happy. Lady Anne has told her all, and has had the goodness to introduce me to her as we walked, unobserved by the ladies who/ were with us. I have kissed her hand as a seal of my pardon. That moment! O Mordaunt![b] with what difficulty did I restrain the transport of my soul!

Yes, my friend, she forgives me, a sweet benign serenity reigns in her lovely eyes; she approves my conduct; she is pleased with the concern I show[c] at giving pain to the heart which loves me; her chearfulness is returned, and has restored mine; she rules every movement of my heart as she pleases: never did I pass so happy a day. I am all joy; no sad idea can enter; I have scarce room even for the tender compassion I owe to her I have made wretched. I am going to bed,[d] but without the least expectation of sleep: joy will now have the same effect as I last night found from a contrary cause. Adieu!

H. MANDEVILLE.[e]/

To Col. BELLVILLE.

THURSDAY Morning.

I Have reconciled the friends: the scene was amazingly pathetic and pretty: I am only sorry I am too lazy to describe it. He kissed her hand, without her showing[f] the least symptom of anger; she blushed indeed, but, if I understand blushes – in short, times are prodigiously changed.

The strange misses were of infinite use, as they broke the continuity of the tender scene (if I may be allowed the expression) which, however entertaining to Les Amies,[173] would have been something sickly to my Ladyship, if it had lasted.

And now having united, it must be my next work to divide them; for seriously I am apt to believe, the dear creatures are/ in immense danger of a kind of partiality[g] for each other, which would not be quite so convenient.

I have some thoughts, being naturally sentimental and generous, of taking Harry myself, meerly[h] from companion to Lady Julia. Widows, you know, are in some degree the property of handsome young fellows, who have more merit than fortune; and there would be something very heroic in devoting myself to

Volume I 37

save my friend. I always told you, Bellville, I was more an antique Roman than a Briton. But I must leave you: I hear Lady Julia coming to fetch me: we breakfast à Trio in a bower of roses.

O heavens![a] the plot begins to thicken – Lucretia's dagger– Rosamonda's bowl[174] – Harry has had a letter from his charmer – vows she can't live without him – determined to die unless the barbarous man relents./ – This cruel Harry will be the death of us all.

Did I tell you we were going to a ball to-night[b], six or seven miles off? She has heard it, and intends to be there: tells him she shall there expect the sentence of life or death from his lovely eyes: the signal is appointed: if his savage heart is melted, and he pities her sufferings, he is to dance with her, and be master of her divine person and eighty thousand pounds, to-morrow; if not – but she expires at the idea – she entreats him to soften the cruel stroke, and not give a mortal wound to the tenderest of hearts by dancing with another.

You would die to see Harry's distress, – so anxious for the tender creature's life, so incensed at his own wicked attractions, so perplext[c] how to pronounce the fatal sentence – for my part I have had the utmost/ difficulty to keep my countenance. – Lady Julia, who was to have been his partner, sighing with him over the letter, intreating him not to dance, pitying the unhappy love-sick maid, her fine eyes glistening with a tear of tender sympathy.

The whole scene is too ridiculous to be conceived, and too foolish even to laugh at: I could stand it no longer, so retired, and left them to their soft sorrows.

You may talk of women, but you men are as much the dupes of your own vanity as the weakest amongst us can be. Heaven and earth! that, with Harry's understanding and knowledge of the world, he can be seriously alarmed at such a letter.[d] I thought him more learned in the arts 'of wilful woman laboring for her purpose.'[175] Nor is she the kind of woman; I think I know more of the nature of love, than to imagine her capable of it. If there/ was no other lover to be had indeed, – but he is led astray by the dear self-complacency of contemplating the surprizing effects of his own charms.

I see he is shocked at my insensibility, and fancies I have a most unfeeling heart; but I may live to have my revenge. Adio! I am going to my toilet. 'Now awful beauty puts on all its arms.'[176]

Five o'Clock.

The coach is at the door: Harry is drest[e] for execution; always elegant, he is to-day studiously so; a certain proof, to be sure, that his vanity is weaker than his compassion: he is however right; if she must die, he is to be commended for looking as well as he can, to justify a passion which is to have such fatal effects: he sees I observe his dress, and has the grace to blush a little. Adio! Caro![177] Votre[178f]

A. WILMOT.[g]/

38   *The History of Lady Julia Mandeville*

To Col. BELLVILLE.

FRIDAY Morning.

WE are again at Belmont. But Oh, how changed![a] all our heroicks[b] destroyed –
poor Harry![c] I can't look at him without laughing.

Our journey thither was pensive, our conversation sentimental; we entered
the ball-room trembling with apprehension; where the first object which struck
our eyes was the tender, lovesick[d], dying maid, listening with the most eager
attention to Fondville, who was at the very moment kissing her hand; her whole
soul in her eyes, her heart fluttering with a pleasure which she could not conceal,
and every feature on the full stretch coquetry.

An involuntary frown clouded the lovely countenance of my Harry, which
was not/ lessened by his observing a malicious smile on mine: he advanced however towards her, when she, not doubting his design was to ask her to dance, told
him, in a faltering voice, with a mixed air of triumph and irresolution, her eyes
fixed on her fan, that she was engaged to Lord Fondville.

Harry was thunderstruck: a glow of indignation flushed his cheek, and he
left her without deigning to make her any reply; which I observing, and fearing
she might misinterpret his silence, and that the idea of his supposed disappointment might flatter the creature's vanity, took care to explain to her that he was
engaged to Lady Julia before we came; a piece of information which made her
feel to the quick, even through the pleasure of dancing with a Lord; a pleasure
which has inconceivable charms for a citizen's daughter, and which love itself, or
what she pleases/ to call love, could not enable her to resist.

The attention of all the company was now turned on Harry and Lady Julia,
who were dancing a minuet: the beauty of their persons, the easy dignity of their
air, the vivid bloom of their cheeks, the spirit which shone in their eyes, the inimitable graces of their movement, which received a thousand additional charms
from (what I hope no one observed but myself) their desire of pleasing each other,
gave me an idea of perfection in dancing, which never before entered my imagination: all was still as night; not a voice, not a motion, through the whole assembly.
The spectators seemed afraid even to breathe, lest their attention should be one
moment suspended:[e] Envy herself seemed dead, or to confine her influence to the
bosom of Miss Westbrook. The minuet ended, a murmur of applause ran through
the room,/ which, by calling up her blushes, gave a thousand new charms to Lady
Julia, which I observed to the cit, adding also aloud that it was impossible any body
should think of dancing minuets after them;[f] in which sentiment[g] every body con-
curring, we began country dances, Harry never looked so lovely; his beauty, and
the praises lavished on him, having awakened a spark of that flame, which her
ambition had stifled for a moment, the girl endeavor'd,[h] at the beginning of the
evening, to attract his notice, but in vain: I had the pleasure to see him neglect all

Volume I 39

her little arts, and treat her with an air of unaffected indifference, which I knew must cut her to the soul. She then endeavoured to pique him by the most flaming advances to Fondville, which, knowing your capricious sex as I do, rather alarmed me; I therefore determined to destroy the effect of her arts by playing off, in opposition, a more refined species of coquetry, which/ turned all Fondville's attention on myself, and saved Harry from the snare she was laying for him, a snare of all others the hardest to escape.

When I saw I had by the most delicate flattery chained Fondville to my carr for the night, and by playing off a few quality airs inspired him with the strongest contempt for his city partner, I threw myself into a chair; where, affecting an excess of languor and fatigue, and wondering at the amazing constitutions of the country ladies, I declared my intention of dancing no more.

Sir Charles Mellifont, who danced with me, sat down on one side, and Fondville on the other, pouring forth a rhapsody of tender nonsense,[179] vowing all other women were only foils to me, envying Sir Charles's happiness, and kissing my hand with an affection of transport, which pleased me,/ as I saw it mortified the cit, who sat swelling with spite in a window near us, in a situation of mind which I could almost have pitied.

I sat a full hour, receiving the homage of both my adorers, my head reclined, and my whole person in an attitude of the most graceful negligence and inattention; when, observing the Cittadina ready to faint with envy and indignation, turning my eye carelessly on her, O, Heavens! Fondville, said I, you are an inhuman creature; you have absolutely forgot your partner:[a] then[b], starting with Sir Charles, rejoined the dance with an air of easy impertinence, which she could not stand, but burst into tears, and withdrew.

You must know this affair was all of my contriving; I was determined to try the reality of the girl's passion, to quiet Harry's conscience as to the cruelty of rejecting/ her suit, and remove those apprehensions for her life, which seemed so infinitely to distress him.

Full of these ideas, I wrote by one of my servants to Fondville, immediately after Harry communicated to us the Cittadina's tragedy-letter, commanding him to be at this ball, drest for conquest, to enquire out Miss Westbrook, whom he had never seen, to pretend a sudden and violent passion for her, and to entreat[c] the honor of being her partner: that it was a whim I had taken into my head; that I would explain my reasons another time, but insisted on his implicit obedience.

'He came, he saw, he conquered,'[180] as I imagined he would: I knew her rage for title, tinsel, and 'people of a certain rank,'[d] and that Fondville was exactly calculated for the meridian of her taste, understanding and education. The overcharged/ splendor of his dress and equipage must have infinite advantages, with one who had so long breathed city air, over the genuine elegance of Harry Mandeville's; nor was it possible in the nature of things for the daughter of an

40 *The History of Lady Julia Mandeville*

exchange-broker[a] to prefer even personal perfection to the dazzling blaze of a coronet; [181b] Harry's charms gave way before the flattering idea of a title, and the gentle God resigned his place to the greater power, Ambition.

Things to be sure have taken rather a disagreeable turn; but she must thank her own inconstancy, and be content for the future with making love to one man at a time.

I have only one more scene of mortification in view, for her, and my malice will be satisfied; I would invite her to a ball at Belmont, let Harry dance with/ Lady Julia, take Fondville myself, and pair her with the most disagreeable fellow in the room.

You have no notion how Harry's vanity is hurt, though he strives all he can to hide it; piqued to death; just like one of us, who are pleased with the love, though we dislike the lover: he begins to think it possible she may survive his cruelty.

Lady Julia is all astonishment, had no idea of such levity – the amiable ignorant[c] – how little she knows us – the character of half the sex. Adio! I am going with Lady Julia, to pay some morning visits in the environs.

Three o'Clock.

Till this morning I had no notion how much Lord and Lady Belmont were beloved, or, to speak with more propriety,/ adored in their neighborhood[d]: the eager enquiries of the good ladies after their return, their warm expressions of esteem and veneration, are what you can scarce conceive: the swell of affection, which their presence restrained, now breaks forth with redoubled impetuosity.

There are really a great many agreeable people hereabouts: Belmont is the court of this part of the world, and employs its influence, as every court ought to do, in bringing virtue, politeness, and elegant knowledge into fashion. How forcible, how irresistible are such examples in superior life! who can know Lord and Lady Belmont, without endeavoring[e] to imitate them? and who can imitate them without becoming all that is amiable and praise-worthy?[f]

Do you know, Bellville, I begin extremely to dislike myself? I have good/ qualities, and a benevolent heart, but have exerted the former so irregularly, and taken so little pains to rule and direct the virtuous impulses of the latter, that they have hitherto answered very little purpose either to myself or others. I feel I am a comet, shining, but useless, or perhaps destructive, whilst Lady Belmont is a benignant star.

But, for heaven's sake, how came the spirit of reflexion to seize me? There is something in this air. – O Cielo! una Carrozza![182] – my dear Lord Belmont. I fly – Adio!/

June 23d.[g]

To George Mordaunt, Esq;

THEY art come; the impatient villagers crowd the hall, eager to behold them, transport in every eye, whilst the noble pair scarce retain the tender tear of glowing benevolence. How lovely a picture was the audience they come from giving! how sweet the intercourse of warm beneficence and ardent gratitude! my[a] heart melted at the sight. This evening is devoted to joy – I alone – O Mordaunt! have I known this paradise only to be driven for ever from it?

I cannot to-night[b] mention leaving Belmont; to-morrow[c] I will propose it; I am in doubt where to go; my father is absent from camp on a visit of a fortnight to the Duke of –, his Colonel. I/ have some thoughts of going to Lord T –'s, till his return: perhaps I may come to town; all places but this are equal to me: yet I must leave it; I am every moment more sensible of my danger: yes, Mordaunt, I love her, I can no longer deceive myself; I love her with the fondest passion; friendship is too cold a name for what I feel, too cold for charms like hers to inspire: yet, heaven is my witness, I am incapable of a wish to her disadvantage; her happiness is my first, my only object – I know not what I would say, – why does fortune for ever oppose the tender union of hearts?[d] Farewel![e]

H. Mandeville.[f]/

To Col. Bellville.

Saturday.

MY Lord has brought us a thousand presents, a thousand books, a thousand trinkets, all in so exquisite a taste – He is the sweetest man in the world certainly – Such delight in obliging – 'Tis happy for you he is not thirty years younger and disengaged; I should infallibly have a passion – He has brought Harry the divinest horse; we have been seeing him ride, 'spring from the ground like feather'd[g] Mercury'[183] – you can have no conception how handsome he looks on horseback – poor Lady Julia's little innocent heart – I can't say I was absolutely insensible myself – you know I am infinitely fond of beauty, and vastly above dissembling it: indeed it seems immensely absurd that one is allowed to be charm'd[h] with living perfection in every species but our own, and/ that there one must admire only dead colours: one may talk in raptures of a life-less Adonis,[184] and not of a breathing Harry Mandeville. Is not this a despicable kind of prudery? For my part, I think nature's coloring[i] vastly preferable to the noblest attempts of art, and am not the less sensible to the graces of a fine form because it is animated. Adieu! we are going to dine at the hermitage; Lord Belmont is to be my Cecisbeo.

To George Mordaunt, Esq;

HOW inconsistent is the human mind! I cannot leave Belmont, I cannot give up the delight of beholding her: I fancy a softness in her manner which raises the most flattering ideas; she blushes when her eyes meet mine – Tho'[a] I see the madness of hope, I indulge it in spite of myself. No one can deserve her; yet, as Lord/ Belmont honors me with his esteem, I would persuade myself fortune alone forbids – I will struggle with impossibilities; I have many and powerful friends; we have a Prince[b] in the early prime of life, the season of generous virtue; a Prince[c] to whom the patriot glow, and that disinterested loyalty, which is almost my whole inheritance, cannot but be the strongest recommendations; to him it may be merit to have suffered, when the basest of the people rose on the ruins of their country. Those ample possessions, which would have descended to me, and might have raised my hopes to the most angelic of womankind, were gloriously spent in endeavouring[d] to support the throne, when shook by the rage of faction and narrow-minded bigoted enthusiasm; the younger branch of our family escaped the storm by having a minor at it's[e] head: to this accident, the partiality of an ancestor, and the military talents of his father, lord Belmont owes/ the affluence he so nobly enjoys, and which I only, of all mankind, have cause to regret.

These circumstances raise a flattering hope – my views are confused, but I will pursue the track. If I succeed, I may openly avow my passion; if not, the secret of my love shall die with me: never, my friend, will I attempt her heart by unworthy means: let me endeavour to deserve, and leave to heaven, to determine whether I shall possess, the noblest gift it has to bestow. Farewel.[f]

H. Mandeville.[g]

To George Mordaunt, Esq;

August 1st.

I Have heard from my father on the subject of Lady Mary's intended settlement, who extremely disapproves my intention of entirely declining it, which he thinks cannot be founded on any motives/ worthy of me, but on a false pride of disdaining to be obliged, which is in this case unjust, and greatly below my character: that I might as well object to receiving a part of his estate, which he intends to settle on me at the same time: he says Lord Belmont acts properly, and consistently with himself, and does not at all mean to break in on that independence which can never be too highly valued: that Lady Julia would scarce perceive such an addition to her already splendid fortune, whilst this settlement fixes in some degree of affluence the elder branch of the family, which lost its superiority, by the injustice of an ancestor, and that heroic loyalty which has ever characterized our house. That[h] he will talk further with me on this subject when we meet, but in the mean time advises me, as a friend zealous for my interest, yet not the less attentive to my honor, and the propriety of my conduct, to accept the immediate settlement of 500*l*.[a]/ a year, which will enable me to be serviceable to my country; but to postpone to some distant time settling the whole, and to insist that Lady Mary be convinced I deserve her friendship before she lavishes it so profusely on me.

This advice gives me pleasure, as it coincides with my own present sentiments:[b] eager to pursue my scheme of rising to such consequence as may justify my hopes of the only event desirable to me in this world, I am happy in the thought of appearing in every light in which I can attract the notice of my Prince; and, by steadily serving him and my country, whose true interest must ever be the same, deserve that favor on which all my designs are founded.

The time not being yet arrived when I can serve the noblest cause in the senate, I will go to Germany, and endeavour[c] first to signalize myself in the manner most suited/ to my period of life, the season of action, not of counsel: it is shameful, at my age, to recline in the flowery bower of indolence, when the whole world is in arms; I have not yet begun to live; my time has hitherto been less pass'd[d] in acting, than in preparing to act, my part on the great theatre of human life.[185]

Oh[e], Mordaunt! should I succeed in my views! should the hour come when I may openly avow my passion for the most lovely of womankind! this is the sweet hope which fires my soul, and animates me to the glorious pursuit. Why do closeted moralists, strangers to the human heart, rail indiscriminately at love? when inspired by a worthy object, it leads to every thing that is great and noble; warmed by the desire of being approved by her, there is nothing I would not attempt. I will to-day write to my father for his consent,/ and embark immediately for the army.

I have just received your letter: you call my design madness, the light in which every animated purpose will appear to minds inactive, unimpassioned, and sunk in the lethargic calm of lifeless tranquillity. – Mordaunt, you speak the cold language of a heart at rest: talk not of impossibilities; nothing is impossible to a soul impelled by the most lively of all passions, and ardent in a pursuit on which its whole happiness depends; nothing is impossible to him who aspires to please the most lovely, the most amiable, the most exalted of her sex.

I feel, I know[f] I shall be successful. I ask not advice, but declare my settled purpose: I am already determined, and, if your friendship be warm as mine, you will not torture me by further opposition. My father alone has power to change my resolution,/ but it is a power he will not exert: I shall ask his permission, but inform him at the same time, that, by refusing, he cuts off all the hope of my future days, and chains me down to a life of tasteless insensibility.

I know him well; he will advise, he will remonstrate, if he disapproves; but he will leave me that freedom of choice which is the inherent right of every rational

44   *The History of Lady Julia Mandeville*

being, and which he never, in one instance,[a] invaded, when I was much less capable of judging for myself.

Fearful however lest he should disapprove my passion for Lady Julia, I shall not declare it to him at present; but, as I never will even tacitly deceive him, I shall tell him I have a motive to this design, which I beg his leave to conceal from him till I have a prospect of success./

I this morning mentioned leaving Belmont, but my Lord insists on my staying a few days longer, which are devoted to domestic happiness. I cannot refuse without making him suspect some latent cause; nor will it make any difference in my plan, since I must wait somewhere an answer from my father, which will reach Belmont about the time I shall now leave it. Tomorrow[b] se'nnight[186c] expect me in town:[187] I shall stay but two nights: I need little preparation: my equipage and attendance are already greatly beyond my fortune, and rather suited to what you call the madness of my expectations: my[d] father, the most generous of mankind, has always proportioned my expences more to my birth than his moderate income: as my companions have ever been of the first rank, he has supported me greatly above myself, and on a full equality with them, lest I should be dazzled to mean compliances with their faults, by the false splendor/ they might receive from a superiority in these outward distinctions.

Did I tell you Lord Belmont had presented me with a beautiful Arabian horse, which he bought when in town? What delight has he in giving pleasure to others! What addition, if that can admit addition, to the happiness of the man who is blest with Lady Julia, will it be to be so nearly allied to worth like Lord Belmont's!

O Mordaunt! were it possible! – it is, it must – I will not give room to the faintest idea of disappointment.

Adieu! I have this moment a letter from my father, which I must answer to-night.

H. MANDEVILLE./

To HENRY MANDEVILLE, Esq;

Roseberry-House.

TUESDAY.

IT gives me the warmest pleasure, my dear son, to find you are pleased with the expensive education I have given you, though it reduces your fortune considerably below what it might otherwise have been: I considered that wealth, if necessary to happiness, which I do not believe, might be acquired; but that the flying hours of youth, the season of instruction, are never to be recalled.

I have the happiness to see you reward and justify my cares by a generous freedom of thinking, and nobleness of sentiment, which the common methods of education might have crampt,[e] or perhaps totally destroy'd[f]. It has always

Volume I

appeared to me, that/ our understandings are fettered by systems,[188] and our hearts corrupted by example: and that there needs no more to minds well disposed than to recover their native freedom,[189] and think and act from themselves. Full of this idea, I have instructed you how, but never what to think; I have pointed out the road which leads to truth, but have left you to discover her abode by your own strength of mind:[190] even on the most important of all subjects, I have said no more, than that conviction must be on the side of that religion, which teaches the purest and most benevolent morality, is most conducive to the general happiness of mankind, and gives the most sublime idea of the Deity.

Convinced that the seeds of virtue are innate,[191] I have only watched to cherish the rising shoots[a], and prune, but with a trembling hand, the too luxuriant branches./

By virtue I would here be understood to mean, not a partial attention to any one duty of life, but that rectitude of heart, which leads us to fulfil all, as far as the frailty of human nature will permit, and which is a constant monitor of our faults. Confucius[192] has well observed, that virtue does not consist in never erring, which is impossible, but in recovering as fast as we can from our errors.[b]

With what joy, my dearest Harry, did I early see in you that warmth of temper, which is alone productive of every extraordinary exertion of the human mind, the proper soil of genius and the virtues; that heat from which light[193] is inseparable!

I have only one fear for you; inured to a habit of profuse expence, I dread your being unable to practice that frugality, which will now be indispensable. To lady Mary's intended settlement, I will add a/ third of my estate, but even that is below your birth, and the manner of life to which you are habituated. But why do I doubt you![c] I know your generosity of spirit, and scorn of every species of slavery; that you will not descend to be indebted, to with-hold[d] a moment the price of laborious industry, or lessen the honest profit of the trader, by a delay yet more destructive to yourself than to him.

Intended to become a part of the legislative power, you are doubly bound to keep your self from all temptation of corruption or dependence, by living within your income; the amplest estate is wretched penury, if exceeded by the expences of its possessor.

Need I say more to recommend œconomy to a spirit like yours, than that it is the fountain of liberality, and the parent of independence?

You enquire after the place where I am: it is, except Belmont, the sweetest spot I/ ever beheld, but in a different style: the situation is rather beautiful than magnificent. There is a mild elegance, a refined simplicity in the air all around, strongly expressive of the mind of its amiable possessor; a poetic wildness, a luxuriant glow, like that of primeval nature, adorned by the hand of the Graces.

46   *The History of Lady Julia Mandeville*

The same spirit of liberty breathes here as with you: we are all perfectly at home; our time is subject to no restraint but that which our desire of obliging each other makes a voluntary imposition.

I am now alone, sitting in an arbour,[a] attentive to the lively chant of the birds, who swell their little throats with a morning hymn of gratitude to their Creator: whilst I listen, I think of those sweet lines of Cowley:

> 'All round the little winged choir,
> Pathetic tender thoughts inspire:/
> With ease the inspiration I obey,
> And sing as unconcern'd and as well pleas'd as they.'[194]

'Tis yet early day: the flocks and herds are spreading over the distant meadows, and joining the universal song of praise to the beneficent Lord of nature.

Rejoicing in the general joy, I adore the God who has expanded so wide the circle of happiness, and endeavour to regulate my own desires by attending to the simplicity of theirs.

When I see the dumb creation,[195] my dear Harry, pursuing steadily the purposes of their being, their own private happiness, and the good of their peculiar species, I am astonished at the folly and degeneracy of man, who acts in general so directly contrary to both; for both are invariably united.

The wise and benevolent Creator has placed the supreme felicity of every individual/ in those kind domestic social affections, which tend to the well-being[b] of the whole. Whoever presumes to deviate from this plan, the plan of God and nature, shall find satiety, regret or disappointment his reward.

I this moment receive your letter: you judge perfectly well in saying, there is an activity and restlessness in the mind of man, which makes it impossible for him to be happy in a state of absolute inaction:[196] some point of view, some favourite pursuit is necessary to keep the mind awake. 'Tis on this principle alone one can account for what seems so extraordinary to the eyes of impartial reason, that avarice and ambition should be the vices of age, that men should most ardently pursue riches and honours[c] at the time when they have the least prospect of enjoying them; the lively passions of youth subsiding, some active principle must be found to replace them; and where that warm benevolence of heart is wanting,/ which is a perpetual source of ever-new[d] delight, I do not wonder they engage in the chace of wealth and power, though sure so soon to melt from their grasp.

The first purpose of my heart, next to that superior and general one of making myself acceptable to my Creator, was to render the most angelic of women, your lovely mother, happy; in that, heaven was pleased to disappoint my hopes, by taking her to itself. My second has been to make you the most amiable of

Volume I   47

men; in which, I am not afraid to say to yourself, I have been successful, beyond my most sanguine wishes.

Adieu, my dear son! may you succeed in every purpose of your soul as fully as I have done in this, and be as happy as your virtues have made your father!

I am, &c.

J. MANDEVILLE.[a]/

To Col. BELLVILLE.

O Heavens! Bellville! Nay, there is absolutely no resisting a man that carries one off. Since you have mentioned the thing, I shall not abate you a scruple. There is no saying how charming it will be: let common beauties inspire whining, submissive, respectful passions; but let me – heaven! earth![b] to be run away with at four-and-twenty[c] – a paragraph in the papers.[d] – 'Yesterday the celebrated lady Anne Wilmot was forcibly carried off by a gentleman who had long in vain deprecated her pity: if any thing can excuse so atrocious an action, the unrivalled beauty of the lady' – Dear Bellville! when do you begin your adventure?

But, in sober sadness, how come you so flippant on the sudden?[e] Thus it is with/ you all; use you ill, and not a spaniel can be more under command: but the least encouragement quite ruins you. There is no saying a civil thing, but you presume upon one's favour so intolerably.–[f]

Why, yes, as you say, the hours past pleasantly enough at Sudley farm. Pretty rural scenes, tender Platonic chat, perfect confidence, the harmony of souls in unison; infinite flattery on your side, and implicit belief on mine: the sprightly god of love gave wings to the rapid hours. The gentle Muses too. – I think, Bellville, you are a pretty enough poet for a man of fashion; flowery, mild, not overburdened with ideas.

'O, can you forget the fond hours,
When all by yon fountain we stray'd.'[197][g]

I wish could remember the rest; but you are a cruel creature, never will leave me a/ copy of any thing, dreading the severity of my criticism: nay, you are right; yours are excellent verses, as Moliere says, to lock up in your bureau.[198]

Nine at Night.

Peace to the gentle spirit of him who invented cards! the very bond of peace, and cement of society.

After a philosophical enquiry into the *fummum bonum*,[199] I find it to consist in play: the more sublime pleasures require relaxation, are only for holyday wear, come but now and then, and keep the mind too much expanded: all other delights, all other amusements, pall; but play, dear, divine, seraphic[200] play, is always new, the same to-day, to-morrow, and for ever./

48   *The History of Lady Julia Mandeville*

It reconciles parties, removes distinctions, and restores what my lord calls the natural equality of mankind.

I have only one fault to find with it; that for the time it extremely weakens, or rather totally suspends, the impressions of beauty: the finest woman in the world, whilst at the card-table, is regarded by the most susceptible man only as a being which is to lose its money.

You will imagine success produced these wise reflexions: yes, we have been playing a most engaging pool at quadrille in the wood, where I have with the utmost composure won an immensity. If I go on thus, all objections to our union will be removed: I shall be literally a fortune in myself.

Without vanity, I have some little skill in the game; but, at present, there is no/ great degree of merit in winning of the friends, who happened to be of my party, with an absurd conceited squire, who loves quality, and thinks it the greatest honor in the world that I will condescend to win his money. We had four tables under the shade of a spreading oak.

I can no more. –

Adieu![a]

A. WILMOT.[b]

We have had a penitential letter from the Cittadina, with another from Papa, offering 30,000*l.*[c] at present, and 50,000*l.*[d] at his death, on condition lord Belmont will get Harry an Irish title: knows it is a bad match, but won't baulk his girl's fancy; and besides, considers Harry has good blood in his veins: we[e] rejected it politely, but with a little of the Mandeville stateliness.

O Heavens! Fondville's valet[f] – A billet-doux.[201] – I shall be cruel, – This murderous/ form – I must absolutely hide myself, or wear a mask, in pity to mankind. – My Lord has taken the letter – He brings it me – He is on the stairs – How! gone on to lady Belmont's apartment! – A billet, and not to me! – What can it mean? – Can the dear man be false?

The infidel! Yes, he has left me – forgot his vows. – This bewitching lady Julia; it is really an heroic exertion of virtue not to hate her. Could you have thought it possible[g] – but read, his cruel letter.[h]/

To the Earl of BELMONT.

My LORD,[i]

YOUR Lordship will be perhaps surprized – Yet[j] why surprized? Lady Julia is absolutely an immense fine creature: and though marriage, to those who know life, cannot but seem an impertinent affair, and what will subject me to infinite ridicule; yet custom, and what one owes to one's rank, and keeping up a family! –[k]

Volume I   49

In short, my Lord, people of a certain consequence being above those romantic views which pair the vulgar, I chose rather to apply to your Lordship than the Lady, and flatter myself my estate will bear the strictest inspection: not but that, I assure your Lordship, I set a due value on Lady Julia's charms; and, though I have visited every court in Europe, and/ seen all that is lovely in the Beau sexe, never yet beheld the fair whom I would so soon wish to see fill the rank of Lady Viscountess Fondville as her Ladyship.

If my pretensions are so happy as to be favorably[a] received by your Lordship, I will beg leave to wait on Lady Julia tomorrow, and my lawyer shall attend your Lordship's[b] wherever and whenever you please to appoint. Believe me, my Lord, with the most perfect devotion,

Your Lordship's
most Obedient and
very Humble Servant,
Fondville./

To Lord Viscount FONDVILLE.

My Lord,

I Am the last man in the world to whom it was necessary to apologize for an intention of entering into a state which, I have experienced, is productive of such exquisite felicity.

My daughter's choice is perfectly free; nor shall I ever do more than advise her, in an affair of such consequence to herself; but, from what I know of her character, think it highly improbable she should approve the pretensions of a man, who professes being above those tender affections which alone can make happy sensibility like hers.

Allow me to take the liberty of observing, in answer to the latter part of your/ Lordship's letter, that there are few ranks which Lady Julia Mandeville has not a right to fill. I am, my Lord,

Your Lordship's
most Obedient and
devoted Servant,
BELMONT.

Don't come to Belmont, I charge you; I shall have this invincible Lady Julia seduce you too. Besides, I have some reasons why I chuse our attachment should not yet come to a crisis; till when, I will take Lady Belmont's advice and be prudent: obey in silence; let me have no more sighs till the milder influence of the heavens dispose me to be gracious. I am always in good humor in Autumn; your fate may possibly be determined in little more than a month: ask no questions:/

50   *The History of Lady Julia Mandeville*

suspend your passion, or at least the outward expression of it, and write to me in Amico.[202] Adieu!

To George Mordaunt, Esq;

I Have been riding alone with Lord Belmont this morning, a pleasure I very often enjoy, and on which I set infinite value: in those hours of perfect confidence, I am certain of being instructed and amused, by a train of ideas uncommon, enlarged, noble, benevolent; and adapted to inspire me with a love of virtue, by showing her in her native charms: I shall be all my life the wiser and worthier man, for the hours I have passed at Belmont./

But, O Mordaunt![a] shall I be the happiest?[b] That is in the bosom of futurity: a thousand times have I been tempted, in these hours of indulgent friendship, to open all my heart to Lord Belmont.

I know his contempt of wealth, and how little he thinks it conducive to happiness. 'Heaven,' said he to me this very morning, 'has blest me with affluence: I am thankful, and endeavor to deserve, by applying an ample portion of it to the purposes of beneficence. But for myself, my pleasures are of so unexpensive and simple a kind, that a diminution of fortune would take very little from my private felicity:[c] Health, content, the sweets of social and domestic life, the only enjoyments[d] suited to the nature of man, are and ought to be within the reach of all the species: yes[e], my dear Mr. Mandeville; it gives a double relish to all my pleasures,/ to reflect that they are such as every man may enjoy if he will.'

Can this man, my dear Mordaunt, sacrifice the real happiness of his[f] child, the calm delight of domestic friendship on which he sets such value himself, to the gaudy trappings of tasteless grandeur? Did she approve my passion, I should hope every thing from the most indulgent of fathers.

He has refused Lord Fondville for Lady Julia, whose fortune is as large as avarice itself could desire: Good heaven,[g] that such a man, without one other recommendation, without a soul to taste even the charms of her person, can aspire to all that can be imagined of perfection![h]

Adieu!

H. Mandeville.[i]/

To Col. Bellville.

Thursday Afternoon.

O Ciel! I faint! what a world do we live in! How[j] many unavoidable enemies to enjoyment! It is sometimes too cold, sometimes too hot to be happy! One[k] is never pleased a week together. I shall absolutely grow a snarling philosopher, and find fault with every thing.

Volume I 51

These unconscionable lovers have dragged me cross an open meadow, exposed to the sun's burning rays – no mercy on my complexion – Lady Julia sure, for her own sake, – yet she is laughing at my distress. I am too languid to say more. – Oh! for a cooling breeze![a]

'The whispering zephyr, and the purling rill.'[203]/

We are going to have an addition to our group of friends: Emily Howard, daughter to the late dean of –, a distant relation, and rector of the parish, being expected to-morrow at Belmont: she is Lady Julia's friend in the most emphatical sense of the word. Do you know, I feel extremely inclined to be jealous of her;[b] and am angry with my self for such meanness?

A. WILMOT.[c]
TUESDAY[d] 3[d].

To Col. BELLVILLE.

SHE is come, this redoubtable Emily Howard; and, I find I have only a second place in Lady Julia's friendship: I would hate her if I could, but it is really impossible: she is so gentle, she steals one's affection imperceptibly, and one has the/ vexation to be forced to love her in spite of one's self.

She has been here three days, and in that short time she has gained amazingly upon my heart: her person is little, finely proportioned, and delicate almost to fragility; her voice and manner soft and timid: her countenance a mixture of innocence and sweetness which would disarm the rage of a tyger:[d] her heart is tender, kind, compassionate; and tremblingly awake to friendship, of which she is universally the object:[e] Lady Julia doats on her, nor am I surprised at it: she appears so weak, so helpless, so exquisitely feminine, it seems cruelty not to be her friend: no one ever saw her without wishing her happiness: the love one has for her seems of a peculiar species, or most nearly resembles that instinctive fondness one feels for a beautiful child: it is independent of esteem, for one loves her before one knows her. It is the/ pleasantest kind of affection that can be conceived.

Yet, though she is extremely handsome, or rather, to suit the expression to her form, extremely pretty, she is very little the taste of men; her excessive modesty renders both her beauty and understanding in some degree useless to her; 'not obvious, not obtrusive,'[204] she escapes the observation of common eyes; and though infinitely lovely, I never heard she was beloved.

For this very reason, the women do her ample justice; she is no woman's rival, stands in nobody's way, which cannot fail of exciting a general good will towards her, in her own sex; they even allow her more beauty than she really has, and take a delight in setting her charms in opposition to every impertinent thing the

52   *The History of Lady Julia Mandeville*

men are fond of. 'Yes, the[a] girl is very well,/ but nothing to Emily Howard,' is the common cry on the appearance of a new beauty.

There is another strong reason for loving her; tho' exact in her own conduct, she has an indulgence to that of others, which is a consequence of her excessive gentleness of temper, and her seeing every action on the favourable[b] side: one could own one's greatest weakness to her almost without blushing, and at this very moment I dare say Lady Julia is confessing to her her passion for Harry Mandeville, who is riding out with my Lord. I dare say she would find an excuse for my indiscretion in regard to you, and see only the delicacy of our friendship.

She sings and dances angelically, but she blushes to death if you tell her so./

Such gentle unassuming characters as these, make the most agreeable friends in the world; they are the mild green of the soul, on which it rests itself from more glaring objects: one may be absurd, one may be vain, one may be imprudent, secure of being heard with indulgence: I know nothing which would make her more what I mean but her being a fool: however the indulgent sweetness of her temper answers almost the same purpose.

I am disconsolate that the Caro Enrico is going to desert us; but the cruel man is inflexible to all my soft perswasions[c], and determined to leave us on Wednesday.

Adieu!

The sweet Emily is going on Thursday for ten days to Sir George Martin's, and then returns to finish the summer here./

O,[d] do you know that I am credibly informed, her favorite Suivante[205] having told it to one, who told it to another, who told it to a good old gossiping lady, who told it to me, that the Cittadina, who has in vain wrote[e] Harry a penitential letter, is playing off the same arts, the same dying airs, to Fondville, which had such extreme ill success with him; the[f] siege is at present suspended, not by his addressing Lady Julia, which is a profound secret to her and every body without these walls, but by his mother's death, which has called him hastily to town; and which, by the way, adds 2000*l.* a year to his income. Do you know, that I think the thing may do, if Lady Julia continues cruel; they[g] are absolutely formed for each other, and it would be a thousand pities to part them.

Ever yours,
A. WILMOT.[h]/

To Col. BELLVILLE.

August 6.

CERTAINLY next to a new lover the pleasantest thing upon earth is a new friend: let antediluvians[206] take seven years to fix,[207] but for us insects of an hour,[208] noth-

Volume I 53

ing can be more absurd: by the time one has try'd[a] them on these maxims, one's taste for them is worn out. I have made a thousand friendships at first sight, and sometimes broke them at the second: there is a certain exertion of soul, a lively desire of pleasing, which gives a kind of volatile spirit to a beginning acquaintance, which is extremely apt to evaporate. Some people make a great merit of constancy, and it is to be sure a very laudable virtue; but for my part, I am above dissembling: My friendships wear out like my clothes, but often much faster./

Not that this is the case in regard to Emily Howard; no, really, I think this Penchant[209] is very likely to be lasting; may probably hold out the summer.

To-morrow, when Harry leaves us, my Lord, to divert our chagrin, takes us, with three strange belles, and five most engaging beaux, a ramble I cannot tell whither.

Saturday Morning.

O heavens![b] one of our male animals has disappointed us. Absolutely I shall insist on Harry's attendance; he shall defer his journey, I am resolved: there is no supporting a scarcity of beaux.

He goes with us; Lady Julia's eyes have prevailed; she had seduced him before I went down: his chaise is ordered back to wait for ours.

Adio, Carissimo.[210]/

To George Mordaunt, Esq;

Saturday Night.

I AM still here; when shall I have strength of mind to go? not having heard from my father in the time I expedited, I was determined to go to Lord T –'s, whose zeal for my interest, and great knowledge of mankind, makes him the properest person I can consult. My chaise was this morning at the door, when my Lord told me, Lady Julia intreated my stay a few days longer: she blush'd,[c] and with the loveliest confusion confirm'd[d] my Lord's assertion: all my resolution vanished in a moment; there is enchantment in her look, her voice – enchantment which it is not in man to resist./

Sunday Morning.[e]

I am every hour more unhappy: Lord Fondville's proposal gives me infinite uneasiness; not that I fear such a rival; but it has raised the idea of other pretensions, which may be accepted before it is time for me to avow my designs: I have pass'd[f] this night in forming schemes to prevent so fatal a blow to all my hopes; and am determined to own my passion to the lovely object of it, and entreat her, if no other man is so happy as to possess her heart, to wait one year the result of those views which that love, which has inspired may perhaps prosper.

54   *The History of Lady Julia Mandeville*

Not certain I shall have courage to own my tenderness in her presence, I will write, and seize some favourable opportunity to give her the letter on which all my happiness depends: I will ask no answer/ but from her eyes. How shall I meet them after so daring an attempt?

We are going to the parish church; the coach is at the door: Adieu! she[a] comes! What[b] graces play around that form! What divinity in those eyes! O[c] Mordaunt, what task will be difficult to him who has such a reward in view!

To Col. BELLVILLE.

Sunday Evening.

OUR ramble yesterday was infinitely agreeable; there is something very charming in changing the scene; my Lord understands the art of making life pleasurable by making it various.

We have been to the parish church, to hear Dr. H.[d] preach; he has that spirit in/ his manner without which the most sensible sermon has very little effect on the hearers. The organ, which my Lord gave, is excellent. You know I think musick[e] an essential part of public worship, used as such by the wisest nations, and commanded by God himself to the Jews; it has indeed so admirable an effect in disposing the mind to devotion, that I think it should never be omitted.

Our Sundays here are extremely pleasant: we have, after evening service, a moving rural picture from the windows of the saloon, in the villagers, for whose amusement the gardens are that day thrown open.

Our rustic Mall[211f] is full from five till eight, and there is an inexpressible pleasure in contemplating so many groups of neat, healthy, happy-looking people, enjoying the diversion of walking in these lovely/ shades, by the kindness of their beneficent Lord, who not only provides for their wants, but their pleasures.

My Lord is of opinion that Sunday was intended as a day of rejoicing not of mortification; and meant not only to render our praises to our benevolent Creator, but to give rest and chearful relaxation to the industrious part of mankind, from the labors of the week.

On this principle, tho' he will never suffer the least breach of the laws in being, he wishes the severity of them softened, by allowing some innocent amusements after the duties of the day are past: he thinks this would prevent those fumes of enthusiasm which have had here such fatal effects, and could not be offensive to that gracious Power who delights in the happiness of his creatures, and who, by the royal poet,[212g] has commanded them to praise him in the cymbals and dances.[h]/

For my own part, having seen the good effect of this liberty in catholic countries, I cannot help wishing, though a zealous protestant, that we were, to imitate them in this particular.

Volume I 55

It is worth observing, that the book of sports[213] was put forth by the pious, the religious, the sober Charles the 1st,[a] and the law for the more strict observation of Sunday passed in the reign, of the libertine Charles the 2d.[214b]

Love of pleasure is natural to the human heart,[215] and the best preservative against criminal ones, is a proper indulgence in such as are innocent.

These are my sentiments, and I am happy in finding Lord Belmont of the same opinion. Adio!

A. Wilmot.[c]/

To George Mordaunt, Esq;

Monday.

MORDAUNT, the die is cast, and the whole happiness of my life hangs on the present moment. After having kept the letter confessing my passion two days without having resolution to deliver it, this morning in the garden, being a moment alone with Lady Julia in a summer-house, the company at some distance, I assumed courage to lay it on a table whilst she was looking out at a window which had a prospect that engag'd[d] all her attention: when I laid it down, I trembled, a chillness seized my whole frame, my heart dy'd[e] within me; I withdrew instantly, without even staying to see if she took it up: I waited at a little distance hid in a close arbour[f] of woodbines, my heart throbbing with apprehension, and,/ by the time she staid in the summer-house, had no doubt of her having seen the letter. When[g] she appeared I was still more convinced; she came out with a timid air, and looked round as if fearful of surprize: the lively crimson flushed[h] her cheek, and was succeeded by a dying paleness; I attempted to follow, but had not courage to approach her. I suffered her to pass the arbor where I was, and advance slowly towards the house: when she was out of sight I went back to the summer house, and found the letter was gone. I have not seen her. I am called to dinner: my limbs will scarce support me: how shall I bear the first sight of Lady Julia! how be able to meet her eyes![i]

I have seen her, but my fate is yet undetermined; she has avoided my eyes, which I have scare dar'd[j] to raise from the ground; I once look'd[k] at her when she did/ not observe me, and saw a melancholy on her countenance which stab'd[l] me to the soul. I have given sorrow to the heart of her, whom I would wish to be ever most happy; and to whose good I would sacrifice the cleared hope of my soul. Yes, Mordaunt, let me be wretched, but let every blessing heaven can bestow, be the portion of the loveliest of her sex.

How little did I know of love, when I gave that name to the shameful passion I felt for the wife of my friend! The[m] extreme beauty of the countess Melespini, that unreserved manner which seldom fails to give hope, the flattering preference she seemed to give me above all others, lighted up in my soul a more violent

56   *The History of Lady Julia Mandeville*

degree of youthful inclination, which the esteem I had for her virtues refined to an appearance of the noblest of affections, to which it had not the remotest real resemblance./

Without any view in my pursuit of her but my own selfish gratification, I would have sacrificed her honor and happiness to a transient fondness, which dishonored my character, and, if successful, might have corrupted a heart naturally full of probity; her amiable reproofs, free from that severity which robs virtue of half her charms, with the generous behaviour of the most injured of mankind, recalled my soul to honor, and stopped me early in the career of folly; time wore out the impression of her charms, and left only a cold esteem remaining, a certain proof that she was never the object of more than a light desire, since the wounds which real love inflicts are never to be intirely[a] healed.

Such was the infamous passion which I yet remember with horror: but my tenderness for Lady Julia, more warm, more animated, more violent, has a delicacy of which those only who love like me can/ form any idea: independent of the charms of her person, it can never cease but with life; nor even then if in another state we have any sense of what has passed in this; it is eternal, and incorporated with the soul. Above every selfish desire, the first object of my thoughts and wishes is her happiness which I would[b] die, or live wretched, to secure: every action of my life is directed to the sole purpose of pleasing her: my noblest ambition is to be worthy her esteem. My dreams are full of her; and when I wake, the first idea which rises in my mind is the hope of seeing her, and of seeing her well and happy: my most ardent prayer to the supreme[c] Giver of all good is for her welfare.

In true love, my dear Mordaunt, there is a pleasure abstracted from all hope of return; and were I certain she would never be mine, nay, certain I should never behold her more, I would not, for all the/ kingdoms of the world, give up the dear delight of loving her.

Those who never felt this enlivening power, this divinity of the soul, may find a poor insipid pleasure in tranquillity, or plunge into vicious excesses to animate their tedious hours; but those who have, can never give up so sweet, so divine a transport, but with their existence, or taste any other joy but in subordination.

O Mordaunt![d] when I behold her, read the soft language of those speaking eyes, hear those harmonious sounds – who that has a soul can be insensible! – yet there are men dead to all sense of perfection, who can regard that angel form without rapture, can hear the music of that voice without emotion! I have myself with astonishment seen them, inanimate as the trees around them, listen coldly to those melting/ accents – There is a sweetness in her voice, Mordaunt, a melodious softness, which fancy cannot paint: the enchantment of her conversation is inexpressible.

Volume I 57

Four o'clock.

I am the most wretched of mankind, and wretched without the right of complaining: the baseness of my attempt deserves even the pangs I suffer. Could I, who made a parade of refusing to meet the advances of the daughter of almost a stranger descend to seduce the heiress of him on earth to whom I am most obliged? O Mordaunt![a] have we indeed two souls? Can[b] I see so strongly what is right, yet want power to act up to my own sentiments? The torrent of passion bears down all before it. I abhor myself for this weakness. I would give worlds to recall that fatal letter: her coldness, her reserve, are more than I can support. My madness has undone me. – My assiduity is importunate./ I might have preserved her friendship. I have thrown away the first happiness of my life. Her eyes averted shun me as an object of hatred. I shall not long offend her by my presence. I will leave her for ever. I am eager to be gone, that I may carry far from her – O Mordaunt![c] who could have thought that cruelty dwelt in such a form? She hates me, and all my hopes are destroyed for ever.

Monday Evening.

BELMONT.

This day, the first of my life; what a change has this day produced! These few flying hours have raised me above mortality. Yes: I am most happy; she loves me, Mordaunt: her conscious blushes, her downcast eyes, her heaving bosom, her sweet confusion, have told me what her tongue could not utter: she loves me, and all else is below my care: she loves me, and I will pursue her. What are the mean/ considerations of fortune to the tender union of hearts? Can wealth or titles deserve her? No, Mordaunt, love alone. – She is mine by the strongest ties, by the sacred bond of affection. The delicacy of her soul is my certain pledge of happiness: I can leave her without fear; she cannot now be another's.

I told you my despair this morning; my Lord proposed an airing; chance placed me in lady Julia's chaise. I entered it with a beating heart: a tender fear of having offended, inseparable from real love, kept me some time silent; at length, with some hesitation, I beg'd[d] her to pardon the effect of passion and despair, vowed I would rather die than displease her; that I did not now hope for her love, but could not support her hate.

I then ventured to look up to the loveliest of women; her cheeks were suffused/ with the deepest blush; her eyes, in which was the most dying languor, were cast timidly on the ground, her whole frame trembled, and with a voice broken and interrupted, she exclaimed, 'Hate you, Mr. Mandeville, O heaven!'[e] she could say no more; nor did she need, the dear truth broke like a sudden flash of light on my soul.

58 *The History of Lady Julia Mandeville*

Yet think not I will take advantage of this dear prepossession in my favor, to seduce her from her duty to the best of parents; from Lord Belmont only will I receive her: I will propose no engagements contrary to the rights of an indulgent father, to whom she is bound by every tie of gratitude and filial tenderness: I will pursue my purpose, and leave the event to heaven, to that heaven which knows the integrity, the disinterested purity of my intentions: I will evince the reality of my/ passion by endeavoring[a] to be worthy of her. The love of such a woman, is the love of virtue itself: it raises, it refines, it ennobles every sentiment of the heart; how different from that fever of selfish desire I felt for the amiable countess![b]

O Mordaunt![c] had you beheld those blushes of reluctant sensibility, seen those charming eyes softened with a tenderness as refined as that of angels[d] – She loves me – let me repeat the dear sounds. – She loves me, and I am happier than a god!

I have this moment a letter from my father: he approves my design, but begs me for a short time to delay it: my heart ill bears this delay: I will carry the letter to lady Julia.

She approves my father's reasons, yet begs I will leave Belmont: her will is the/ law of my heart; yet a few days I must give to love. I will go on Tuesday to lord T –'s. His friendship will assist me in the only view which makes life supportable to me; he will point out, he will lead me to the path of wealth and greatness.

Expect to hear from me when I arrive at Lord T –'s. I shall not write sooner: my moments here are too precious.

Adieu.[e]

Your faithful

H. MANDEVILLE.[f]/

To HENRY MANDEVILLE, Esq;

Aug. 6th.[g]

HAPPY in seeing in my son that heroic spirit, which has ever distinguished our house, I should with pleasure consent his design, were this a proper time to execute it, provided he went a volunteer, and determined to accept no command but as a reward of real services, and with a resolution it should never interfere with that independence to which I would have him sacrifice every other consideration; but, when there is so strong a probability of peace, his going would appear like making a parade of that courage which he did not expect would be tried.

Yes, my son, I am well allured we shall have peace; that the most amiable of/ princes, the friend of humankind, pitying the miseries of his species, and melting with compassion at the wide extended[h] scene of desolation, meditates such a peace as equally provides for the interest and honor of Britain, and the future quiet of mankind. The terms talked of are such as give us an immense addition of empire, and strengthen that superiority of naval force on which our very being depends, whilst they protect our former possessions, and remove the source of future wars, by securing all, and much more than all, for which this was undertaken; yet, by their just moderation, convince the world a British monarch is governed only-by the laws of honor and equity, not by that impious thirst of false glory, which actuates the laurel'd scourges of mankind.

After so long, so extensive and bloody a war, a war which has depopulated our/ country, and loaded us with a burden of debt, from which nothing can extricate us but the noble spirit of public frugality, which, if steadily and uniformly pursued, will rank the name of our Prince with those of Elizabeth, and Henry the great.[216a] All ardently wish for peace, but those who gain by the continuance of war; the clamors of those are inconceivable; clamors which can be founded only in private interest, because begun before they could even guess at the terms intended, and continued when such are mentioned as reason herself would dictate: but such ever will be the conduct of those in whom love of wealth is the primary passion.

Heaven and earth! can men wearing the form, and professing the sentiments of humanity, deaf to the cries of the widow and the orphan, labor to perpetuate the dreadful carnage, which has deluged the world/ with the blood of their fellow creatures, only to add to the mass of their already unwieldy wealth, and prey longer on the distresses of their country!

These clamors are as illegal as they are indecent: peace and war are the prerogative[b] of the crown, sacred as the liberties of the people, nor will ever be invaded by those who understand and love our happy constitution: let[c] us strengthen the hands of our sovereign by our warm approbation during the course of this arduous work; and if his ministers abuse their trust, let them answer it, not to the noise of unthinking faction, or the unfeeling bosom of private interest, but to the impartial laws of their country.

Heaven forbid I should ever see a British King independent on his people collectively; but I would have him raised above/ private cabals, or the influence of any partial body of men, however wealthy or respectable.

If the generous views of our Prince do not meet with the success they merit, if France refuses such a peace as secures the safety of our colonies,[217] and that superiority, as a naval power, so necessary to the liberties of Europe, as well as our own independence, you shall join the army in a manner becoming your birth, and the style of life in which you have been educated: till then, restrain within just bounds that noble ardor so becoming a Briton, and study to serve that country with your counsels in peace, which will not, I hope, have occasion for your sword in war. Adieu.[d]/

WEDNESDAY, August 11th.[e]

To Miss HOWARD.

MY Emily, your friend, your unhappy Julia, is undone. He knows the tenderness which I have so long endeavored[a] to conceal. The trial was too great for the softness of a heart like mine; I had almost conquered my own passion, when I became a victim to his: I could not see his love, his despair, without emotions which discovered all my soul.[b] I am not formed for deceit: artless as the village maid, every sentiment of my soul is in my eyes; I have not learnt, I will never learn, to disguise their expressive language. With what pain did I affect a coldness to/ which I was indeed a stranger! But why do I wrong my own heart? I did not affect it. The native modesty of my sex gave a reserve to my behavior, on the first discovery of his passion, which his fears magnified into hate. O, Emily! Do I indeed hate him![c] you to whose dear bosom your Julia confides her every thought, tell me if I hate this most amiable of mankind?[d] You know by what imperceptible steps my inexperienced heart has been seduced to love: you know how deceived by the sacred name of friendship – But why do I seek to excuse my sensibility? Is he not worthy all my tenderness?[e] are we not equal in all but wealth, a consideration below my care? is not his merit above titles and riches? How [f] shall I paint his delicacy, his respectful fondness? Too plainly convinced of his power over my heart, he disdains to use that power to my disadvantage; he declares he will never receive me but from my father, he consents/ to leave me till a happier fortune enables him to avow his love to all the world; he goes without asking the least promise in his favor. Heaven sure will prosper his designs, will reward a heart like his. O, my Emily,[g] did my father see with my eyes! what is fortune in the ballance with such virtue! Had I worlds in my own power, I should value them only as they enabled me to show more strongly the disinterestedness of my affection.

Born with a too tender heart, which never before found an object worthy its attachment, the excess of my affection is unspeakable. Delicate in my choice even of friends, it was not easy to find a lover equal to that idea of perfection my imagination had formed; he alone of all mankind rises up to it; the speaking grace, the easy dignity of his air, are the natural consequences of the superiority of his soul. He/ looks as if born to command the world. I am interrupted. Adieu.

AUGUST 15th.

To Col. BELLVILLE.

YOU never were more mistaken: you will not have the honor of seeing me yet in town. My Lord thinks it infinitely more respectful to his royal Master to celebrate this happy event[218] in the country.

'My congratulations, says he, would[h] be lost in the crowd of a drawing room, but here I can diffuse a spirit of loyalty and joy through half a county, and impress all around me with the same veneration and love for the most amiable of Princes which burns in my own bosom'.[a]/

Our entertainment yesterday was magnifique,[219] and in the Gusto[220] Belmonto: there is a beautiful lake in the park, on the borders of which, on one side, interspersed amongst the trees, which form a woody theatre round it, at a distance of about three hundred yards, tents were fixed for the company to dine in, which consisted of all the gentlemen's families twenty miles round. Westbrook and his daughter were there, as my Lord would not shock them by leaving them only out when the whole neighbourhood were invited; though he observed smiling, this was a favor, for these kind of people were only gentlemen by the courtesy of England.[b] Streamers of the gayest colors waved on the tops of the tents, and glittered in the dancing sunbeams: the[c] tables were spread with every delicacy in season, at which we placed ourselves in parties, without ceremony or distinction, just as choice or accident directed. On a little island in the midst of/ the lake, an excellent band of music was placed, which played some of the finest compositions of Handel[221] during our repast; which ended, we spread ourselves on the borders of the lake, where we danced on the verdant green, till tea and coffee again summoned us to the tents; and when evening 'had in her sober livery all things clad,'[222] a superb supper, and grand ball in the saloon finished our festival.

Nor were the villagers forgot: Tables[d] were spread for them on the opposite side of the lake, under the shade of the tallest trees, and so disposed as to form the most agreeable points of view to us, as our encampment must do to them.

I am ill at describing, but the feast had a thousand unspeakable charms.

Poor Harry! How I pity him! His[e] whole soul was absorbed in the contemplation/ of Lady Julia, with whom he danced. His eyes perpetually followed her; and, if I mistake not, his will not be the only heart which aches at parting on Tuesday, for so long is Harry's going postponed. He may go, but, like the wounded deer, he carries the arrow in his breast.

Adio![f]/

Tuesday, August 17th:[g]

To Miss HOWARD.

HOW, my sweet Emily, shall I bear his absence;[h] an absence embittered by the remembrance of those lively impassioned hours which love alone can give?[i] What joy have I found in owning the sentiments of my soul to one so worthy of all my tenderness![j] Yes, Emily, I love him – words can but ill paint what I feel – he, he alone, – yet he leaves Belmont – leaves it by my command, leaves it this very hour, leaves it perhaps for ever – Great Heaven! can I support that thought?

If you love, if you pity your unhappy friend, return immediately to Belmont, let me repose my sorrows in that faithful breast: Lady Anne is tenderly my friend, but the sprightliness of her character intimidates me: I do not hope find in her/ that sweet indulgence to all my faults, as in the gentle soul of my Emily.

I have entreated[a] him to take no leave of me; I shall only see him with the family: The moment draws near – my fluttering heart – How shall I hide my concern?[b] – Lady Anne is coming to my apartment: I must go with her to the saloon, where he only waits to bid us adieu: his chaise is in the court. O Emily![c] my emotion will betray me. –[d]

He is gone, the whole house is in tears: never was man so adored, never man so infinitely deserved it. He pressed my hand to his lips, his eyes spoke unutterable love. I leaned almost fainting on Lady Anne, and hid my tears in her bosom: she hurried me to my apartment, and left me to give vent to my full heart! She sees my weakness, and kindly strives/ to hide it from others, whilst her delicacy prevents her mentioning it to myself: she has a tender and compassionate heart, and my reserve is an injury to her friendship.

Lady Anne has sent to ask me to air; I shall be glad to avoid all eyes but hers; perhaps I may have courage to tell her – she merits all my confidence, nor is it distrust but timidity which prevents – she is here – I am ashamed to see her. Adieu! my dearest, my beloved friend!/

To Col. BELLVILLE.

FRIDAY Night.

WE have lost our lovely Harry; he left us this morning for Lord T –'s. Poor Lady Julia! how I adore her amiable sincerity! she has owned her passion to me as we aired, and mentioned hopes which are founded in madness: I ventured gently to remonstrate, but there is no reasoning with a heart in love. Time and absence may effect a cure: I am the confidente[e] of both: I am perplexed how to proceed: I must either betray the trust reposed in me, or abuse Lord Belmont's friendship and hospitality.

In what a false light do we see every thing through the medium of passion! Lady Julia is heiress to 14,000*l*,[f] a year, yet/ thinks Harry's merit may raise him to a situation which will justify his pretending to her, and that this stupendous rise may be brought about in a twelvemonth: he too thinks it possible, nay the scheme is his. Heaven and earth! yet they are not fools, and Harry has some knowledge of mankind.

At present there is no talking reasonably to either of them. I must soothe them, to bring them off this ruinous inclination by degrees.

As idleness is the nurse of love, I will endeavour[g] to keep Lady Julia continually amused: a new lover might do much, but there is nobody near us that is tolerable: indeed the woman who has loved Harry Mandeville, will be somewhat hard to please./

Volume I 63

Chance favors my designs; my Lord has proposed a visit of a fortnight to a neighbouring nobleman, Lord Rochdale, whose house is generally full of gay people; his son too, Lord Melvin, with whom I was acquainted abroad, and who is only inferior to Harry Mandeville, is hourly expected from his travels.

Since I wrote the last paragraph an idea has struck me; from a very particular expression in a letter I once received from Lady Belmont, in France, I have a strong suspicion Lord Melvin is intended for Lady Julia; I wish he might be agreeable to her, for her present passion is absolute distraction.

We go to-morrow: when we come back you shall hear from me: or, perhaps, for I am something variable in my determinations,[a] as soon as I get thither. Expect nothing however: if I do you the honor,/ you must set an immense value on my condescension, for I know we shall not have a moment to spare from amusements.

Adieu!

A. WILMOT.[b]

To George Mordaunt, Esq;

I Have at length left Belmont, and left it certain of Lady Julia's tenderness: I am the happiest of mankind; she loves me, she confesses it, I have every thing to hope from time, fortune, perseverance, and the constancy of the most amiable of her sex.

All cold reserve is banished from that charming bosom; above the meanness of suspicion, she believes my passion noble and disinterested as her own; she hears my vows with a pleasure which she cannot,/ nay which she does not wish to conceal; she suffers me to swear eternal tenderness – We dined on Wednesday at the hermitage. The company dispersed, the most delicate of women, not from coquetry, but that sweet impulsive modesty, not obvious, not obtrusive,[c] which gives to beauty its loveliest charm, avoided an opportunity, which eager watchful love at last obtained: alone with her in those sweet shades, – O Mordaunt![d] let not the gross unloving libertine talk of pleasure: how tasteless are the false endearments, the treacherous arts of the venal wanton, to the sweet unaffected downcast eye of virgin innocence, the vivid glow of artless tenderness, the native vermilion[223] of blushing sensibility, the genuine smile of undissembled love!

I write this on the road to Lord T –'s, where I shall be to-night, I shall expect to hear from you immediately. Adieu!

H. MANDEVILLE.[e]/

64　　　　　　　*The History of Lady Julia Mandeville*

To HENRY MANDEVILLE, Esq;

Mount Melvin,
THURSDAY.

I Never so strongly relish the happiness of my own manner of living, as when I compare it with that of others. I hear perpetual complaints abroad of the tediousness of life, and see in every face a certain weariness of themselves, from which I am so happy as to be perfectly free. I carry about me an innate disposition to be pleased, which is the source of continual pleasure.

That I have escaped what is in general the fate of people of my rank, is chiefly owing to my fortunate choice in marriage: our mutual passion, the only foundation on which sensible souls can build happiness, has been kept alive by a delicacy of behaviour, an angel purity, in Lady Belmont,/ to which words cannot do justice. The transports of youthful passion yield its[a] sweetness to the delight of that refined, yet animated sensation which my heart feels for her at this moment. I never leave her without regret, nor meet her without rapture, the lively rapture of love,

'By long experience mellowed[b] into friendship,'[224]

We have been married thirty years. There[c] are people who think she was never handsome; yet to me she is all loveliness. I think no woman beautiful but as she resembles her; and even Julia's greatest charm, in my eye, is the likeness she has to her amiable mother.

This tender, this exquisite affection, has diffused a spirit through our whole lives, and given a charm to the most common occurrences; a charm, to which the dulness/ of apathy, and the fever of guilty passion, are equally strangers.

The family where we are furnish a striking example of the impossibility of being happy without the soft union of hearts. Though both worthy people, having been joined by their parents, without that affection which can alone make so near a connexion supportable, their lives pass on in a tedious and insipid round: without taste for each other's conversation, they engage in a perpetual series of diversions, not to give relish to, but to exclude, those retired domestic hours, which are the most sprightly, and animated of my life; they seek, by crowds and amusements, to fly from each other and from themselves.

The great secret of human happiness, my dear Mr. Mandeville, consists in finding such constant employment for the mind, as,/ without over-fatiguing, may prevent its languishing in a painful inactivity. To this end I would recommend to every man, to have not only some important point in view, but many subordinate ones, to fill up those vacant hours, when our great purpose, whatever it is, must be suspended: our very pleasures, even the best, will fatigue, if not relieved by variety: the mind cannot always be on the stretch, nor attentive to the same object, however pleasing: Relaxation[d] is as necessary as activity, to keep the soul in its due equipoise. No innocent amusement, however trifling it may seem to the rigid or the proud, is below the regard of a rational creature, which keeps the mind in play, and unbends it from more serious pursuits.

Volume I

I often regard at once with pity and astonishment, persons of my own rank and age, dragged about in unwieldy state, forging for themselves the galling fetters of/ eternal ceremony, or the still heavier chains of ambition; their bodies bending under the weight of dress, their minds for ever filled with the idea of their own dignity and importance; to the fear of lessening which, they sacrifice all the genuine pleasures of life.

Heaven grant, my dear friend, I may never be too wise, or too proud, to be happy!

To you, my amiable friend, who are just entering on the stage of life, I would recommend such active pursuits as may make you an useful member of society, and contribute to raise your own fortune and consequence in the world, as well as secure the esteem of your fellow citizens, and the approbation of your Prince.

For my own part, like the Roman veterans, I may now be excused, if I ask/ my discharge from those anxious pursuits, which are only becoming in the vigor of our days, and from those ceremonial attentions, which are scarce bearable even then. My duty as a senator, and my respect to my king, nothing but real inability shall ever suspend; but for the rest, I think it time at sixty to be free, to live to one's self, and in one's own way; and endeavour[a] to *be*, rather than to *seem* happy.

The rest of my days, except those I owe to my country and my prince, shall be devoted to the sweets of conjugal and paternal affection, to the lively joys of friendship. I have only one wish as to this world, to see Julia married to a man who deserves her, who has sensibility to make her happy, and whose rank and fortune are such as may justify us to the world, above which the most philosophic mind cannot entirely rise; let me but see this, and have a hope that they will pursue my/ plan of life, let me see them blest in each other, and blessing all around them, and my measure of earthly felicity will be complete.

You know not, my dear Mr. Mandeville, how much my happiness in this world has been owing also to the lively hope of another: this idea has given me a constant serenity, which may not improperly be called the health of the mind, and which has diffused a brightness over all my hours.

Your account of Lord T – made me smile; his fear of being dismissed at seventy from the toilsome drudgery of business, is truly ridiculous: rich, childless,[b] infirm, ought not ease and retirement to be the first objects of his wishes? But such is the wretched slavery of all who are under the absolute dominion of any passion, unguided by the hand of reason./

The passions of every kind, under proper restraints, are the gentle breezes which keep life from stagnation; but, let loose, they are the storms and whirlwinds which tear up all before them, and scatter ruin and destruction around.

Adieu. I ought to apologize for the length of this; but age is the season of garrulity.

Your affectionate
BELMONT.[c]/

To the Earl of BELMONT.

HOW happy would it be for mankind, if every person of your Lordship's rank and fortune governed themselves by the same generous maxims!

It is with infinite pain I see Lord T – pursuing a plan, which has drawn on him the curse of thousands, and made his estate a scene of desolation: his[a] farms are in the hands of a few men, to whom the sons of the old tenants are either forced to be servants, or to leave the country to get their bread elsewhere. The village, large, and once populous, is reduced to about eight families; a dreary silence reigns over their deserted fields; the farm houses, once the seats of chearful smiling industry, now useless,/ are falling in ruins around him; his tenants are merchants and ingrossers, proud, lazy, luxurious, insolent, and spurning the hand which feeds them.

Yesterday one of them went off largely in his debt: I took that occasion of pressing him on his most vulnerable side, and remonstrating the danger of trusting so much of his property in one hand: but I am afraid all I can say will have no effect, as he has, by this narrow selfish plan, a little encreased his rents at present, which is all he has in view, without extending his thoughts to that future time, when this wretched policy, by depopulating the country, will lower the price of all the fruits of the earth, and lessen, in consequence, the value of his estate.

With all my friendship for Lord T –, I cannot help observing in him another fault greatly below his rank and understanding,/ I mean a despicable kind of pride, which measures worth by the gifts of fortune, of which the largest portion is too often in the hands of the least deserving.

His treatment of some gentlemen, whose fortunes were unequal to their birth and merit, yesterday, at his table, almost determined me to leave his house: I expostulated warmly, tho'[b] not impolitely, with him on the subject, and almost got him to confess his error. My friendship for him makes me feel sensibly what must lessen his character in the eyes of all whose esteem is desirable. I wish him to pass a month at Belmont, that he may see dignity without pride, and condescension without meanness; that he may see virtue in her loveliest form, and acknowledge her genuine beauty.

I am, my Lord, &c.[c]

H. MANDEVILLE./

To GEORGE MORDAUNT, Esq;

FRIDAY.

I Have past[d] a tedious fortnight at Lord T –'s, without tasting any pleasure but that of talking of Lady Julia, with some ladies in the neighbourhood who know her. I estimate the merit of those I converse with, by the distinction of being known to her: those who are so happy as to be of her acquaintance have, in my eye, every charm, that polished wit or elegant knowledge can give; those who want that advantage scarce deserve the name of human beings: all conversation, of which she is not the subject, is lifeless and insipid; all, of which she is, brilliant and divine.

My Lord rallies me on my frequent visits to these Ladies, and, as one of them is extremely handsome, supposes it a beginning passion: the Lady herself, I am/ afraid, is deceived, for, as she is particularly warm in her praises of Lady Julia, my eyes sparkle with pleasure at her approach, I single her out in every company, and dance with her at all our little parties; I have even an attention to her superior to that of common lovers, and feel for her a tenderness for which I want a name.

Lady Anne has had the goodness to write twice to me, from Lord Rochdale's, whither my Lord went, with his amiable family, two days after I left Belmont: Lady Julia is well, she loves me, she hears of me with pleasure. Ought I at present to wish more?[a]

I have hinted to Lord T – my purpose, though not the dear motive which inspired it; he is warmly my friend, if there is truth in man. I will be more explicit the first time I see him alone: shall[b] I own to you one weakness of my heart? I would be/ served by any interest but Lord Belmont's. How can I pretend to his daughter, if all I have is, in a manner, his gift? I would be rich independently of his friendship.

Lord T – is walking in the garden alone, I will go to him, and explain all my designs: his knowledge of mankind will guide me to the best road to wealth and honor, his friendship will assist me to the ample extent of his power. Adieu!/

To Henry Mandeville, Esq;

OH,[c] do you know I have a little request to make you? but[d] first, by way of preface, I must inform you, Lady Belmont has been reading me a serious lecture about the Caro Bellville, who has wrote to her to beg her intercession in his favor.

I find fools have been impertinent in regard to our friendship: there are so few pleasures in this world, I think it extremely hard to give up one so lively, yet innocent, as that of indulging a tender esteem for an amiable man. But to our conversation:

'My dear Lady Anne, I am convinced you love Colonel Bellville.'[e]

Love him, Madam? no, I rather think not; I am not sure: The man is not shocking, and dies for me: I pity him, poor creature;/ and pity, your Ladyship knows, is a-kin[f] to love.[225]

Will you be grave[226] one moment?

A thousand, if your Ladyship desires it: nothing, so easy to me; the gravest creature in the world naturally.

You allow Colonel Bellville merit?

Certainement.[227]

That he loves you?

To distraction.

And you return it?

68 *The History of Lady Julia Mandeville*

Why as to that – he flatters agreeably, and I am fond of his conversation on that account: and let me tell you, my dear Lady Belmont, it is not every man that can flatter; it requires more genius than one would suppose./

You intend some time or other to marry him?

Marry? O heavens!ᵃ How did such a thought enter your Ladyship's imagination? Haveᵇ not I been married already? And is not once enough in conscience, for any reasonable woman?

Will you pardon me if I then ask, with what view you allow his address?

I allow? Heavens, Lady Belmont! I allow the addresses of an odious male animal? If fellows will follow one, how is it to be avoided?ᶜ it is one's misfortune to be handsome, and one must bear the consequences.

But, my dear Lady Anne, an unconnected life –

Is the pleasantest life in the world. Have not I 3000*l.*ᵈ a year? am not I a widow? mistress of my own actions? with youth, health, a tolerable understanding,/ an air of the world, and a person not very disagreeable?

All this I own.

All this? yes, and twenty times more, or you do nothing. Have not these unhappy eyes carryedᵉ destruction from one climate to another? Haveᶠ not the sprightly French, the haughty Romans, confestᵍ themselves my slaves? Haveʰ not – But it would take up a life to tell you all my conquests.

But what is all this to the purpose, my dear?

Now I protest I think it is vastly to the purpose. And all this you advise me to give up, to become a tame, domestic, inanimate – reallyⁱ, my dear Madam, I did not think it was in your nature to be so unreasonable.

It is with infinite pain, my dearest Lady Anne, I bring myself to say any thing/ which can give you a moment's uneasiness. But it is the task of true friendship –

To tell disagreeable truths: I know that is what your Ladyship would say: and, to spare you what your delicacy starts at mentioning, you have heard aspersions on my character, which are the consequences of my friendship for Col. Bellville.

I know and admire the innocent chearfulness of your heart, but I grieve to say, the opinion of the world –

As to the opinion of the world, by which is meant the malice of a few spiteful old cats, I am perfectly unconcerned about it; but your Ladyship's esteem is necessary to my happiness: I will therefore to you vindicate my conduct: which, though indiscreet, has been really irreproachable. Though a widow, and accountable to nobody, I have ever lived/ with Colonel Bellville, with the reserve of blushing apprehensive fifteen, whilst the warmth of my friendship for him, and the pleasure I found in his conversation, have let loose the baleful tongue of envy, and subjected my resolutionʲ to the malice of an ill-judging world, a world I despise for his sake, a world, whose applause is too often bestowed on the cold, the selfish, and the artful, and denied to that generous unsuspecting openness and warmth of heart, which

Volume I 69

are the strongest characteristicks[a] of true virtue. My friendship, or, if you please, my love, for Colonel Bellville, is the first pleasure of my life; the happiest hours of which have been past[b] in his conversation; nor is there any thing I would not sacrifice to my passion for him, but his happiness; which, for reasons unknown to your Ladyship, is incompatible with his marrying me./

But is it not possible to remove those reasons?

I am afraid not.

Would it not then, my dear Madam, be most prudent to break off a connexion, which can answer no purpose but making both unhappy?

I own it would, but prudence was never a part of my character. Will you forgive and pity me, Lady Belmont, when I say, that, though I see in the strongest light my own indiscretion, I am not enough mistress of my heart to break with the man to whom I have only a very precarious and distant hope of being united? There is an enchantment[c] in his friendship, which I have not force of mind to break through; he is my guide, my guardian, protector, friend; the only man I ever loved, the man to whom the last recesses of my heart are open: must[d] I give up the tender exquisite, refined delight of his conversation,/ to the false opinion of a world, governed by prejudice, judging by the exterior, which is generally fallacious, and condemning, without distinction, those soft affections without which life is scarcely above vegetation?

Do not imagine, my dear Lady Belmont, I have really the levity I affect: or, had my prejudices against marriage been ever so strong, the time I have passed here would have removed them: I see my Lord and you, after an union of thirty years, with as keen a relish for each other's conversation as you could have felt at the moment which first joined you: I see in you all the attention, the tender solicitude of beginning love, with the calm delight and perfect confidence of habitual friendship. I am therefore convinced marriage is capable of happiness, to which an unconnected state is lifeless and insipid; and, from observing the lovely delicacy of your/ Ladyship's conduct, I am instructed how that happiness is to be secured; I am instructed how to avoid that tasteless, languid, unimpassioned hour, so fatal to love and friendship.

With the man to whom I was a victim, my life was one continued scene of misery; to a sensible mind, there is no cold medium in marriage; its sorrows, like its pleasures, are exquisite. Relieved from those galling chains, I have met with a heart suited[e] to my own; born with the same sensibility, the same peculiar turn of thinking: pleased with the same pleasures, and exactly formed to make me happy:[f] I will believe this similarity was not given to condemn us both to wretchedness: as it is impossible either of us can be happy but with the other, I will hope the bar, which at present seems invincible, may be removed: till then indulge me, my dear Lady Belmont, in the innocent/ pleasure of loving him, and trust to his honor for the safety of mine.'

70   *The History of Lady Julia Mandeville*

The most candid and amiable of women, after a gentle remonstrance on the importance of reputation to happiness, left me, so perfectly satisfied, that she intends to invite Bellville down. I send you this conversation as an introduction to a request I have to make you, which I must postpone to my next. Heavens! how perverse! interrupted by one of the veriest cats in nature, who will not leave us till ages after the post is gone. Adieu! for the present!ᵃ it is prettily enough contrived, and one of the great advantages of society, that one'sᵇ time, the most precious of all possessions, is to be sacrifised,ᶜ from a false politeness, to every idle creature who knows not what else to do. Every body complains of this, but nobody attempts to remedy it./

Am not I the most inhuman of women, to write two sheets without naming Lady Julia?ᵈ She is well, and beautiful as an angel: we have a ball to-night on Lord Melvin's return, against which she is putting on all her charms. We shall be at Belmont to-morrow, which is two or three days sooner than my Lord intended.

Lady Julia dances with Lord Melvin, who is, except two, the most amiable man I know: she came up just as I sat down to write, and looked as if she had something to say: she is gone, however, without a word; her childish bashfulness about you is intolerable.

The ball waits for us. I am interrupted by an extreme pretty fellow, Sir Charles Mellifont, who has to-night the honor of my hand. Adio!ᵉ

A. WILMOT.ᶠ/

To Lady ANNE WILMOT.

'WE have a ball to-night on Lord Melvin's return, against which she is putting on all her charms.'

Oh, Lady Anne!ᵍ can you indeed know what it is to love, yet play with the anxiety of a tender heart? I can scarce bear the thought of her looking lovely in my absence, or in any eyes but mine; how then can I support the idea of her endeavouringʰ to please another, of her putting on all her charms to grace the return of a man, young, amiable, rich, noble, and the son of her father's friend? aⁱ thousand fears, a thousand conjectures torment me: should she love another – the possibility distracts/ me. – Go to her, and ask her if the tenderest, most exalted passion, if the man who adores her – I know not what I would say – youʲ have set me on the rack – If you have pity, my dearest Lady Anne, lose not a moment to make me easy.

Yours, &c.
H. MANDEVILLE.ᵏ

The END *of the* FIRST VOLUME.ˡ

VOLUME II

To Miss HOWARD.

BELMONT, TUESDAY.

O EMILY! How inconsistent is a heart in love!ᵃ I entreated Mr. Mandeville not to write to me, and am chagrined at his too exact obedience: I think, if he loved as I do, he could not so easily obey me. He writes to Lady Anne; and, though by my desire,/ I am ashamed of my weakness; – but I wish he wrote less often:ᵇ there is an air of gaiety in his letters which offends me – He talks of balls, of parties with ladies – Perhaps I am unjust, but the delicacy of my love is wounded by his knowing a moment's pleasure in my absence; to me all places are equal where he is not; all amusements without him are dull, and tasteless. Have not I an equal right to expect, Emily!ᶜ He knows not how I love him.

Convinced that this mutual passion is the designation of heaven to restore him to that affluence he lost by the partiality of an ancestor, and the generous loyalty of his family, I give way to it without reserve; I regard my love as a virtue; I am proud of having distinguished his merit without those trappings of wealth, which alone can attract common eyes. His idea is for ever before me; I think with transport of those enchanting moments/ – Emily, that week of tender confidence is all my life, the rest is not worth numbering in my existence.

My father to-night gives a ball to Lord Melvin, with whom I am again, unwillingly, obliged to dance. I wish not to dance at all; to make this sacrifice to the most beloved of men: Why have I not courage to avow my sentiments, to declare he alone – This Lord Melvin too, I know not why, but I never see him without horror.

O Emily! How do all men sink on the comparison!ᵈ He seems of a superior rank of beings. Your Julia will never give her hand to another; she swears this to the dear bosom of friendship.

This detested Lord Melvin is at the door; he will not let me proceed; he tells me it is to a lover I am writing; he says/ this in a manner, and with a tone of voice – he looks at me with an earnestness – Lady Anne has alarmed me – Should my

72   *The History of Lady Julia Mandeville*

father intend – yet why should I fear the most cruel of all acts of tyranny from the most tender and indulgent of parents?[a]

I feel a dejection of spirits on this subject, which does injury, to my father's goodness: perhaps it is no more than the natural effects of absence on, a tender and unexperienced heart.

Adieu! I am forced to finish my letter. All good angels guard and preserve my Emily![b]

Yours,

JULIA MANDEVILLE.[c]/

To the Earl of BELMONT.

WITH all my affection for Lord T –, I am hourly shocked by that most unworthy of all faults, his haughtiness to inferior fortune, however distinguished by virtue, talents, or even the more shining advantage of birth. Dress, equipage, and the over-bearing assurance which wealth inspires, strike him so forcibly, that there is no room in his soul for that esteem which is a debt to modest merit;

We had yesterday to dine Mr. Herbert, one of the most amiable men I ever saw; his person was genteel, his countenance at once expressive of genius and worth, which were rendered more touching to me, by that pensive look and irresolute air, which are the constant attendants on an adverse fortune. Lord T – returned his bow/ almost without looking at him, and continued talking familiarly to a wretch with whom no gentleman would converse, were he not master of six thousand a year: the whole company, instructed in his situation by the supercilious air of the master of the house, treated him with the same neglect, which I endeavoured to console him for by every little civility in my power, and by confining my attention intirely[d] to him; when we parted, he asked me to his house with a look full of sensibility; an invitation I shall take the first opportunity of accepting.

When the company were gone, I asked Lord T – the character of this stranger. Why, really, says[e] he, I believe he is in himself the most estimable man in my neighbourhood; of a good family too; but one must measure one's reception of people by the countenance the world shews them; and he is too poor to be greatly caressed/ there. Besides I am not fond of being acquainted with unhappy people; they are very apt to ask favours.[f]

Is it possible, said I, my Lord, interrupting him hastily, you can avow sentiments like these? Why[g] are you raised by Providence above others? Why entrusted with that wealth and consequence which might make you a guardian angel to the unhappy? Where is my chaise?[h] I will return to Belmont, where affliction ever finds a ready audience; where adversity is sure of being heard, though pomp and equipage wait.

Volume II 73

Lord T – smiled at my earnestness, and praised the generosity of my senti-ments, which he assured me were his at my age: he owned he had been to blame; but in the world, said he, Harry, we are carried away by the torrent, and act wrong every moment mechanically meerly[1] by seeing others do the same. However I/ stand corrected, and you shall have no future reason to complain of me.[a]

He spoke this with an air of good humour which reconciled us, and has promised to accompany me in my visit to Mr. Herbert, which I have insisted shall be the first we pay, and that he shall beg his pardon for the behaviour of yesterday.

Is it not strange, my Lord, that men whose hearts are not bad, can avoid those whose characters do honor to their species, only because fortune denies them those outward distinctions which wealth can give to the lowest and most despic-able of mankind?

Surely of all human vices, Pride is the most detestable![2]

I am, &c.

H. MANDEVILLE.[b]/

To HENRY MANDEVILLE, Esquire.

CAN I play with the anxiety of a tender heart? Certainly, or I should not be what I am, a coquet[c] of the first order. Setting aside the pleasure of the thing, and I know few pleasanter amusements, Policy dictates this conduct; for there is no possibility of keeping any of you without throwing the charms of dear variety into one's treatment of you: nothing cloys like continual sweets; a little acid is absolutely necessary.

I am just come from giving Lady Julia some excellent advice on the subject of her passion for you. Really, my dear, said I, you are extremely absurd to blush and look foolish about loving so pretty a fellow as Harry Mandeville, handsome, well made, lively, elegant; in the true classical stile,[d]/ and approved by the connois-seurs, by Madame le Comtesse de – herself, whom I look upon to be the greatest judge of male merit on the face of the globe.

It is not for loving him I am angry with you, but for entertaining so ridicu-lous a thought as that of marrying him. You have only one rational step to take; marry Lord Melvin, who has title and fortune, requisites not to be dispensed with in a husband, and take Harry Mandeville for your Cecisbeo.

The dear creature was immensely displeased, as you, who know the romantic turn of her imagination, will easily conceive.

O,[e] I had almost forgot: yes, indeed, you have great right to give yourself jealous airs: we have not heard of your coquetry with Miss Truman. My corre-spondent tells me there is no doubt of its being a real passion on both sides, and/

74   *The History of Lady Julia Mandeville*

that the Truman family have been making private enquiries into your fortune. I shewed Lady Julia the letter, and you cannot conceive how prettily she blushed.

But to be grave, I am afraid you have nothing, to fear from Lord Melvin. You must forgive my making use of this expression; for, as I see no possibility of surmounting the obstacles which oppose your union with Lady Julia, I am too much a friend to both, not to wish earnestly to break a connexion which has not a shadow of hope to support it.

But a truce to this subject, which is not a pleasant one to either of us.

I told you in my last I had something to say to you. As I am your confidente[a], you must consent to be mine, having a little present occasion for your services. You are to know, my dear Harry, that, with all/ my coquetry, I am as much in love as yourself, and with almost as little prospect of success: this odious money is absolutely the bane of us true lovers, and always contrives to stand in our way.

My dear spouse then, who in the whole course of our acquaintance did but one obliging thing, being kindly determined I should neither be happy with him nor without him, obligingly, though nobody knows this but myself and the Caro Bellville, made my jointure what it is, on condition I never married again: on observance of which condition, it was to be in my power to give the estate to whoever I pleased at my death; but, on a proof of my supposed future marriage, it was to go immediately to a niece of his, who at his death was in a convent in France, who is ignorant of this condition, and whose whole present fortune scarce amounts to fifteen hundred pounds. She is both in person and mind one of the/ most lovely of women, and has an affection for me, which inclines me to think she would come into measures for my sake, which I shall make it her interest to acquiesce in for her own.

Bellville's fortune is extremely moderate; and, if I marry him at present, I shall not add a shilling to it; his income will remain in statu-quo,[b] with the incumbrance of an indigent woman of quality, whose affairs are a little derangé,[3] and amongst whose virtues œconomy was never one of the most observable. He would with transport marry me to-morrow, even on these hard conditions; but how little should I deserve so generous a passion, if I suffered it to seduce him to his ruin?[c] I have wrote to my niece to come to England, when I shall tell her my passion for Bellville, and propose to her a private agreement to divide the fortune, which will be forfeited to her on my marriage, and which it is in my/ power by living single to deprive her of forever. Incapable, however, of injustice, I have at all events made a will, dividing it equally between her and Bellville, if I die unmarried: I have a right to do this for the man I love, as my father left thirty thousand pounds to Mr. Wilmot, which in equity ought to be regarded as mine,[4] and which is all I desire, on the division: she, therefore, by my will, has all she ever can expect, even from the strictest justice: and she can never, I think,

Volume II 75

hesitate between waiting till my death and at my mercy, and receiving the utmost she could hope then, at the present.[a]

I have heard from the lady to whom I enclosed[b] my letter, which she has returned, my niece having left France a year ago, to accompany a relation into Italy. What I, therefore, have to ask of you is, to endeavour[c] to find her out, by your Italian friends, as I will by mine at the same time, that I/ may write to her to return immediately to England, as I will not run the hazard of mentioning the subject in a letter. She is the daughter of the late colonel Hastings, once abroad in a public character, and is well known in Italy.

Bellville is not at all in the secret of my scheme; nor did I ever tell him I would marry him, though I sometimes give him reason to hope.

I am too good a politician[5] in love matters ever to put a man out of doubt till half an hour before the ceremony. The moment a woman is weak enough to promise, she sets the heart of her lover at rest; the chace, and of consequence the pleasure, is at an end; and he has nothing to do but to seek a new object, and begin the pursuit over again./

I tell you, but I tell it in confidence, that if I find Bell Hastings, if she comes into my scheme, and my mind does not change, I may, perhaps, do Bellville the honor. And yet, when I reflect on the matter; on the condition of the obligation, 'so long as ye both shall live' – Jesu Maria! Only think of promising to be of the same mind as long as one lives.[d] My dear Harry, people may talk as they will, but the thing is utterly impossible.

Adieu!

Mon cher Ami,[6]

A. Wilmot.[e]

To George Mordaunt, Esquire.

I Have already told you I came hither with a view of engaging Lord T –'s interest in support of those views, on which all my hopes of happiness depend. The friendship he has ever professed for me has been warm as that of a father. I was continually with him at Rome, and he there/ prest[f] me to accept those services I then never expected to have occasion for. Till now content with my situation, love first raised in me the spirit of ambition, and determined me to accept those offers. In a former letter I told you I was going to follow Lord T – into the garden, to communicate to him my purpose of pushing my fortune in the world; on which I had before given general hints, which he seemed to approve, as a kind of spirit becoming a young man, warm with hope, and not destitute of merit.

On revolving my scheme as I approached him, it appeared so romantic, so void of all rational hope, that I had not resolution to mention it, and determined at least to suspend it till better digested, and more fitted to bear the cool eye of impartial reason: in these sentiments I should still have remained, had not a letter from Lady Anne Wilmot, by giving me jealousy, determined/ me not to defer one moment a design on which all my happiness depended.

I, therefore, with some hesitation, this morning opened all my heart, and the real state of my circumstances, to Lord T –, concealing only what related to Lady Julia. He heard me with great coolness, carelessly lolling[7] on a settee;[8] his eyes fixed on a new Chinese summer-house,[9] opposite the window near which he sat, and made me the following answer; 'Your views, Mr. Mandeville, seem rather romantic, for a man who has no party connexions, and so little parliamentary interest. However, you are of a good family, and there are things to be had in time if properly recommended. Have you no friend who would mention you to the minister?'[10] He then rang the bell hastily for his valet, and retired to dress, leaving me motionless with astonishment and indignation./

We met no more till dinner, when he treated me with a distant civility, the meaning of which was easily understood. He apologized with an air of ceremony on his being forced to go for a fortnight to Scarborough, with a party, who, being all strangers, he was afraid would not be agreeable to me; but at his return he should be glad of the honor of seeing me again, I bowed coldly, and took no other notice of what he said, than to order my chaise immediately on which he pressed my stay to-night, but in vain. The servants leaving the room, he was a little disconcerted, but observed, he was sorry for me; my case was really hard; he always thought my fortune much larger; wondered at my father's indiscretion in educating me so improperly – People[a] ought to consider their circumstances – It[b] was pity I had no friend – Lord Belmont, if he pleased, but he was so absurdly fond of his independence.[c]/

During this[d] harangue I intirely[e] recovered my presence of mind, and with an air of great ease and unconcern told his Lordship, I was much obliged to him for curing me of a pursuit so improper for a man of my temper: that the liberal offers of service he had formerly made me at Rome had betrayed me into a false opinion of the friendship of great men; but that I was now convinced of what value such professions are, and that they are only made where it seems certain they will never be accepted. That[f] it was impossible his Lordship could judge properly of the conduct of a man of my father's characters; that[g] I was proud of being son to the most exalted and generous of mankind; and would not give up that honor to be first minister to the first prince on earth. That[h] I never so strongly felt the value of independence as at that moment, and did not wonder at the value Lord Belmont set on so inestimable a blessing.[i]/

I came away without waiting for an answer, and stopped at an inn about ten miles off, where I am now waiting for one of my servants, whom I left behind to bring me a letter I expect to-day from Lady Anne Wilmot.

And now, my dear Mordaunt, what will become of your unhappy friend? The flattering hopes I fondly entertained are dispersed like a flitting cloud. Lord T –'s behaviour has removed the veil which love had spread over the wildness of my design, and convinced me that success is impossible. Where or to whom shall I now apply? Lord T –[a] was him on whose friendship I most depended; whose power to serve me was greatest, and whose professions gave me most right to expect his services.

I here for ever give up all views – Can I then calmly give up the hopes of Lady/ Julia? I will go back, confess my passion to Lord Belmont, and throw myself on that goodness whose first delight is that of making others happy. Yet can I hope he will give his daughter, the heiress of such affluence – Disinterested and noble as he is, the false maxims of the world – Mordaunt, I am born to wretchedness – What have I gained by inspiring the most angelic of women with pity? I have doomed to misery her for whose happiness I would sacrifice my life.

The servant I left at Lord T –'s, is this moment arrived; he has brought me a letter – I know not why, but my hand trembles, I have scarce power to break the seal./

To Henry Mandeville, Esquire.[b]

Summon all your resolution, my dear Mr. Mandeville – Sure[c] my fears were prophetic – do not be too much alarmed – Lady Julia is well; she is in tears by me; she disapproves her father's views; she begs me to assure you her heart is not less sensible than yours will be to so cruel a stroke; begs you not to return yet to Belmont, but to depend on her affection, and leave your fate in her hands.

The inclosed letters will acquaint you with what I have been for some time in apprehension of. With such a design for his daughter, why did my Lord bring you to Belmont? So[d] formed to inspire love as you both are, why did he expose you to danger it was scarce possible for you to escape?/

But it is now too late to wish you had never met; all my hopes are in your resolution; I dare expect nothing from Lady Julia's.

To the Earl of Belmont.[e]

September 10.

My Lord,

YOUR Lordship's absence, and the death of my mother, which renders my estate more worthy Lady Julia, has hitherto prevented my explanation of an unguarded expression, which I find has had the misfortune to displease you. I am far from intending – Your Lordship intirely[f] mistakes me – No[g] man can be more sensible of the honor of your lordship's alliance, or of Lady Julia's uncommon perfections: but a light way of talking, which one naturally acquires in the

78   *The History of Lady Julia Mandeville*

world, has led me/ undesignedly into some appearance of disrespect to a state, of the felicity of which I have not the least doubt.

I flatter myself your Lordship will, on cooler reflexion, forgive an unguarded word, and allow me to hope for the honor of convincing you and the lady, by my future conduct, that no man has a higher idea of matrimonial happiness, than,

My Lord,
Your Lordship's
Most devoted, and very
obedient Servant,
FONDVILLE./

To Lord Viscount FONDVILLE.[a]

My LORD,

I Readily admit your Lordship's apology; as I am under no apprehension any man can intend to slight the alliance of one who has always endeavoured[b] his character should be worthy his birth, and the rank he has the honor to hold in his country.

As I love the plainest dealing in affairs of such consequence, I will not a moment deceive your Lordship, or suffer you to engage in a pursuit, which, if I have any influence over my daughter, will be unsuccessful; not from any disesteem of your Lordship, but because I have another view for her, the disappointment of which would destroy all my hopes of a happy evening of life, and embitter my last hours. I have long intended her, with her own approbation, which her filial piety gives me/ no room to doubt, for the son of my friend, the heir of an earldom, and of an affluent fortune; and, what I much more value, of uncommon merit; and one of the first families in the kingdom.

I am sure your Lordship will not endeavour[c] to oppose a design, which has been long formed, is far advanced, and on which I have so much set my heart.

I am, my Lord,

With great Regard, your
Lordship's very obedient,
And devoted Servant,

BELMONT.

I have long, my dear Mr. Mandeville, suspected my Lord's design in favour of Lord Melvin, of which there is not now the least doubt. Our coming away from his father's, on his arrival, was a circumstance/ which then struck me extremely. Lady Julia's stay there, on this supposition, would have been ill suited to the delicacy of her sex and rank. Yet I am astonished my Lord has not sooner told her of it; but there is no accounting for the caprice of age. How shall I tell my dear Mr.

Mandeville my sentiments on this discovery! How[a] shall I, without wounding a passion which bears no restraint, hint to him my wishes, that he would sacrifice that love, which can only by its continuance make him wretched, to Lady Julia's peace of mind! That[b] he would himself assist her to conquer an inclination which is incompatible with the views which the most indulgent of parents entertains for her happiness![c] Views, the disappointment of which, he has declared, will embitter his last hours?[d] Make one generous effort, my amiable friend: it is glorious to conquer where conquest is most difficult: think of Lord Belmont's friendship; of his almost/ parental care of your fortune; of the pleasure with which he talks of your virtues; and it will be impossible for you to continue to oppose that design on which his hopes of a happy evening of life are founded. Would you deny a happy evening to that life to which thousands owe the felicity of theirs?

It is from you, and not Lady Julia, I expect this sacrifice: the consideration which will most strongly influence you to make it, will for ever prevent her; it pains me to wound your delicacy, by saying I mean the difference of your fortunes. From a romantic generosity, she will think herself obliged to that perseverance, which the same generosity now calls loudly on you to decline. If you have greatness of mind to give up hopes which can never be accomplished, time and absence may assist Lady Julia's filial sweetness, and bring her to a compliance with her father's will. Believe,/ that, whilst I write, my heart melts with compassion for you both; and that nothing but the tenderest friendship could have urged me to so painful a task.

I am, &c.

A. Wilmot.[e]

O Mordaunt! till now I was never truly wretched. I[f] have not even a glimpse of hope remaining. I must give up the only wish for which life is worth my care, or embitter the last hours of the man, who with unequalled generosity has pleaded my cause against himself, and declined a noble acquisition of fortune, that it might give consequence, and, as he thought, happiness to me.

But Lady Julia[g] – Heaven is my witness, to make her happy, I would this moment give up all my rights in her heart. I would myself lead her to the altar, though the same hand the next moment – Mordaunt, I will promise, if she requests/ it, to consent to her marriage; but I will not to survive it. My thoughts are all distraction – I cannot write to Lady Anne – I will write to the most lovely of women – She knows not the cruel request of her friend – Her love disdains the low consideration of wealth – Our hearts were formed for each other – She knows every sentiment of my soul – She knows, that, were I monarch of the world – O Mordaunt[h] is it possible – Can[i] the gentle, the indulgent Lord Belmont – but all conspires to undo me: the best, the most mild of mankind is turned a tyrant to make me wretched. I will know from herself if she consents;

80   *The History of Lady Julia Mandeville*

I will give up my own hopes to her happiness; but let me first be convinced it is indeed her happiness, not the prejudices of her father, to which I make so cruel a sacrifice.

I have wrote[a] to Lady Julia, and am more calm: I have mentioned Lady Anne's/ request. I have told her, that, though without hope, if I am still blest in her affection, I will never resign her but with life: but if she can be happy with Lord Melvin, if she asks it, she is this moment free. I have entreated her to consult her own heart, without a thought of me; that I would die this moment to contribute to her peace; that the first purpose of my life is her happiness, with which my own shall never come in competition; that there is nothing I will ever refuse her, but to cease to think of her with adoration; that if she wishes to marry Lord Melvin (Great[b] Heaven! is it possible she can wish it?[c]) I will return to Italy, and carry far from her a passion which can never cease but in the grave.

I will wait here an answer, and then determine where to go./

To Col. BELLVILLE.

THURSDAY.

EMILY HOWARD came last night. Lady Julia and she are reading natural history[11] with my Lord, and examining butterflies wings in a microscope;[12] a pretty innocent amusement to keep young ladies out of mischief.[d] I wish my Lord had thought of it sooner, it might have been of great use to Lady Julia: if one is but amused, it is of no great consequence whether by a butterfly or a lover.

Vastly severe that last sentence; it must be allowed I have a pretty genius for satire.

My Lord certainly intends Lady Julia for Lord Melvin. I have wrote Harry a ridiculous wise letter, perswading[e] him to sacrifise[f]/ his own passion to my Lord's caprice; and giving him advice, which I should hate him, if I thought him capable of following. How easy it is to be wise for any body but ones[g] self! I suppose Harry could with great calmness preach on the imprudence of my attachment to you.

We are going to a strolling play[13] to-night. My Lord encourages diversions on his estate, on the same principle that a wise prince protects the fine arts, to keep his people at home.

We had a family to dine here yesterday, who are very agreeable people, and to whom my Lord shewed a particular attention. Mr. Barker, the father, is the most bearable man I have seen in this country; and the daughters vastly above the stile of the misses here: Lady Belmont intends to take them this winter with her to town,/ as she does, every year, some gentleman's daughter in her neighbourhood.

Adieu! I am peevish beyond measure, and scarce know what I would be at. Have you never these kinds[h] of feels? Never[i] fretful, you cannot tell why? It is well for you, you are not here: a lover and a favourite lap-dog have a dreadful life on these occasions; or indeed any animal one can use ill with impunity. Strangely severe to-day; do not you perceive it?

Six o'clock.

Ten thousand times more peevish than ever: we have just had a visit from 'the best kind of woman in the world,' and her daughter, 'an amiable and accomplished young lady,' who writes verses and journals, paints, makes shell-flowers, cuts paper,[14] and has 'every qualification to render the marriage state happy;'/ talks of the charms of rural retirement, the pleasures of reflexion, the beauties of the mind; and sings, 'Love's a gentle generous passion.'[15] It was not in nature to have stood it a quarter of an hour. Heaven be praised! the play hour is come, and the coaches are at the door.

Eleven o'Clock.

We have seen them enact Juliet and Romeo. Lady Julia seemed to sympathize with the heroine.

'I'll not wed Paris, Romeo is my husband.'[16]

Buona Notte.[17]/

To Colonel BELLVILLE.

WE have been all extremely busy today, celebrating a harvest home;[18a] a long procession of our village youths, all drest gaily in fine shirts, adorned with ribbands, paired with the handsomest of the country girls, in white jackets and petticoats, garlands of flowers and wheat-ears on their heads, their rakes streaming with various coloured[b] ribbands, which glittered in the sun-beams, preceded the harvest cart; on which, in a bower of green boughs, stood a beautiful little girl, drest in the rural stile, with inimitable elegance, by the hands of Lady Julia herself. The gay procession walked slowly through the village; a tabor[19] and pipe playing before them, till they came before the house, where they danced a thousand little rustic dances, the novelty of which charmed me extremely:/ they then adjourned to the hall, where a plentiful feast was provided, and where the whole village were that night my Lord's guests.

Lord Belmont is extremely fond of all these old customs, and will suffer none of them to be left off on his estate. The prospect of this festivity, he says, chears them in their labor, and is a laudable tribute of gladness to that beneficent Being, to whose bounty we owe the full reward of our toil, the plenteous harvest, and who rejoices in the happiness of his creatures.

Besides, says my Lord, all these amusements encourage a spirit of matrimony, and encrease[c] the number of my people.[d]

82 *The History of Lady Julia Mandeville*

And pray, my dear Lord, do they encourage no other spirit?[a]/

No, Madam; Lady Belmont's anger and mine would, in such a case, they know, contrary to that of the world, fall chiefly where it ought, on the seducer, who would be for ever expelled from my estate, the heaviest punishment I could possibly inflict. Then, as I am a declared enemy to interested marriages, the young people are allowed to chuse for themselves, which removes the temptation to vice, which is generally caused by the shameful avarice of parents.

Our example too is of great service, and allures them to a regular behaviour; they think that must be the happiest life, which we, who have the power of chusing, prefer; and therefore it is the fashion amongst them to be regular, and seek their happiness, as we do, at home.

I believe my Lord is right: I am well pleased too, he throws the blame on you he-wretches,[20] and excuses the poor lasses./ In the eye of the world it is to be sure 'toute au contraire;'[21] but my Lord and Lady Belmont are so singular as to see with their own eyes.

Adieu! We are all to go down one dance with the villagers, and I hear the tabor and pipe.

O Heavens! a coach and six, the Mandeville livery;[b] a running footman;[c] it must be Lady Mary; I will enquire: it is herself; my Lord flies to receive her in the court; Lady Belmont and Lady Julia are at the door; she alights; I never saw her before; her figure is striking, full of dignity, and that grace which is almost lost in this generation; she enters the house leaning on my Lord. I am grieved Harry is gone; I wished her to be some time with him; she only just saw him as he came through London in his way to Belmont./

But I must go to pay my respects. Adieu!

To George Mordaunt, Esquire.

Tuesday, September 14.

AS I was sitting alone this morning at the inn looking out at a window, I saw ride into the yard Mr. Herbert, the gentleman to whom I took so strong an inclination at Lord T –'s, and for whose character I have the highest esteem. He saw me, and, springing eagerly from his horse, sent to know if I would admit him. He came, and, after expressing some surprize at seeing me there, on my telling him I had left Lord T –'s, and waited there a few days for letters, he insisted on my spending that time at his house, in a manner which it was impossible for me to refuse. As we rode, he apologized for the entertainment/ I should meet with; wished for a larger share of the gifts of fortune, that he might receive his friends in a manner more suited to his desires; but said, if he knew me, the heart of the host was all I should care for; and that I should relish the homely meat of chearful friendship, as well as the splendid profusion of luxury and pride.[d]

Volume II

We arrived at a neat house, with a little romantic[22] garden behind it, where we were received by Mrs. Herbert with that hospitable air which is inseparable from real benevolence of heart. Her person was extremely pleasing, and her dress elegantly plain. She had a little boy sitting by her, lovely and playful as a Cupid.

Neatness and propriety presided at our frugal meat; and, after a little desert of excellent fruit from their garden, Mr. Herbert took me the tour of his estate, which consists of about seventy acres, which he cultivates/ himself, and has embellished with every thing that can make it lovely: all has the appearance of content and peace: I observed this to him, and added, that I infinitely envied his happiness. He stopped and looked earnestly at me; I am indeed, said he, happy in many things, and though my fortune is greatly below my birth and hopes, I am not in want; things may be better, till then I bear them as I can: my wife, whose worth outweighs all praise, combats our ill fate with a spirit I cannot always imitate; for her, Mr. Mandeville, for her, I feel with double keenness the stings of adversity.

I observed him too much affected to pursue the subject farther; I therefore changed it, and returned to the house: but I will not leave him till I am instructed how to draw the worm of discontent[23] from one of the worthiest of human bosoms./

Write to me here. I shall stay till I know when my father will be in the country. Adieu!

To Colonel BELLVILLE.

WEDNESDAY.

I AM charmed with Lady Mary, her address is easy, polite, attentive; she is tall, brown, well made, and perfectly graceful; her air would inspire awe, if not softened by the utmost sweetness and affability of behaviour. She has great vivacity in her looks and manner; her hair is quite white; her eyes have lost their lustre, yet it is easy to see she has been very handsome; her hand and arm are yet lovely, of which she is not a little vain: take her for all in all, she is the finest ruin I ever beheld.

She is full of anecdotes of the Queen's time, chose with judgment, and told with/ spirit, which make her conversation infinitely amusing. She has been saying so many fine things of Harry, who by the way strongly resembles her, that I begin to think the good old lady has a matrimonial design upon him: really not amiss such a scheme; fine remains, an affluent fortune, and as to years, eighty is absolutely the best age I know for a wife, except eighteen. She thinks him, what is extremely in his favor, very like her brother, who was killed at the battle of Almanza.[24]

She has the talkativeness of age, which, where there is sense and knowledge of the world, I do not dislike; she is learned in genealogy, and can tell you not

84   *The History of Lady Julia Mandeville*

only the intermarriages, but the family virtues and vices of every ancient house in the kingdom; as to the modern ones, she does not think them worth studying. I am high in her favor, because my blood has never been contaminated by a city marriage.[25] She/ tells me the women of my family have always been famous for a certain ease and bon air, which she is glad to see is not lost; and that my grandmother was the greatest ornament of Queen Mary's court.[26]

She has a great contempt for the present race of beauties, says the very idea of grace is almost lost, and that we see nothing now but meer[a] pretty women; that she can only account for this, by supposing the trifling turn of their minds gives an insignificance to their persons; and that she would advise them to learn to think and act, in order to their being able to look and move, with dignity. 'You, nephew, she says, who remember each bright Churchill[27] of the Galaxy, will readily come into my opinion.' She does me the honor, however, to say I am the most graceful woman she has seen since the Queen's time./

She is a great politician and something inclined to be a tory, though she professes perfect impartiality; loves the King, and idolizes the Queen, because she thinks she sees in her the sweet affability so admired in her favourite Queen Mary – Forgives the cits[28] for their opposition to peace, because they get more money by war, the criterion by which they judge every thing: but is amazed nobles, born guardians of the just rights of the throne, the fountain of all their honors, should join these interested Change-alley politicians, and endeavour,[b] from private pique,[29] to weaken the hands of their sovereign: But[c] adds, with a sigh, that mankind were always alike, and that it was just so in the Queen's time.

'But pray, nephew, this Canada; – I remember when Hill[30] was sent against it in the Queen's time, it was thought of great consequence; and two or three[d] years ago pamphlets were wrote, I am told, by/ men very well born, to prove it was the only point we ought to have in view; but a point in which we could scarce hope to succeed. Is it really so trifling an acquisition?[e] And how comes the nature of it to be so changed now we are likely to keep it?'

'The terms of peace[31] talked of, madam, said Lord Belmont, if we consider them in the only just light, their relation to the end for which war was undertaken, are such as wisdom and equity equally dictate. Canada, considered merely as the possession of it gives security to our colonies, is of more national consequence to us than all our Sugar-islands[32] on the globe: but if the present inhabitants are encouraged to stay by the mildness of our laws, and that full liberty of conscience which every rational creature has a right; if they are taught by every honest art a love for that constitution which makes them free, and a personal attachment/ to the best of princes; if they are allured to our religious worship, by seeing it in its genuine beauty, equally remote from their load of trifling ceremonies, and the unornamented forms of the dissenters: if population is encouraged; the waste

Volume II 85

lands settled; and a whale fishery set on foot, we shall find it, considered in every light, an acquisition beyond our most sanguine hopes.'

O Ciel! I am tired. Adieu!

A WILMOT.[a]

To GEORGE MORDAUNT, Esq;

I AM still with Mr. Herbert, whose genius, learning, and goodness of heart, make him an honour to human nature itself: I shall never know peace till I find a way to render his situation more worthy of his character./

It was with great difficulty I drew from him the following short account of himself.

There is nothing in my past life but what is, I fear, too usual to be worth relating.[b] Warmth of temper, and the vanity of youth, seduced me into a circle of company not to be kept up, by one of my fortune, at a less price than ruin; and the same vanity, with inexperience, and a false opinion of mankind, betrayed me into views not less destructive.

My father unhappily died when I was about nineteen, leaving me at college, master of my own actions, of the little estate you see, and of four thousand pounds; a sum I then thought inexhaustible. The reputation of such a sum in my own power, drew about me all the worthless young men of fashion in the university, whose persuasions and examples led me into a train of expence/ to which my fortune was far from being equal; they flattered those talents of which I thought but too well myself, and easily persuaded me I only wanted to be known in the great world to rise to what height I pleased. I accompanied them to town, full of the idea of raising my fortune, to which they assured me nothing so much contributed as the appearance of being perfectly at ease. To this end I launched into every expence they proposed, dress, equipage, play, and every fashionable extravagance. I was well received every where,[c] and thought my designs in a prosperous way. I found my fortune however decaying at the end of two years, but had not courage to enquire into particulars; till, drawing upon my banker for money to pay some debts I had unwarily contracted, he told me he had already paid the whole.

It was some time before he could convince me of this; but, finding his accounts/ had all the appearance of exactness, I was obliged to acquiesce, and went home in an agony of despair. Unable to quit a way of life which was become habitual, and which it was now impossible to support without dishonesty, there is no describing my feelings. After revolving a thousand different schemes in my imagination, I determined to conceal the situation of my affairs, to sell my estate, and, before that money was gone, press my great friends to serve me.

86   *The History of Lady Julia Mandeville*

I applied to my banker, who undertook to send me a purchaser; but before I had compleated[a] my design I received by the post a bank note of five hundred pounds,[33] the sum I was indebted in town; with a letter, in a hand unknown to me, representing, in the most delicate manner, the imprudence of my past conduct, the madness of my views, and the certain consequences of my parting with this my last stake: intreating me, by the memory of my parents, to preserve/ this sacred deposit, this little remain of what their tender care had left me.

Melted with this generosity, struck with the just reproof, yet chained down to that world which had undone me; convinced, yet irresolute; I struggled with my own heart to determine on retiring into the country; but, to postpone as long as possible a retreat, which I could not bear to think of, resolved first to try my great friends, and be certain of what I had to hope for. I represented to them the necessity of immediately attempting in earnest to push my fortune, and pressing them closely found their promises were air. They talked in general terms of their esteem for me, of my merit, and each of them expressed the warmest desire of seeing me served by any means but his own. As a means[b] to animate their languid friendship, I discovered to them the real state of my affairs; and from that moment found myself avoided by them all;/ they dropped me by degrees; were never at home when I called; and at length ceased even to bow to me in public; ashamed[c] of their own baseness in thus cruelly deferring me, after leading me into ruin, most of them fought to excuse it by blackening my character; whilst the best of them affected coldly to pity me, as a vain foolish fellow, who had undone himself by forgetting his own primeval situation, and arrogantly presuming to live with them.

Burning with indignation, I determined at once to break the bands which held me captive. I sold my equipage, discharged my debts, and came down to this place, resolved to find out to whom I had been so obliged; and, by living on half my income, to repay this generous benefactor.

I took lodgings in a farm-house, and soon found that peace of mind to which I/ had long been a stranger. I tried every method to find out to whom I was indebted for an act of such exalted friendship, but in vain; till one day, a relation being present, of whom I had some suspicion, I related the story, as of another, keeping my eyes fixed upon him; he remained perfectly unmoved; but happening to turn my head, I saw a confusion in the air of a young lady in the room, with whom I had been bred in the greatest intimacy, which excited all my attention. She saw me observe her, and a blush overspread her cheek, which convinced me I had found the object of my search. I changed the subject; and the next morning made her a visit, when I with great difficulty drew from her a confession, that, having long had a tender esteem for me, she had, by a friend in a town,[d] watched all my actions: that my banker had applied to that very friend to purchase my estate; on which, seeing me on the brink of absolute ruin, she/ had taken what

Volume II 87

appeared to her the most probable means to prevent it; and was so happy as to see she had succeeded.

I dare say I need not tell you this noble creature was my dear Mrs. Herbert, the smallness of whose fortune added infinitely to the generosity of the action, what she had sent me being within a trifle her all.

I loved, I addressed her, and at length, was so happy as to call her mine. Blest in the most exalted passion for each other, a passion which time has rather encreased[a] than abated, the narrowness of our circumstances is the only ill we have to complain of; even this we have borne with chearfulness in the hope of happier days. A late accident has, however, broke in upon that tranquillity with which Heaven has hitherto blest[b] us. It is now about six months since a lady, who tenderly esteemed us both, sent for me, and acquainted me she had/ procured for me of a gentleman, whose family had been obliged to her, a living of above three hundred pounds a year, in a beautiful situation; and desired I would immediately take orders. As I was originally educated with a view to the church, I consented with inexpressible joy, blessing that Heaven, which had thus rewarded my Sophia's generous affection, and given us all that was wanting to compleat our happiness. I set out for London with an exulting heart; where, after being ordained, I received the presentation, and went down to take possession. The house was large and elegant, and betrayed me into furnishing it rather better than suited my present circumstances; but, as I determined on the utmost frugality for some years, I thought this of little consequence. I set men to work in the garden; and wrote my wife an account of our new residence, which made her eager to hasten her removal. The day of my coming for my family was fixed,/ when my patron came down to his seat, which was within sight of the rectory; I waited on him, and found him surrounded by wretches, to whom it was scarce possible to give the name of human; profligate, abandoned, lost even to the sense of shame; their conversation wounded reason, virtue, politeness, and all that mankind agree[c] to hold sacred. My patron, the wealthy heir of a West Indian,[34] was raised above them, only by fortune, and a superior degree of ignorance and savage insensibility. He received me with an insolence, which I found great difficulty in submitting to: and, after some brutal general reflexions on the clergy, dared to utter expressions relating to the beauty of my wife,[35] which fired my soul with indignation; breathless with rage, I had not power to reply: when one of the company speaking low to him, he answered aloud, Hark you, Herbert, this blockhead thinks a parson a gentleman; and wonders/ at my treating, as I please, a fellow who eats my bread.[d]

I will sooner want bread, Sir, said I, rising, than owe it to the most contemptible of mankind. Your living is once more at your disposal; I resign all right to it before this company.[e]

The pleasure of having acted as I ought swelled my bosom with conscious delight, and supported me till I reached home; when my heart sunk at the thought of what my Sophia might feel from the disappointment. Our affairs too were a little embarassed,[a] from which misery I had hoped to be set free, instead of which my debts were encreased.[b] Mr. Mandeville, if you never knew the horrors of being in debt, you can form no idea of what it is to breathe the air at the mercy of another; to labor, to struggle to be just, whilst the/ cruel world are loading you with the guilt of injustice.

I entered the house, filled with horrors not to be conceived. My wife met me with eager enquiries about our future residence; and with repeated thanks to that God who had thus graciously bestowed on us the means of doing justice to all the world. You will imagine what I felt at that moment: instead of replying, I related to her the treatment I had met with, and the character of him to whom we were to be obliged; and asked her, what she would wish me to do? Resign the living, said she, and trust to that Heaven whose goodness is over all his creatures.[c] I embraced her with tears of tender transport, and told her I had already done it. We wrote to the lady to whose friendship we had been obliged for the presentation; and she had the greatness of mind not to disapprove my conduct. We have since practised a more severe frugality,/ which we are determined not to relax till what we owe is fully discharged: time will, we hope, bring about this end, and remove the load which now oppresses my heart. Determined to trust to Heaven and our own industry, and to aim at independence alone, I have avoided all acquaintance which could interfere with this only rational plan: but Lord T –, seeing me at the house of a nobleman, whose virtues do honor[d] to his rank, and imagining my fortune easy from my cordial reception there, invited me earnestly to his seat; where, having, as I suppose, been since undeceived as to my situation, you were a witness of his unworthy treatment of me; of one descended from a family noble as his own, liberally educated, with a spirit equally above meanness and pride, and a heart which feels too sensibly to be happy in a world like this.

Oh[e] Mr. Mandeville! What can you think of him, who, instead of pouring out his/ soul in thankfulness to Heaven for those advantages he enjoys by its[f] goodness above his fellow-creatures, makes use of them to wound the bosom of the wretched, and add double bitterness to the cup of adversity?

The real evils of a narrow fortune are trifling; its worst pangs spring from the unfeeling cruelty of others; it is not always that philosophy can raise us above the proud man's contumely,[36] or those thousand insults

'Which patient merit of th' unworthy takes.'[37]

You, Mr. Mandeville, are young, and full of probity; your own heart will mislead you, by drawing too flattering a picture of others; the world is gay before you; and, blinded by prosperity, you have never yet seen it as it is. I have heard you with infinite concern hint designs too like my own; let me intreat, let me conjure/ you to profit by my example; if peace is worth your care, be content with your paternal fortune, however small; nor, by rashly launching on the flattering sea of hope, hazard that shipwreck which I have suffered.

Mordaunt!^a Is not this the voice of Heaven? I will return to the bosom of independence, and give up designs in which it is almost impossible for modest worth to succeed.

My father is in town; I will go to him when he returns; his advice shall determine my future conduct.

A letter from Lady Julia: my servant has this moment brought it from Lord Lord T –'s, whither I desired it to be directed, not chusing to let them know I have put an end to my visit, lest Lord Belmont should insist on my return./

To HENRY MANDEVILLE, Esquire.[b]

IN what words shall I assure the most amiable of men he has nothing to fear from Lord Melvin? If he knows my heart, he knows it incapable of change; he knows, not his own generous spirit more disdains the low consideration of fortune; he knows I can have but one wish, that this accidental advantage was on his side, that he might taste the transport of obliging her he loves.

My duty, my gratitude to the best of parents, forbids my entering into present engagements without his knowledge; nor will I make future ones, which would have in view an event on which I cannot think without horror: but his commands, were he capable of acting so inconsistently with his past indulgent goodness, would be insufficient to make me give my hand to Lord Melvin, when my heart is fixedly another's./

I may, perhaps, assume courage to own my sensibility, a sensibility justified by such merit in the object, to the tenderest of mothers and friends: in the mean time[38] defer your return to Belmont, and hope every thing from time, my father's friendship, and my unalterable esteem – Esteem did I say? Where did I learn this coldness of expression? Let me own,[c] though I am covered with blushes whilst I write, it is from my love, my ardent love, from a passion which is the pride and boast of my life, that the most charming of mankind has every thing to hope;[d] if his happiness depends on my affection, he is happy.

You shall hear from[e] me by Lady Anne and my beloved Emily; at present you will not ask to hear from[f] me.

Adieu!

O[g] Mordaunt! How[h] shall I restrain the wild transports of my heart! Her love, her/ most ardent love[i] – How[j] could I suspect her truth? – No,[k] my friend, I ask no more, I will not return to Belmont; certain of her tenderness, I submit, without repining, to her commands.

Unable, however, to resist: the desire of being near her, I will go privately to a little farm, four miles from Belmont, of which it has a view, which is rented by an old servant of my father's, whose son is in love with one of Lady Belmont's maids, and from whom I shall hear daily accounts of Lady Julia; as it is near the road, I may even have a chance of seeing her pass by.

I shall leave my servants at the inn, and order all my letters hither: Mr. Herbert will convey them to me, and keep the secret of my retreat.

Great heaven! I shall to-night be near her, I shall behold the turrets of Belmont!/ It is even possible I may see the dear object of all my wishes. A thousand sweet ideas rise in my mind. My heart dances with pleasure.

Mordaunt! she loves me, she will never be another's.

This passion absorbs me wholly: I had almost forgot my friend; go to my banker's, take a hundred pounds, and send it by the post to Mr. Herbert, without letting him know from whom it comes. Why is this trifle all that is in my power to do for worth like his? If a happier fate – But let me not encourage the sanguine hopes of youth.[39]

I will introduce him to Lord Belmont, the friend of virtue, the support of the unhappy, the delegate of Heaven itself.

Adieu! your faithful
H. MANDEVILLE./[a]

To Colonel BELLVILLE.

THURSDAY.

A Pretty sentimental letter your last, and would make an admirable figure in a true history of Celadon and Urania.[40b] Absolutely though, Bellville, for people who have sensibility, and so little prospect of coming together in an honorable[c] way, we are a most extraordinary pair of lovers. And yet the world – apropos[41d] to the world, a French author I am reading, says, a wise writer, to divert the fury of criticism from his works, should throw in now and then an indiscretion in his conduct to play with, as seamen do a tub to the whale.[42e]

Do not you think this might be a useful hint to us beauties? If I treat the good old ladies sometimes with a little, imprudence/ in regard to you, my complexion may escape the better for it.

We are just returned from a party on the water, which, like most concerted parties, turned out exceedingly dull: we had gilded barges, excellent musick,[f] an elegant repast, and all that could invite pleasure amongst us; but whether her ladyship be a true coquette, flying fastest when pursued, or what is the reason I know not, but certain it is, one seldom finds her when one goes to seek her; her visits are generally spontaneous and unexpected; she rejects all invitations, and comes upon you in her own way, by surprize. I set off in high spirits, my heart

Volume II 91

beating with expectation, and never past[a] a more languid day; I fancied every moment would be pleasanter, but found the last hour as spiritless as the first. I saw chagrin and disappointment in the eyes of half the company, especially the younger part of it. Lady Julia seemed to/ say, 'All this would be charming if Harry Mandeville was here.' My own ideas were something similar, I could not keep my imagination from wandering a little to Grosvenor-street;[43] most of the misses were in the same situation, whilst the good old people seemed perfectly satisfied; which convinces me that at a certain time of life there is no pleasure without the heart; where that is untouched, and takes no part in your amusements, all is still life and vegetation: it is in vain to expect enjoyment from outward objects, where the soul is from home.

I missed my sweet Harry exceedingly, for though not a lover, he is a divine fellow; and there is something vastly amusing in having so agreeable an object before one's eyes./

Whenever I make a party of pleasure, it shall consist all of lovers, who have not met for a twelvemonth.

Who should we meet on our return, but Fondville, in a superb barge, full of company, dying at the feet of the Cittadina, who was singing a melting Italian air.[b] Yes, we are to be Lady Viscountess Fondville, all is agreed, the clothes bespoke, our very garters interwoven with coronets. I shall get off before the days of visitation, for there will be no supporting Madame la Viscomtesse.

I have been taking half an hour tete à tete with Lady Mary; and have let her into the secret of little Westbrook's passion for Harry: She drew up at the very mention, was astonished, that a creature of yesterday, could think of mixing his[c] blood with that of Mandeville, declared she knew but twenty houses in Europe into which she should ever consent to Harry's marrying./

I took this opportunity of giving a hint of his inclination for Lady Julia, but am doubtful whether she understood me. Oh! that he had Lord Melvin's expectations! But why do I wish for impossibilities? Let me rather wish, what is next to impossible, that Lord Belmont would overlook the want of them!

Adieu!

To Colonel BELLVILLE.

THURSDAY Evening.

O CIEL! Une avanture![44] Making use of the sweet liberty of Belmont, which has no rule but that of the Thelemites,[45] 'Do what thou wilt,' I left them after dinner to settle family affairs, and ordered my chariot, to take a solitary airing: an old cat, however, arriving just as it/ came to the door, who is a famous proficient in scandal, a treat I am absolutely deprived of at Belmont; I changed my mind, and

92   *The History of Lady Julia Mandeville*

asked her to accompany me, that I might be amused with the secret history of all the neighbourhood.

She had torn to pieces half a dozen of the prettiest women about us, when, passing through a little village about six miles from Belmont, I was struck with the extreme neatness of a small house and garden near the road; there was an elegant plainness in the air of it, which pleased me so much, that I pulled the string,[46] and ordered the coachman to stop, that I might examine it more at leisure. I was going to bid him drive on, when two women came out of an arbor, one of whom instantly engaged all my attention.

Imagine to yourself in such a place all that is graceful and lovely in woman; an/ elegance of form and habit; a dignity of deportment; an air of delicate languor and sensibility, which won the heart at a look; a complexion inclining to pale; the finest dark eyes; with a countenance in which a modest sorrow and dignified dejection gave the strongest indications of suffering merit.

My companion, seeing the apparent partiality, with which I beheld this amiable object, began to give me a history of her, embittered by all the virulence of malice; which, however, amounted to no more, than that she was a stranger, and that, as nobody knew who she was, they generously concluded she was one whose interest it was not to be known.

They now drew nearer to us; and the charming creature, raising her eyes, and then first seeing us, exclaimed, Good Heaven! Lady Anne Wilmot! Is it possible!ᵃ/ I now regarded her more attentively, and, though greatly changed since I saw her, knew her to be Bell Hastings, Mr. Wilmot's niece, whom I had been long endeavouringᵇ to find. I sprung from the chariot to meet her, and need not tell you my transport at so unexpected a rencounter.[47]

After the common enquiries on meeting, I expressed my surprize at finding her there, with a gentle reproach at her unkindness in being in England without letting me know it. She blushed, and seemed embarrassed at what I said; on which I changed the subject, and pressed her to accompany me immediately to Belmont, the place on earth where merit like hers was most sure of finding its best reward, esteem. She declined this proposal in a manner which convinced me she had some particular reason for refusing, which I doubted not her taking a proper time to explain, and therefore gave it up for the present./ I insisted, however, on her promising to go with me to town; and that nothing but a matrimonial engagement should separate her from me. There is no describing the excess of her gratitude; tears of tender sensibility shone in her eyes; and I could see her bosom swell with sensations to which she could not give utterance.

An hour passed without my having thought of my meagre companion at the gate. I was not sorry for having accidentally mortified the envious wretch for her spite to poor Bell. However, as I would not designedly be shocking, I sent to her, and apologized for my neglect, which I excused from my joy at meeting

Volume II 93

unexpectedly with a relation for whom I had the tenderest friendship. The creature alighted at my request; and, to make amends for the picture she had drawn of my amiable niece, overwhelmed her with civilities and expressions of esteem, which would have/ encreased[a] my contempt for her, if any thing in nature could.

After tea we returned, when I related my adventure, and, though so late, could scarce prevail on Lady Belmont to defer her visit to Bell till to-morrow. She hopes to be able to prevail on her to accompany us back to Belmont.

To GEORGE MORDAUNT, Esquire.

I Write this from my new abode, a little sequestered farm, at the side of a romantic wood: there is an arbor in the thickest grove of intermingled jessamines and roses. Here William meditates future happy hours, when joined to his lovely Anna: he has adorned it with every charm of nature, to please the mistress of his soul: here I pass my sweetest hours: here William/ brings me news of Lady Julia; he is this moment returned; he saw her walking to the rustic temple, leaning on Emily Howard: he tells me she sighed as she past[b] him. O[c] Mordaunt! was that sigh for me?

Not certain Lady Julia would forgive my being so near her, or a concealment which has so guilty an air, I have enjoined William secrecy even to his Anna, and bribed it by a promise of making him happy. My letters therefore come round by Mr. Herbert's, and it is three days before I receive them. I have not yet heard from Belmont, or my father. I am supposed to be still at Lord T –'s.

Ever an enthusiast, from warmth of heart and imagination, my whole soul is devoted to Lady Julia. I pass my days in carving that loved name on the rinds of the smoothest trees:[48] and, when the good old man retires to his rest, William and I steal/ forth, and ride to the end of Belmont Park, where, having contemplated the dear abode of all that earth contains of lovely, and breathed an ardent prayer to Heaven for her happiness, I return to my rustic retreat, and wait patiently till the next evening brings back the same pleasing employment.

Since I left Belmont, I have never known happiness like what I now feel. Certain of her tenderness, tranquillity is restored to my soul: for ever employed in thinking of her, that painful restraint which company brought is removed; the scenes around me, and the dear solitude I enjoy, are proper to flatter a love-sick heart; my passion is soothed by the artless expression of William's;[d] I make him sit hours talking of his Anna: he brings me every day intelligence of my angel; I see every hour the place which she inhabits. Am I not most happy? Her idea is perpetually before me; when/ I walk in these sweet shades, so resembling those of Belmont, I look round as if expecting to behold her; I start at every sound, and almost fancy her lovely form in my view.

94 *The History of Lady Julia Mandeville*

Oh! Mordaunt! what transport do I find in this sweet delirium of love! How[a] eagerly do I expect, the return of evening! Could[b] I but once again behold her! Once[c] again swear eternal passion – I have a thousand things to say./

To Col. BELLVILLE.

TUESDAY Morning.

I Have this moment a letter from Bell Hastings, which I send you: I wish her here, yet know not how to press it, after so rational an apology.

To Lady ANNE WILMOT.[d]

BEFORE I absolutely accept or refuse your Ladyship's generous invitation, allow me to account to you for my being in a place where you so little expected to find me; but which I am convinced you will acquiesce in my continuing in, when you know the motives which induced me to make choice of it./

When my uncle married your ladyship, you remember he left me in a convent at Paris, where I staid till his death. I should then have returned, but having contracted a very tender[e] friendship for a young lady of the first quality in England, she pressed me to continue there till her return, which was fixed for the year following. About three months before we intended to leave Paris, her brother arrived, on which occasion she left the convent, and went to spend her remaining time with an aunt who then resided in France, and who, being told I had staid the last year in complaisance to her amiable niece, insisted on my accompanying her: to[f] spare a long narrative of common events, the brother of my friend became passionately in love with me, and I was so unhappy as to be too sensible to his tenderness: he intreated[g] me to conceal our attachment from his sister for the present; professed the most honorable[h] designs; told me he did not doubt of bringing his father to/ consent to a marriage, to which there could be no objection that was not founded in the most sordid avarice, and on which the happiness of his life depended.

The time of our intended return to England drawing near, he employed, and successfully, the power he had over my heart, to influence my acceptance of an invitation given me, by a friend of my mother's, to accompany her to Florence, where I promised to stay till his return from Rome.

Too much in love, as he said, and I weakly believed, to support a longer absence, he came in a few months to Florence; we were then in the country with a Florentine nobleman, whose lady was related to my friend, to whom he was strongly recommended, and who gave him an invitation to his villa; which I need not tell you he accepted. We saw each other continually, but under a restraint, which, whilst it encreased[i]/ our mutual passion, was equally painful to both. At length he contrived to give me a letter, pressing me to see him alone in the garden at an hour he mentioned. I went, and found the most beloved of men waiting for me in a grove of

Volume II　　　　　　　95

oranges. He saw me at a distance: I stopped by an involuntary impulse; he ran to me, he approached me with a transport which left me no room to doubt of his affection.

After an hour spent in vows of everlasting love, he pressed me to marry him privately, which I refused with an air of firmness but little suited to the state of my heart, and protested no consideration should ever induce me to give him my hand without the consent of his father.

He expressed great resentment of a resolution, which, he affirmed, was inconsistent with a real passion; pretended jealousy of a young nobleman in the house, and artfully/ hinted at returning immediately to England; then, softening his voice, implored my compassion, vowed he could not live without me; and so varied his behaviour from rage to the most seducing softness, that the fear of displeasing him, who was dearer to me than life, assisted by the tender persuasive eloquence of well-dissembled[a] love, so far prevailed over the dictates of reason and strict honor, that, unable to resist his despair, I consented to a clandestine marriage: I then insisted on returning immediately to the house, to which he consented, though unwillingly, and, leaving me with all the exulting raptures of successful love, went to Florence to prepare a priest to unite us, promising to return with him in the morning: the next day passed, and the next, without my hearing of him; a whole week elapsed in the same manner: convinced[b] of his affection, my fears were all for his safety; my imagination presented danger in every form, and, no longer able to support/ the terrors of my mind filled with a thousand dreadful ideas, I sent a servant to enquire for him at the house, where he lodged, who brought me word he had left Florence the very morning on which I expected his return. Those only who have loved like me can conceive what I felt at this news; but judge into what an abyss of misery I was plunged, on receiving a few hours after a letter from his sister, pressing me to return to her at Paris, where she was still waiting, in compliance with orders from home, for her brother, who was to accompany her to England directly, to marry an heiress for whom he had been long intended by his father; she added that I must not lose a moment, for that her brother would, before I could receive the letter, be on the road to Paris.

Rage, love, pride, resentment, indignation, now tore my bosom alternately. After a conflict of different passions, I determined/ on forgetting my unworthy lover, whose neglect appeared to me the contemptible insolence of superior fortune: I left the place the next day, as if for Paris; but, taking the nearest way to England, came hither to a clergyman's widow, who had been a friend of my mother's; to whom I told my story, and with whom I determined to stay concealed, till I heard the fate of my lover. I made a solemn vow, in the first heat of my resentment, never to write to him, or let him know my retreat, and, though with infinite difficulty, I have hitherto kept it. But what have I not suffered for this conduct, which, though my reason dictates, my heart condemns! A thousand times have I been on the point of discovering myself to him, and at least

96   *The History of Lady Julia Mandeville*

giving him an opportunity of vindicating himself. I accuse myself of injustice in condemning him unheard, and on appearances which might be false. So weak is a heart in love, that, though, when I chose my place of retreat, I was ignorant/ of that circumstance, it was with pleasure, though a pleasure I endeavoured to hide from myself, that I heard it was only ten miles from his father's seat. I ought certainly to have changed it on this knowledge, but find a thousand plausible reasons to the contrary, and am but too successful in deceiving myself.

Convinced of the propriety of my conduct in avoiding him, I am not the more happy. My heart betrays me, and represents him continually to my imagination in the most amiable light, as a faithful lover, injured by my suspicions, and made wretched by my loss.

Torn by sentiments which vary every moment; the struggles of my soul have impaired my health, and will in time put an end to a life,[a] to the continuance of which, without him, I am perfectly indifferent./

Determined, however, to persist in a conduct, which, whatever I suffer from it, is certainly my duty, I cannot, as I hear he is returned, consent to come to Belmont; where it is scarce possible I should fail meeting a man of his rank, who must undoubtedly be of Lord Belmont's acquaintance.

Till he is married, or I am convinced I have injured him, I will not leave this retreat; at least I will not appear where I am almost certain of meeting him whom I ought for ever to avoid.

O[b] Lady Anne! How[c] severe is this trial! How painful the conquest over the sweetest affections of the human heart! How[d] mortifying to love an object which one has ceased to esteem! Convinced of his unworthiness, my passion remains the same, nor will ever cease but with life: I at once despise and adore him: yes, my tenderness is, if possible, more lively than ever; and,/ though he has doomed me to misery, I would die to contribute to his happiness.

You, Madam, will, I know, pity and forgive the inconsistencies of a heart ashamed of its own weaknesses, yet too sincere to disguise or palliate them. I am no stranger to your nobleness of sentiment; in your friendship and compassion all my hopes of tranquillity are founded. I will endeavour to conquer this ill-placed prepossession, and render myself more worthy your esteem. If his marriage with another makes it impossible for him to suppose I throw myself designedly in his way, I will go with you to town in the winter, and try if the hurry of the world can erase his image from my bosom. If he continues unconnected, and no accident clears up to me his conduct, I will continue where I am, and for ever hide my folly in this retreat

I am, &c.

A. HASTINGS.[e]

Poor Bell! how I pity her! Heaven certainly means love for our reward in another world, it so seldom makes us happy in this. But why do we blame heaven? It

Volume II

is our own prejudices, our rage for wealth, our cowardly compliance with the absurd opinions of others, which robs us of all the real happiness of life.

I should be glad to know who this despicable fellow is: though really it is possible she may injure him. I must know his name, and find out whether or not she is torturing herself without reason. If he bears scrutinizing, our plans may coincide, and my jointure make us all happy; if not, he shall have the mortification of knowing she has an easy fortune; and of seeing her, what it shall be my business to make her next winter, one of the most fashionable women, and celebrated toasts, about town.[49]/

After all, are we not a little in the machine style,[50] not to be able to withdraw our love when our esteem is at an end? I suppose one might find a philosophical reason for this in Newton's Laws of Attraction.[51] The heart of a woman does, I imagine, naturally gravitate towards a handsome, well-dressed, well-bred fellow, without enquiry into his mental qualities. Nay, as to that, do not let me be partial to you odious men; you have as little taste for mere internal charms as the lightest coquette in town. You talk sometimes of the beauties of the mind; but I should be glad, as somebody has said very well, to see one of you[a] in love with a mind of threescore.[52]

I am really sorry for Bell, but hope to bring her out of these heroics[53] by Christmas. The town air, and being followed five or six weeks as a beauty, will do wonders. I know no specific for a love-fit like a constant crowd of pretty fellows./

The world, I dare say, will soon restore her to her senses; it is impossible she should ever regain them in a lonely village, with no company but an old woman.

How dearly we love to nurse up our follies! Bell, I dare say, fancies vast merit in this romantic constancy[54] to a man who, if he knew her absurdity, would laugh at it.

I have no patience with my own sex, for their want of spirit.

Friday Night.

O Heavens! who could have thought it? Of all the birds in the air, find me out Lord Melvin for Bell Hastings's lover: Nothing was ever so charming: I tell the story, which does his business here in a moment; serves my lovely Harry, and punishes the/ wretch's infidelity as it deserves. Adieu! I fly to communicate.

Saturday Morning.

All this is very strange to me. Lord Belmont, to whom I last night mentioned Lord Melvin's connexion with Bell, as a reason against his marrying Lady Julia, assures me no such thing was ever intended; that he was amazed how I came to think so; that Lord Rochdale has other views for his son, to which, however, he is averse. I am glad to hear this last circumstance, and hope Bell has wronged him by her suspicions.

98   *The History of Lady Julia Mandeville*

But who can this be that is intended for Lady Julia? I do not love to be impertinent, but my curiosity is rather excited; I shall not sleep till I am in this secret; I must follow my Lord about till I get a clue to direct me. How shall I begin the attack? 'Really, my Lord, says I, this surprizes/ me extremely, I could have sworn Lord Melvin was the person your Lordship meant; if it is not him, who can it be?'

Yes, this will do; I will go to him directly – Cruel man! how he plays with my anxiety! He[a] is gone out in a post-chaise with Lady Julia; the chaise drove from the door this moment.

I can say not a word more; I am on the rack of expectation; I could not be more anxious about a lover of my own.

'The heir of an earldom, and of an affluent fortune.'[b] I have tortured my brain this hour, and not a scruple[55] the nearer.

To George Mordaunt, Esq;

Saturday Morning.

O[c] Mordaunt! I have seen her; have heard the sound of that enchanting voice; my Lord was in the chaise with her; they stopped to drink fresh cream; William presented her a nosegay;[56] she thanked him with an air of sweetness; which would have won the soul of a savage. My heart beat with unutterable transport; it was with difficulty I restrained myself.

Mordaunt! I must return; I can no longer bear this absence: I will write this moment to Lord Belmont, and own my passion for his daughter; I will paint in the most lively colors my love and my despair: I will tell him I have nothing to hope from the world, and throw myself intirely[d] on his friendship. I know the indiscretion of/ this proceeding; I know I ought not to hope success; but I have too long concealed my sentiments, and pursued a conduct unworthy of my heart.

I have wrote;[e] I have sent away the letter. I have said all that can engage his heart in my favor; to-morrow he will receive my letter – to-morrow[f] – O Mordaunt! how soon will my fate be determined! A chilliness seizes me at the thought,[g] my hand trembles, it is with difficulty I hold the pen. I have entreated[h] an immediate answer; it will come inclosed to Mr. Herbert, to whom I have wrote to bring the letter himself. On Wednesday I shall be the most happy or most lost of mankind. What a dreadful interval will it be! My[i] heart dies within me at the thought./

Volume II 99

To HENRY MANDEVILLE, Esq;

BELMONT, 18th September.

I AM commissioned by Lady Anne, my dear Mr. Mandeville, to insist on your immediate return; she declares she can no longer support, the country without you, but shall die with chagrin[57] and ennui;[58] even play itself has lost half its charms in your absence. Lady Mary, my wife, and daughter join in the same request, which I have a thousand reasons to press your complying with, as soon as is consistent with what politeness exacts in regard to Lord T –.

One, and not the weakest, is the pleasure I find in conversation, a pleasure I never taste more strongly than with you, and a pleasure which promiscuous visitors have for some time ceased to give me. I have not lost my relish for society, but it grows,/ in spite of all my endeavors, more delicate; I have as great pleasure as ever in the convention of select friends; but I cannot so well bear the common run of company. I look on this delicacy as one of the infirmities of age, and as much a symptom of decay, as it would be to lose my taste for roast beef, and be able only to relish ortolans.[59]

Lord Fondeville is next week to marry Miss Westbrook; they have a coach making which is to cost a thousand pounds.

I am interrupted by a worthy man, to whom I am so happy[a] as to be able to do a service: to you I need make no other apology.

Adieu! my amiable friend!/

To Lady ANNE WILMOT.

Saturday, Grosvenor Street.

CAN the most refined of her sex, at the very moment when she owns herself shocked at Mrs. H –'s malicious insinuation, refuse to silence her by making me happy? Can[b] she submit to one of the keenest evils a sensible and delicate mind can feel, only to inflict torment on the man whose whole happiness depends on her, and to whose tenderness she has owned herself not insensible?

Seeing your averseness to marriage, I have never pressed you on a subject which seemed displeasing to you, but left it to time and my unwearied love, to dissipate those unjust and groundless prejudices, which stood in the way of all my hopes: but does not this respect, this submission,/ demand that you should strictly examine those prejudices, and be convinced, before you make it, that they deserve such a sacrifice?

Why will you, my dearest Lady Anne, urge your past unhappiness as a reason against entering into a state of which you cannot be a judge? You were never married; the soft consent of hearts, the tender sympathy of yielding minds, was wanting: forced by the will of a tyrannic father to take on you an insupport-

100   *The History of Lady Julia Mandeville*

able yoke, too young to assert the rights of humanity; the freedom of your will destroyed; the name of marriage is profaned by giving it to so detestable an union.

You have often spoke with pleasure of those sweet hours we past[a] at Sudley-Farm.[b] Can you then refuse to perpetuate such happiness? Are[c] there no charms in the unreserved converse of the man who adores/ you? Or[d] can you prefer the unmeaning flattery of fools you despise, to the animated language of faithful love?[e]

If you are still insensible to my happiness, will not my interest prevail on you to relent? My uncle, who has just lost his only son, offers to settle his whole estate on me, on condition I immediately marry; a condition it depends on you alone whether I shall comply with. If you refuse, he gives it[f] on the same terms to a distant relation, whose mistress has a less cruel heart. Have you so little generosity as to condemn me at once to be poor and miserable; to lose the gifts both of love and fortune?

I have wrote to Lady Belmont to intercede for me, and trust infinitely more to her eloquence than my own./

The only rational objection to my happiness my uncle's estate removes; you will bring me his fortune, and your own will make Bell Hastings happy: if you now refuse, you have the heart of a tygress,[60g] and delight in the misery of others.

Interrupted: my uncle: May all good angels guard the most amiable and lovely of women, and give her to her passionate

BELLVILLE!/

To Colonel BELLVILLE.

MONDAY.

'WILL you marry me, my dear Ally Croaker?'[61] For ever this question, Bellville? And yet really you seem to be not at all in the secret. 'Respect, submission' – I thought you had known the sex better: How[h] should a modest woman ever be prevailed on by a respectful submissive lover? You would not surely have us –

O Heavens! A billet.[62] Some despairing inamorato:[63] Indeed?[i] Lord Melvin? He is not going to make love to me sure.

Very well; things are in a fine train. He writes me here as pretty an heroic epistle as one would desire, setting forth his passion for Bell Hastings, whom he has just/ discovered is my niece, and whom he declares he cannot live without; owning appearances are against him, and begging me to convey to her a long tidi didum[j] letter, explaining the reasons and causes – The story is tedious, but the sum total is this; that[k] he found at Florence the friend on earth he most loved, engaged in an affair of honour,[l] in which he could not avoid taking part as his second; that they went to the last town in the Tuscan state, in order to escape into another, if any accident made it necessary to elude the pursuit of justice; that, to avoid suspicion, he left orders with his people to say he had left Florence: that he wrote to her by his valet, who was unfortunately seized and confined, the affair being suspected: that he was wounded, and obliged to stay some time before he could return to Florence, when he was informed she had left Italy; and though he had omitted no means to find her, had never been so happy as to succeed:/ had made his sister, Lady Louisa, his confident, and by her assistance had almost prevailed on his father to consent.

'Almost prevailed on.'[a] Really these are pretty airs.[b] I shall write him an extreme stately answer, and let him know, if he expects Miss Hastings to do him the honor, his address must be in quite another style: Miss Hastings,[c] in blood, in merit, in education, in every thing truly valuable, and in fortune too, if I please, his equal.[d] I wish the foolish girl was not so madly in love with him, for I long to torture his proud heart: I cannot resist teizing[e] him a little, but, as I know her weakness, and that we must come to[f] at last, I shall be forced to leave a door of mercy open: I shall, however, insist on his family's seeking the match, and on Lord Rochdale's asking her of me in form; I will not yield a scruple of our dignity on this occasion./

But I must carry this letter to Bell.

Adieu!

As to your foolish question, I may perhaps allow you to visit at Belmont; I will promise no more at present.

Did I tell you we all spent yesterday with my niece?[g] She has the honor[h] to please Lady Mary, who, on seeing her at a little distance with Lady Julia and me, (no ill group certainly) insisted on our sitting next winter for a picture of the Graces[64] dancing.

Or suppose, Madam, said I, the three Goddesses on mount Ida, with Harry Mandeville for our Paris?[65i]

Poor little Emily, being equally under size for a Grace or a Goddess, must be content to be a Hebe[66] in a single piece.

Adio!
Yours,
A WILMOT./[j]

To HENRY MANDEVILLE, Esquire.

London, September 19.

THIS event[67] in Russia is most extraordinary: but these sudden and violent revolutions are the natural consequences of that instability which must ever attend despotic forms of government: Happy Britain! where the laws are equally the guard of prince and people, where liberty and prerogative go hand in hand, and mutually support each other; where no invasion can ever be made on any part of the constitution without endangering the whole: where popular clamor, like the thunder-storm, by agitating, clears and purifies the air, and, its business done, subsides.

102 *The History of Lady Julia Mandeville*

If this letter finds you at Lord T –'s, I would have you return immediately to Belmont, where I shall[a] be in a few days./ Lady Mary is already there, and intends to execute the design Lord Belmont mentioned to you, which makes your presence there absolutely necessary.

The tide of fortune, my dear Harry, seems turning in your favor, but let it not harden your heart to the misfortunes of your fellow-creatures, make you insolent to merit in the vale of humbler life, or tempt you to forget that all you possess is the gift of that beneficent Power, in whose sight virtue is the only distinction.

The knowledge I have of your heart makes these cautions perhaps unnecessary; but you will forgive the excessive anxiety of paternal tenderness, alarmed at the near prospect of your tasting the poison most fatal to youth, the intoxicating cup of prosperity./

May Heaven, my dearest Harry, continue you all you are at present! Your father has not another wish![b]

Adieu!

J. MANDEVILLE.[c]

To Col. BELLVILLE.

TUESDAY Morning.

I Staid late last night with Bell; there is no telling you her transport; she agrees with me, however, as to the propriety of keeping up our dignity, and has consented, though with infinite reluctance, not to admit Lord Melvin's visits till his father hath[d] made proposals to me. She is to see him first at Belmont, whither she removes in four or five days. Emily Howard is gone, at my request, to spend that interval with her. We have a divine scheme/ in our heads, which you are not yet to be honored[e] with the knowledge of.

Oh! do you know I have this morning discovered why Lady Mary is a Tory![f] She has been flattered by Bolingbroke,[68] and sung by Atterbury[69]; had Addison[70] tuned his lyre to her praise, she had certainly changed parties. I am seldom at a loss to explore the source of petticoat-politics.[71g] Vanity is the moving spring in the female-machine,[72] as interest is in the male. Certainly our principle of action is by much more noble.

Eleven o'Clock.

'Lord,[h] What is come to my mother?' She is gone smiling into Lady Mary's room; her air is gay beyond measure; it is she must sit for a dancing Grace./

Past Twelve.

There is something in agitation with which I am unacquainted. Lord and Lady Belmont have been an hour in close consultation with Lady Mary: la bella Julia[73]

Volume II 103

is this moment summoned to attend them. This unknown lover: I tremble for Harry: should another –

Almost One.

I Have your letter: this Russian event – true – as you say, these violent convulsions – Yes,[a] you are right, your reflexions are perfectly just, but my thoughts are at present a little engaged. This consultation I fear bodes Harry no good – Should[b] my Lord's authority – I am on the rack of impatience –

The door opens; Lady Julia comes this way; she has been in tears; I tremble at/ the sight – Bellville, they are not tears of sorrow; they are like the dew-drops on the morning rose, she looks a thousand times more lovely through them; her eyes have a melting languishment, a softness inexpressible, a sensibility mixed with transport – There[c] is an animation in her look, a blush of unexpected happiness – She[d] moves with the lightness of a wood-nymph – Lady Belmont follows with a serene joy in that amiable countenance. They approach; they are already in my apartment.

Adio!

Bellville! In[e] what words – How[f] shall I explain to you – I am breathless with pleasure and surprise – My[g] Lord – Harry Mandeville – Lady Julia – They were always intended for each other.

A letter from Harry this morning, confessing his passion for Lady Julia, determined/ them to make an immediate discovery – Read the enclosed[h] letters, and adore the goodness of Providence, which leads us, by secret ways, to that happiness our own wisdom could never arrive at.

To Colonel MANDEVILLE.[i]

Belmont, August 10, 1752.[j]

My dear Col.[k]

BY a clause in the patent, which has been hitherto kept secret in our part of the family, it is provided, that, on default of heirs male in the younger branch, the title of Earl of Belmont should go to the elder: in favour[l] also of this disposition, the greatest part of the estate then in our possession, which is about half what I now enjoy, is, by a deed, in which, however, my lawyer tells me there is a flaw,[m] which/ makes it of no effect, annexed to the title for ever. Julia being the only child we ever had, it is very probable the estate and title will be yours: Heaven having blest[n] you with a son, it would be infinitely agreeable[o] to me, and would keep up the splendor of our name, to agree on an inter-marriage between our children. I would have you educate your son with this view, and at an expence becoming the heir of the titles and possessions of our family: but, as it is possible I may yet have a son, in that case, Lady Mary, our relation, whose heart is greatly

104 *The History of Lady Julia Mandeville*

set on this marriage, will settle her estate on yours, and I will give him my daughter, with twenty thousand pounds.

I insist on being at the whole expence of his education as my heir; as the estate will probably be his own, it is only anticipating his rents a few years, and does not lay him under the shadow of an obligation./

I have mentioned above, that there is a defect in the deed, which puts it in my power to rob you of your right in the estate: but, as the design of our ancestor is clear, I take no merit to myself from not being the most infamous of mankind, which I should be, were I capable of making use of such a circumstance to your disadvantage.

But, could I reconcile so base an action to myself in a private light, no consideration could make it easy to me in a public one: I know nothing so dangerous to our happy constitution as an indigent nobility, chained down to a necessity of court-dependence,[a] or tempted, by making faction the tool of ambition, to disturb the internal peace of their country. Men who are at ease in their fortunes are generally good subjects; the preservation of what they have is a powerful tie of obedience: it is the needy, the dissolute, the Cæsars,[74] the Catalines[75] of the world,/ who raise the storms which shake the foundation of government.

You will imagine, my dear friend, I only intend this alliance to take place, if their sentiments, when of age to judge for themselves, correspond with our intentions for their happiness. That this may be the case, let us educate them, with the utmost care, in every accomplishment of mind[b] and person, which can make them lovely in the eyes of each other.

Let me, my dear Colonel, hear immediately if this proposal is as agreeable to you as to

> Your faithful and affectionate,
> BELMONT./

To the Earl of BELMONT.

My LORD,

I AM greatly obliged to your Lordship for a proposal which does my son such honor; and for a conduct towards us both so noble and worthy your character.

The disposition you mention is what I have sometimes hoped, but knew your Lordship's honor and integrity too well to think it necessary to make any[c] enquiry; convinced, if a settlement was made in my favor, you would in due time make me acquainted with it: till some probability appeared of its taking place, it was, perhaps, better concealed than disclosed.

The alliance your Lordship proposes, if it ever takes place, will make me the happiest of mankind: having, however, observed marriages made by parents in the/ childhood of the parties, to be generally disagreeable to the latter, whether

Volume II 105

from the perverseness of human nature, or the free spirit of love impatient of the least controll,[a] will intreat our design may be kept secret from all the world, and in particular from the young people themselves: all we can do, is to give them such an education as will best improve the gifts of nature, and render them objects of that lively and delicate affection, which alone can make such a connexion happy. Perhaps it may be best to separate them till the time when the heart is most susceptible of tenderness; lest an habitual intercourse should weaken that impression, which we wish their perfections to make on each other. Both at present promise to be lovely; and, if we guard against other attachments, the charm of novelty, added to what nature has done for them, and those acquired graces which it is our part to endeavor to give them, can/ scarce fail of inspiring a mutual passion, which ones[b] seeming to desire it would probably prevent.

If I am so happy as to have your Lordship's concurrence in these sentiments, I will remove my son immediately from your neighbourhood, and educate him in town; at a proper time he shall go, with a private tutor of birth and merit, to the university, and from thence make the tour of Europe,[76] whilst Lady Julia is advancing in every charm, under the eye of the most excellent of mothers.

Men, who act a conspicuous part on the stage of life, and who require a certain audacity and self-possession to bring their talents into full light, cannot, in my opinion, have too public an education: but women, whose loveliest charm is the rosy blush of native modesty, whose virtues blossom fairest/ in the vale, should never leave their houshold[77]gods, the best protectors of innocence.

It is also my request, that my son may be educated in a total ignorance of the settlement in our favor, both because the effect of it may possibly be destroyed by your Lordship's having a son, and because he will taste the pleasures of a distinguished station, if he ever arrives at it, with double relish, if bred with more moderate expectations. He will by this means too escape the pernicious snares of flattery, the servile court of interested inferiors, and all the various mischiefs which poison the minds of young men bred up as heirs to great estates and titles: he will see the hatefulness of pride and arrogance in others before he is tempted to be guilty of them himself; he will learn to esteem virtue without those trappings of wealth and greatness which he will never hope to be possessed of: he will see the world as/ it is by not being of consequence enough to be flattered or deceived.

His education, his company, his expences, shall, however, be suited to the rank he may one day possibly fill; my acquaintance with foreign courts enables me to introduce him every where to those of the first rank and merit; his equipage and attendance shall be such as may secure him general respect.

Your Lordship's generous offer of bearing the expence of his education, deserves my sincerest gratitude; but œconomy will enable me to support it without the least inconvenience to my affairs; half my income, which I will spare to him, with his mother's fortune, which shall all be devoted to this purpose, will be

106   *The History of Lady Julia Mandeville*

sufficient to give him an education becoming the heir of your Lordship's fortune and honors./

May Heaven prosper a design, which has so laudable an end in view, as the future happiness of our children.[a]

I am, my Lord,
Your Lordship's
Affectionate and
Obedient[b] Servant,
J. Mandeville.

To Colonel Bellville.

Wednesday Morning.

THIS joy is a prodigious enemy to sleep. Lady Julia rose this morning with the sun;[78] I dare say she never thought he looked so bright; before he sets she will see the most charming of mankind. My Lord yesterday sent an express to Lord T –'s,/ with orders to follow Harry wherever he was, and bring him this evening to Belmont: Lady Mary is to have the pleasure of making him acquainted with his happiness: the[c] discovery was only delayed, till convinced of their passion for each other.

Colonel Mandeville is in town, directing the drawing of the writings; and comes down in a few days to have them executed.

I have had a second letter from Lord Melvin, as respectful as the pride of woman can desire: a postscript from Lord Rochdale having satisfied me in point of decorum, I allow his son to visit here when he pleases. My niece and Emily Howard come this evening; Lady Julia is now with them; I suppose we shall see Lord Melvin to-morrow: if he is very pressing, they may, perhaps, be married with Lady Julia./

Heavens! Bellville! What[d] a change in all our affairs! The matrimonial star prevails; it would be strange if I should be betrayed into the party: and yet, Lady Mary has drawn so bewitching a plan of a wedding-day, as might seduce a more determined coquette: if[e] one could be married for that day only – Or[f] if one was sure of pleasing for ever like Lady Belmont – 'Dear madam, said I, if your Ladyship would lend one your Cestus.[79]'[g] 'You are already possessed of it, my dear Lady Anne; the delicacy and purity of a bride will always give you the charms of one.'[h]

I believe her Ladyship may be in the right; it is not the state, but the foolish conduct of people who enter into it, that makes it unhappy./

If you should come down with Colonel Mandeville, it is impossible to say what may happen.

Absolutely, Bellville, if I do condescend, which is yet extremely doubtful, we will live in the style of lovers; I hate the dull road of common marriages: no

Volume II 107

impertinent presuming on the name of husband; no saucy freedoms; I will continue to be courted, and shall expect as much flattery, and give myself as many scornful airs, as if I had never honored you with my hand.

I give you warning, I shall make a most intolerable wife; but that is your business, not mine.

This very day se'nnight,[80a] which is Lady Julia's birth-day, is intended for her marriage; the house is to be full of company, invited to celebrate the day, without knowing on what further account; nobody is/ even to suspect them to be lovers; they are to go privately out of Lady Mary's apartment into the chapel, where my Lord chuses the ceremony should be performed. We are to have a masquerade[81] in a grand open pavilion,[b] on Corinthian pillars, built for this happy occasion in the garden, opposite the house, which is to be in view finely illuminated: the intermediate space is to be adorned with lamps, intermixed with festoons of flowers in the trees, round which are to be seats for the villagers, who are never forgot on these days of annual rejoicings.

Lady Mary, who is mistress of the ceremonies, and who insists on joining all our hands that day, has engaged you for the ball to Lady Julia, Harry to Bell Hastings, and Lord Melvin to me: our situation is to be kept secret for a week, which is to be filled up with various scenes of festivity; after which we are to go to/ town to be presented, and from thence on a tour of six months to Italy. This is her scheme, but it depends on Bell Hastings and me whether it shall be executed in full: ten thousand to one but our cruelty spoils the prettiest mysterious plan of a wedding that can be. Absolutely Lady Mary has a kind of an idea of things – I cannot conceive how she came by it – Not[c] the least symptom of an old maid in this plan – Something[d] so fanciful and like a love affair[e] – It is a thousand pities her Ladyship should not be of the party herself. Do you know never a sprightly old courtier of the Queen's time?

My Lord is so pleased with the thought of seeing us all happy, that he has given orders for building a temple to Love and Friendship,[82] at a little villa which the colonel has given him, and which is almost centrical in respect to all our houses; here we/ are to meet once a week, and exclude the rest of the world.

Harry and Lady Julia are to live at Lady Mary's seat, about ten miles from hence, and I have fixed on a house, which is to be sold, at about the same distance.

And now, Bellville, to be very serious, I should be the happiest creature in the world in this prospect, if I was not afraid of my own conduct. I am volatile, light, extravagant, and capricious; qualities ill suited to matrimonial life. I know my faults, but am not able to mend them: I see the beauty of order in the moral world, yet doat to excess on irregularity.

Call on Colonel Mandeville, and concert your journey together. Heaven and earth! What[f] have I not said in that permission? With all my affection for you there is a solemnity in the idea – O Bellville! should I/ ever become less dear to you! should coldness, should indifference ever take place of that lively endearing tenderness – I will throw away the pen for a moment –

The most amiable of men will forgive the too anxious fears of excessive love: I with transport make him the arbiter of my future days. Lady Julia is come back, and has brought me the enclosed[a] bond, by which Bell Hastings engages to pay you thirty thousand pounds on the day of my marriage. Her letter to you will explain this further.

Twelve o'clock.

Ah! cor mio! son confuso![83] Yes, I blush at saying in express words what I have already said by deduction. Your uncle insists on a positive 'I will':[b] How can the dear old man be so cruel? Tell him, if he is not satisfied with this letter, he shall dictate the form of consent himself./

One condition, however, I shall not dispense with; that he comes down to Belmont, and opens the ball with Lady Mary.

Adio!

To Colonel BELLVILLE.

WEDNESDAY, Three o'Clock.

I Really cannot help feeling prodigiously foolish about this marriage; it is a thousand to one but I retreat yet: prepare yourself for a disappointment, for I am exceedingly on the capricioso.[84]

O heavens![c] I forgot[d] to tell you, an old match-making Lady in the neighbourhood, having taken it into her head I have a passion for Harry Mandeville, and designing to win my heart, by persuading me to what she supposes I have a mind to, recommended/ him strongly to me last night for a husband. I heard her with the utmost attention; and, when she had finished her harangue, blushed, looked down, hesitated, and denied the thing with so pretty a confusion, that she is gone away perfectly convinced I am to be Lady Anne Mandeville, and will tell it as a secret all round the country. I am not sorry for this, as it will take away all suspicion of what is really intended, and secure that secrecy we wish on the occasion. The good old lady went away infinitely delighted at being possessed of a quality secret, which in the country gives no little importance; pleased too with her own penetration in discovering what nobody else has suspected: I cannot conceive a happier being than she is at present.

I have just received from town the most divine stomacher[85] and sleeve-knots[86] you ever beheld: 'An interesting event.'[e] Yes,/ creature, and what I can plead authority for mentioning; Did not Mademoiselle, Princess of the blood of France,[87] granddaughter of Henry the Great, write some half a dozen volumes,

Volume II 109

to inform posterity, that, on Saturday the 14th of November 1668, she wore her blue ribbands? Surely, you men think nothing of consequence but sieges and battles: now, in my sentiments, it would be happy for mankind, if all the heroes who make such havock amongst their species, merely because they have nothing to do, would amuse themselves with sorting suits of ribbands for their ladies.

I am in the sweetest good humor[a] to-day than can be imagined, so mild and gentle you would be amazed; a little impatient indeed for the evening, which is to bring my charming Harry.

I have been asking my Lord how, with Harry's sensibility, they contrived to/ keep him so long free from attachments. In answer to which he gave me the enclosed[b] sketch of a letter, from colonel Mandeville to a lady of his acquaintance at Rome, which he said would give me a general notion of the matter.

To the Countess MELESPINI.[c]

Paris, June 24, 1759.

MADAM,

YOU will receive this from the hands of that son I have before had the honor of recomending[d] to your esteem.

I have accompanied him myself hither; where being perfectly satisfied with his behavior,[e] and convinced that generous minds are best won to virtue by implicit confidence, I have dismissed the tutor I intended to have sent with him to Italy, shall return to England/ myself, and depend for his conduct on his own discretion, his desire of obliging me, and that nobleness of sentiment which will make him feel the value of my friendship for him in its utmost extent.

I have given him letters to the most worthy persons[f] in every court I intend he should visit; but, as my chief dependence for the advantages of this tour, are on the count and yourself, I have advised him to spend most of his time at Rome, where, honored by your friendship, I doubt not of his receiving that last finishing, that delicate polish, which, I flatter myself, if not deceived by the fondness of a parent, is all he wants to make him perfectly amiable.

To you, Madam, and the Count, I commit him; defend him from the snares of vice, and the contagion of affectation./

You receive him an unexperienced youth, with lively passions, a warm and affectionate heart, an enthusiastic imagination, probity, openness, generosity; and all those advantages of person and mind, which a liberal education can bestow. I expect him from your hands a gentleman, a man of honor and politeness, with the utmost dignity of sentiment and character, adorned by that easy elegance, that refined simplicity of manner, those unaffected graces of deportment, so difficult to describe, but which it is scarce possible to converse much with you without acquiring.

110   *The History of Lady Julia Mandeville*

Sensible of the irresistible power of beauty, I think it of the utmost consequence with what part of the female world he converses. I have from childhood habituated him to the conversation of the most lovely and polite amongst the best part of the sex, to give him an abhorrence to the indelicacy of the worst. I have endeavoured[a] to impress on/ his mind, the most lively ideas of the native beauty of virtue;[88] and to cultivate in him that elegance of moral taste, that quick sensibility, which is a nearer way to rectitude, than the dull road of inanimate precept.

Continuing the same anxious cares, I send him to perfect his education, not in schools or academies, but in the conversation of the most charming amongst women: the ardent desire of pleasing you, and becoming worthy your esteem, inseparable from the happiness of knowing you, will be the keenest spur to his attainments, and I shall see him return all the fond heart of a parent can wish, from his ambition of being honored with your friendship.

To you, Madam, I shall make no secret of my wish, that he may come back to England unconnected. I have a view for him beyond his most sanguine hopes, to/ which, however, I entreat[b] he may be a stranger; the charms of the Lady cannot fail of attaching a heart which has no prepossession, from which, I conjure you, if possible, to guard him. I should even hear with pleasure you permitted him, to a certain degree, to love you, that he might be steeled to all other charms. If he is half as much in love with you as his father, all other beauties will lay snares for him in vain.

I am, MADAM,

With the most lively Esteem,

Your obedient and devoted,

J. MANDEVILLE.

Oh! Heavens! whilst I have been writing, and thinking nothing of it, the pavillion,[c] which it seems has been some time prepared, is raised opposite the window of the saloon, at the end of a walk leading to the house. We[d] are to sup in it this evening: it is charmante;[89]/ the sight of it, and the idea of its destination, makes my heart palpitate a little. Mon Dieu! that ever I should be seduced into matrimony!

Farewel[e] for an hour or two.

You have no notion what divine dresses we have making for the masquerade; I shall not tell you particulars, as I would not take off the pleasure of surprize, but they are charming beyond conception.

Do not you doat on a masquerade, Bellville?[f] For my own part, I think it is the quintessence of all sublunary joys; and, without flattering my Lord's taste, I have a strange fancy this will be the most agreeable one I ever was at in my life: the scenes, the drapery, the whole disposition of it is enchanting.[g]

Heavens! How little a while will it be that I can write myself,

A. WILMOT./[h]

To George Mordaunt, Esq;

Wednesday Morning.

After four days past[a] in anxiety not to be told, this ardently expected[b] morning is come; I every moment expect Mr. Herbert; I tremble at every sound: another hour, and the happiness of my whole life will be for ever determined: Mordaunt, the idea chills my soul.

It is now a week since I have heard from Belmont; not a line from Emily Howard, or Lady Anne; the unhappy have few friends; Lord Melvin is the minion of fortune;[90] he has taken my place in their esteem.

The time is past, and my friend is not here, he has therefore no letters from Lord Belmont; I rated his disinterestedness too/ high; misled by the mean despicable maxims of the world, he resents my passion for his daughter; he gives her to another, without deigning even to send me an answer: he might surely have respected his own blood. My[c] soul is on fire at this insult: his age, his virtues protect him, but Lord Melvin – Let[d] him avoid my fury.

Yet am I not too rash? May[e] not some accident have retarded my friend? I will wait patiently till evening; I cannot believe Lord Belmont – May[f] he not have seen me, and, suspecting some clandestine design – Yes,[g] my folly has undone me; what can he think of such a concealment? –

Mordaunt! I cannot live in this suspence; I will send William this moment to Belmont.

Five o'clock.

William is come back, and has thrown me into despair: yes, my friend, it is now beyond a doubt./

Lady Julia is intended for Lord Melvin; the most splendid preparations are making; all is joy and festivity at Belmont; a wretch like me is below their thoughts; messengers are hourly coming and going from Lord Rochdale's: it is past, and I am doomed to despair: my letter has only hastened my destruction; has only hastened this detested marriage: over-awed[h] by paternal authority, she gives me up, she marries another; she has forgot her vows, those vows which she called on Heaven to witness: I have lost all for which life was worth my care.

Mordaunt! I am no longer master of myself. Lord Melvin is this moment gone past to Belmont, dressed like a youthful, gay and burning bridegroom; his eyes sparkle with new fire; his cheek has the glow of happy love. This very hour, perhaps, he calls her his – this very hour her consenting blushes – the idea is insupportable/ – First[i] may the avenging bolt of Heaven – but why supplicate Heaven[j] – My[k] own arm – I will follow him – I will not tamely resign her – He shall first – Yes,[l] through my blood alone – What[m] I intend I know not – My thoughts are all distraction.[n]

112   *The History of Lady Julia Mandeville*

To Col. BELLVILLE.

Seven o'clock.

WE expect the caro Enrico[91] every moment: my chariot is gone for Emily Howard and my niece; Lord Melvin too comes this evening by my permission. Lady Julia has just asked me to walk with her in the park; she wants to hear me talk of Harry, whom she cannot mention herself, though her thoughts are full of nothing else; her color comes and goes; her eyes have a double portion of softness; her heart beats with apprehensive pleasure. What an evening of transport will this be! Why are you not here, Bellville? I shall absolutely/ be one of the old people to-night. Can you form an idea of happiness equal to Harry's? Raised[a] from the depth of despair, to the fruition of all his wishes, I long to see how he will receive the first mention of this happy turn of fortune: but Lady Mary has reserved all that to herself.

Adieu!

Great God! to what a scene have I been witness! How[b] shall I relate the shocking particulars?

Lady Julia and I were advanced about a quarter of a mile from the house, blessing Providence, and talking of the dear hope of future happy days; she was owning her passion with blushes, and all the tremor of modest sensibility, when we were interrupted by the clashing of swords behind some trees near us; we turned our heads, and saw Lord Melvin, distraction in his air, his sword bloody, supporting Harry Mandeville,/ pale, bleeding, motionless, and to all appearance in the agonies of death. Lady Julia gave a shriek, and fell senseless in my arms. My cries brought some of the servants, who happened to be near; part of them, with Lord Melvin, conveyed Harry to the house; whilst the rest staid with me to take care of Lady Julia.

Harry was scarce out of sight when she recovered her senses; she looked wildly towards the place where she first saw him, then, starting from me, raising her eyes to Heaven, her hands clasped together – Oh,[c] Bellville! never shall I lose the idea of that image of horror and despair – she neither spoke nor shed a tear – there was an eager wildness in her look, which froze my soul with terror: she advanced hastily towards the house, looking round her every moment, as if expecting again to see him, till, having exhausted all her strength, she sunk down breathless on one of the seats, where I supported her till my Lord's chariot,/ which I had sent for, came up, in which I placed myself by her, and we drove slowly towards the house: she was put to-bed[d] in a burning fever, preceded by a shivering, which gives me apprehensions for her, which I endeavor[e] to conceal from the wretched parents, whose sorrows mock all description.

My Lord is just come from Lord Melvin, who insisted on being his prisoner, till Harry was out of danger; disdaining to fly from justice,[f] since my Lord refuses

Volume II
113

his stay at Belmont, he intreats to be given into the hands of some gentleman near. My Lord has accepted this offer, and named his father Lord Rochdale for the trust. He is gone under the best guard, his own honor, in which Lord Belmont has implicit confidence.

I have been into Lady Julia's room; she takes no notice of any thing. Emily/ Howard kneels weeping by her bedside. Lady Belmont melts my soul when I behold her; she sits motionless as the statue of despair;[a] she holds the hand of her lovely daughter between hers, she presses it to her bosom, and the tears steal silently down her cheeks.

Unable to bear the sight, I am returned to my apartment.

Oh,[b] Bellville! How is this scene of happiness changed![c] Where are now the gay transporting hopes which warmed our hearts this morning?

I have with difficulty prevailed on Lady Mary, who droops under this weight of affliction, and whose years are ill-suited[d] to scenes of horror, to set out this evening for her own seat; my niece, whose sorrow you may easily imagine, is to accompany her thither: if Mr. Mandeville dies, murdered/ by the hand of him with whose fate hers is connected, never must she again enter these[e] hospitable doors.

Bellville! how is the gay structure of ideal happiness fallen in one moment to the ground!

The messenger who was sent to Lord T –'s is returned, and has brought my Lord's letter;[f] he went from thence to Mr. Herbert's, where Mr. Mandeville was supposed to be, but found nobody there but a servant, from whom he could get no information. The family had been gone five days to London, being sent for express to a relation who was dying.

Oh,[g] Bellville! how many accidents have conspired – I myself have innocently contributed to this dreadful event, misled by my Lord's equivocal expressions, which seemed to point so plainly at Lord Melvin/ – If he dies – But[h] I will not give way to so shocking an idea. The servant who went for a surgeon is not yet returned; till his wounds are examined we must be in all the torture of suspence and apprehension.

Eleven o'Clock.

The surgeon is come; he is now with Mr. Mandeville: how I dread to hear his sentence! – The door opens[i] – He[j] comes out with Lord Belmont; horror is in the face of the latter – Oh,[k] Bellville! my presaging heart – they advance towards me – I am unable to meet them – my limbs tremble – a cold dew –

Bellville! his wounds are mortal – the pen drops from my hand[92] –/

A farmer's son in the neighbourhood has just brought the enclosed[l] letter for Mr. Mandeville, which, not knowing the consequence, my Lord has opened.

114   *The History of Lady Julia Mandeville*

To Henry Mandeville, Esquire.[a]

London, Tuesday Morning.

SIR,

THE generous concern you have been pleased to take in my misfortunes, leaves me no room to doubt I shall give you pleasure by informing you that they are at an end; a rich relation, who is just expired, having made a will in my favor, which places me in circumstances beyond my hopes. But you will be still more happy to know you have contributed to this turn of my fortune. The express/ was arrived, with a request from our dying friend, that we would instantly come post to town, and we were lamenting our hard fate in being unable, from our indigence, to undertake a journey on which so much depended, when the post brought me a bill for one hundred pounds, which could come from no hand but yours: I wish the world was such as to make it easy for us to mistake. We set out with hearts filled with the sincerest gratitude to Heaven, and the most worthy of men; and on our arrival[b] found deferring our journey, even a few hours, would have been fatal to all our hopes.

To you, therefore, to whom we owe the means of taking this journey, we owe the ease of fortune which has been the consequence of it. Heaven has been pleased to make the man on earth we most esteem the instrument of its goodness to us./

The hurry of spirits in which we set out prevented my leaving a direction for you with my servant, which I hope has been of no ill consequence. I have to-day sent him a direction, and ordered him to wait on you with this letter. As soon as my affairs here are settled, will[c] replace the money your generous friendship has assisted us with, wherever you please to order.

I am, with the most lively Esteem,

SIR,

Your most affectionate,

And obedient Servant,

W. Herbert.

Bellville! is it not hard the exercise of the noblest virtue should have been attended with such fatal effects? He dies for having alleviated the distresses of his friend, for having sympathized[93] in the affliction of others./

To Colonel Bellville.

Thursday Morning.

THE most lovely of men is no more; he expired early this morning, after having in my presence owned to my Lord, that jealousy was the true cause of his attacking Lord Melvin, who only fought in his own defence, which he intreated him publicly to attest, and to beg Lord Melvin's pardon, in his name, for insults which madness alone could excuse, and which it was not in man to bear; he owned Lord Melvin's behavior[a] in the duel had been noble, and that he had avoided giving him the least wound, till, urged by fury and despair, and aiming at the life of his generous enemy rather than at his own defence, he had rushed on the point of his sword./

He expressed great indifference for life on his own account, but dreaded the effect his death might have on the most tender of fathers: intreated my Lord to soften so painful a stroke by preparing him for it by degrees, and, if possible, to conceal from him the shocking manner of it. 'How ill, said he, has[b] my rashness repaid him for all his anxious cares, his indulgent goodness. I suffer justly; but for him – Great God! support him in the dreadful trial, and pour all thy blessings on his head!'

He then proceeded to expostulate gently with Lord Belmont on his supposed design of forcing the heart of his daughter, and on that neglect of himself which had planted the furies of jealousy in his breast, and occasioned this shocking event. These reproaches brought on an explanation of the situation to which his danger had reduced Lady Julia, of my Lord's intention/ of giving her to him, and of the whole plan of purposed happiness, which his impatience, irritated by a series of unforeseen accidents, had so fatally destroyed.

Till now he had appeared perfectly composed; but from the moment my Lord began to speak, a wildness had appeared in his countenance, which rose before he ended to little less than distraction; he raved, he reproached Heaven itself; then, melting into tears, prayed with fervor unspeakable for Lady Julia's recovery: the agitation of his mind caused his wounds to bleed afresh; successive faintings were the consequence, in one of which he expired.

Lord Belmont is now writing to Colonel Mandeville. How many has this dreadful event involved in misery!

Who shall tell this to Lady Julia,[c] yet how conceal it from her? I dread the most/ fatal effects from her despair, when returning reason makes her capable of knowing her own wretchedness; at present she is in a state of perfect insensibility, her fever is not the least abated; she has every symptom which can indicate danger. Lady Belmont and Emily Howard have never left her bedside a moment. I have with difficulty persuaded them to attempt to rest a few hours, and am going to take Lady Belmont's place by her bedside.

Ten o'clock.

The physician is gone; he thinks Lady Julia in danger, but has not told this to the family: I am going again to her apartment; she has not yet taken notice of any body.

116   *The History of Lady Julia Mandeville*

I had been about half an hour in Lady Julia's room, when, having sent the last attendant away for something I wanted, she looked round, and saw we were alone;/ she half raised herself in the bed, and, grasping my hand, fixed her enquiring eyes ardently on mine. I too well understood their meaning, and, unable to hide my grief, was rising to leave the bedside,[a] when catching hold of me, with a look and air which froze my soul; 'Lady Anne, said she, does he live?'[b] My silence, and the tears which I could not conceal, explained to her the fatal truth, when raising her streaming eyes and supplicating hands to heaven – Oh,[c] Bellville! no words can describe the excess of her sorrow and despair; – fearful of the most fatal instant effects, I was obliged to call her attendants, of whose entrance she took not the least notice. After remaining some time absorbed in an agony of grief, which took from her all power of utterance, and made her insensible to all around her, the tears, which she shed in great abundance, seemed to give her relief: my heart was melted; I wept with her. She saw my tears,[d] and/ pressing my hand tenderly between hers, seemed to thank me for the part I took in her afflictions: I had not opposed the torrent of her despair; but, when I saw it subsiding, endeavored to soothe her with all the tender attention and endearing sympathy of faithful friendship; which so far succeeded, that I have left her more composed than I could have imagined it possible she should so soon have been; she has even an appearance of tranquillity which amazes me; and, seeming inclined to take rest, I have left her for that purpose.

May Heaven restore her to her wretched parents,[e] whose life is wrapt in hers! May[f] it inspire her with courage to bear this stroke, the severest a feeling mind can suffer.[g] Her youth, her sweetness of temper, her unaffected piety, her filial tenderness, sometimes flatter me with a hope of her recovery; but when I think on that melting sensibility, on that exquisitely tender heart,/ which bleeds for the sorrow of every human being, I give way to all the horrors of despair.

Lady Julia has sent to speak with me: I will not a moment delay attending her. How blest should I be if the sympathizing bosom of Friendship[h] could soften by partaking her sorrows!

Oh,[i] Bellville! what request has she made! my blood runs back at the idea.

She received me with a composed air, begged me to sit down by her bedside, and, sending away her attendants, spoke as follows; 'You are, I doubt not, my dear Lady Anne, surprized at the seeming tranquil manner in which I bear the greatest of all misfortunes – Yes,[j] my heart doated on him, my love for him was unutterable – But[k] it is past; I can no longer be deceived by the fond delusion/ of hope. I submit to the will of Heaven. My God! I am resigned, I do not complain of what thy hand has inflicted; a few unavailing tears alone – Lady Anne, you have seen my calmness, you have seen me patient as the trembling victim beneath the sacrificer's knife.[94] Yet think not I have resigned all sensibility: no, were it possible I could live – But[l] I feel my approaching end; Heaven in this is

Volume II 117

merciful. That I bear this dreadful stroke with patience is owing to the certainty I shall not long survive him, that our separation is but for a moment. Lady Anne, I have seen him in my dreams; his spotless soul yet waits for mine: yes, the same grave shall receive us; we shall be joined to part no more. All the sorrow I feel is for my dear parents; to you and Emily Howard I leave the sad talk of comforting them; by all our friendship, I adjure you, leave them not to the effects of their despair: when/ I reflect on all their goodness, and on the misery I have brought on their grey hairs, my heart is torn in pieces, I lament that such a wretch was ever created.

I have been to blame; not in loving the most perfect of human beings;[a] but in concealing that love, and distrusting the indulgence of the best of parents. Why did I hide my passion? Why[b] conceal sentiments only blameable on the venal maxims of a despicable world? Had I been unreserved I had been happy: but Heaven had decreed otherwise, and I submit.

But whither am I wandering?[c] I sent for you to make a request; a request in which I will not be denied. Lady Anne, I would see him; let me be raised and carried to his apartment before my mother returns: let me once more behold/ him, behold him for whom alone life was dear to me: you hesitate, for pity do not oppose me; your refusal will double the pangs of death.'

Overcome by the earnestness of her air and manner, I had not resolution to refuse her; her maids are now dressing her, and I have promised to attend her to his apartment.

I am summoned. Great God! How[d] shall I bear a scene like this? I tremble, my limbs will scarce support me.

Twelve o'Clock.

This dreadful visit is yet unpaid: three times she approached the door, and returned as often to her apartment, unable to enter the room; the third time she fainted away: her little remaining strength being exhausted, she has consented to defer her/ purpose till evening: I hope by that time to persuade her to decline it wholly: faint, and almost sinking under her fatigue, I have prevailed with her to lie down on a couch: Emily Howard sits by her, kissing her hand, and bathing it with her tears.

I have been enquiring at Lady Julia's door; she is in a sweet sleep, from which we have every thing to hope: I fly to tell this to Lady Belmont – She will live;[e] Heaven has heard our prayers. –[f]

I found the wretched mother pouring out her soul before her God, and imploring his mercy on her child – She[g] heard me, and with tears of tender transport – she raised her grateful hands to Heaven –

I am interrupted; Dr. Evelin is at the gate; he is come to my apartment, and desires me to accompany him to Lady Julia./

118   *The History of Lady Julia Mandeville*

We found her still in a gentle sleep, composed as that of an infant; we approached the bed; Dr. Evelin took her hand, he stood some time looking on her with the most fixed attention, when, on my expressing my hopes from her sleep, 'Madam,' said he, 'it is with horror I tell you, that sleep will probably be her last; nature is worn out, and seeks a momentary repose before her last dreadful struggle.'

Not able to bear this, I left the room. – Bellville! is it possible! Can[a] Heaven thus overwhelm with affliction, the best, the noblest of its creatures? Shall[b] the amiable, the reverend pair, the business of whose lives has been to make others happy, be doomed in age to bear the severest of all sorrows? to see all their hopes blasted in one dreadful moment? To believe this, is to blaspheme Providence. No, it is not possible: Heaven will yet restore her: look down, O God of mercy –/

Dr. Evelin is now with the wretched parents, breaking to them the danger of their child: I dread seeing them after this interview; yet he will not sure plunge them at once into despair.

She is awake; I have been with her: her looks are greatly changed: her lips have a dying paleness; there is a dimness in her eyes which alarms me: she has desired to speak a moment with Dr. Evelin; she would know how long he thinks it probable she may live.

Six o'Clock.

She is gone, Bellville, she is gone: those lovely eyes are closed in everlasting night. I saw her die, I saw the last breath quiver on her lips; she expired, almost without a pang, in the arms of her distracted[95] mother./

She felt her approaching dissolution, of which she had been warned, at her own earnest request, by Dr. Evelin; she summoned us all to her apartment; she embraced us with the most affecting tenderness; she called me to her, and, giving me her picture for Col. Mandeville, begged me to tell him, she, who murdered his son, died for him: entreated[c] me to stay some time at Belmont, to comfort her disconsolate parents; conjured Emily to be a child to them, and never to let them miss their Julia.

She begged forgiveness of her wretched parents, for the only instance in which she had ever forgot her duty, and for which she now so severely suffered: entreated them to submit to the hand of Heaven, and not give way to immoderate affliction; to consider that, if they were about to lose a child, thousands were at that moment suffering under the same distress; that death/ was the common portion of humanity, from which youth was not more exempt than age; that their separation was only temporary, whilst their re-union would be eternal: then, raising her blameless hands, prayed fervently to Heaven for them, implored their last blessing; and, turning to her agonizing mother, speechless with excess of sorrow, conjured her to reflect on the past goodness of Heaven, and the many years of happiness she had already past[d] with the best of men; that this was the first misfortune she had ever known; then, embracing her fondly, weeping on her neck, and thanking her for all her goodness, pressed her to her bosom, and expired.

Let me draw a veil over the ensuing scene, to which words cannot do justice. With difficulty have we forced Lady Belmont from the body. I have left Emily Howard with the venerable pair, whose sorrow would melt the most obdurate heart; she kneels by Lady Belmont, she attempts/ to speak, but tears stop her utterance: the wretched mother sees her not; inattentive to all but her grief, her eyes fixed on the ground, stupefaction and horror in her look, she seems insensible of all that passes around her. Sinking under his own distress, and unable to support the sight of hers, my Lord is retired to his apartment. May Heaven look with pity on them both, and enable them to bear this blow to all their hopes!

Bellville! where are now all our gay schemes? Where[a] the circle of happy friends?

How vain are the designs of man![96] unmindful of his transitory state, he lays plans of permanent felicity; he sees the purpose of his heart ready to prosper; the air-drawn building rises, he watches it with a beating heart, it touches the very point at which he aimed, the very summit of imagined perfection,/ when an unforeseen storm arises, and the smiling deceitful structure of hope is dashed in one moment to the ground.

Friday Morning.

Not an eye has been closed this night; the whole house is a scene of horror: the servants glide up and down the apartments, wildness in their look, as if the last day was come.

Scarce have we been able to keep life in Lady Belmont; she asks eagerly for her child, her Julia; she conjures us to lead her to her; she will not believe her dead; she starts up, and fancies she hears her voice: then, recollecting the late dreadful scene, lifts her expostulating hands to Heaven, and sinks motionless into the arms of her attendants./

Six o'Clock.

Worn out by her long watchings, and the violence of her emotions, Lady Belmont is fallen into a slumber: it is now two days and nights since she has attempted rest. May that gracious God, who alone has the power, calm and tranquillize her mind!

Eight o'Clock.

I have been standing an hour looking on the breathless body of my angel friend: lovely even in death, a serene smile sits on that once charming face: her paleness excepted, she looks as if in a tranquil sleep: Bellville, she is happy, she is now a saint in Heaven.

120   *The History of Lady Julia Mandeville*

How persuasive is such a preacher! I gaze on that once matchless form, and all vanity dies within me: who was ever lovely like her,[a] yet she lies before me a clod of senseless clay.[97] Those[b] eyes, which once gave/ love to every beholder, are now robbed of their living lustre; that beauteous bosom is cold as the marble on the silent tomb; the roses of those cheeks are faded; those vermillion[c] lips, from whence truth and virtue ever proceeded – Bellville, the starting tears – I cannot go on[d] –

Look here, ye proud, and be humble! which of you all can vie with her? Youth,[e] health, beauty, birth, riches, all that men call good were hers: all are now of no avail; virtue alone bids defiance to the grave.

Great Heaven! Colonel Mandeville is at the gate; he knows not the cup of sorrow[98] which awaits him; he cannot yet have received my Lord's letter. He alights with a smile of transport; the exultation of hope is in his air. Alas![f] how soon to be destroyed! He comes to attend the bridal-day/ of his son; he finds him a lifeless corse.[99]

The servants bring him this way; they leave to me the dreadful task – Bellville, I cannot go through it.

I have seen the most unhappy of fathers; I have followed him whither my heart shuddered to approach. Too soon informed of his wretched fate, he shot like lightning to the apartment of his son; he kissed his pale lifeless lips; he pressed his cold hand to his bosom; he bathed it with a torrent of tears: then, looking round with the dignity of affliction, waved his hand for us all to retire.[g] We have left him to weep at liberty over the son on whom his heart doated, to enjoy alone and undisturbed the dreadful banquet of despair.

He has been now two hours alone with the body; not an attendant has dared to/ intrude on the sacred rites of paternal sorrow. My Lord is this moment gone to him, to give him a melancholy welcome to Belmont.

Great God! What[h] a meeting! How different from that which their sanguine hopes had projected! The bridal couch is the bed of death![100]

Oh, Bellville! but shall presumptuous man dare to arraign the ways of Heaven!/[i]

To Colonel BELLVILLE.

TUESDAY Morning.

YOUR letter, my dear Bellville, gave me all the consolation it is possible to receive amidst such a scene of wretchedness and despair; the tender sympathy of pitying friendship is the best balm for every woe.

The delicacy with which you decline mentioning a subject so improper for the time, would encrease[j] my esteem for you, if that was possible. I know the goodness, the tender sensibility of your heart, too well to doubt your approving

Volume II　　　　　　　　　　　　　　　　　　　　121

my resolution to give six months to the memory of my angelic friend, and the sad task of endeavoring[a] to soften the sorrows of her parents. Her dying voice adjured me not/ to leave them to their despair: I will not forget the sad task her friendship imposed.

The agony of Lady Belmont's grief begins to give place to a sorrow more reasonable, though, perhaps, not less exquisite. The violence of her emotions abate;[b] she still weeps, but her air is more calm; she raises her eyes to Heaven, but it is with a look of patient resignation, which, whilst it melts my soul to behold, gives me hopes she will not sink under her afflictions. Lord Belmont struggles with his own grief, lest it should encrease[c] hers; he attempts to comfort her; he begs her, with an irresolute air, to consider the hand from whence the stroke proceeded: unable to go on, his voice trembles; his bosom swells with unutterable anguish; he rises; he leaves the room; the tears trickle down his reverend cheeks./

These, Bellville, these are the scenes I have perpetually before my eyes.

Colonel Mandeville indulges his sorrow alone; shut up continually in his apartment, a prey to silent distress, he seems to fly from all human converse: if[d] entreated, he joins our sad party a moment; he enters with a dejected air, his eyes are bent earnestly to the ground; he sits motionless, inattentive, absorbed in reflexion on his own misery: then starting up exclaims, 'All else I could have borne,' and retires to give himself up to his despair.

I am now convinced Emily Howard deserved that preference Lady Julia gave her over me in her heart, of which I once so unjustly complained; I lament, I regret, but am enough myself to reason, to reflect; Emily Howard can only weep./

Far from being consoled for the loss of her lovely friend, by the prospect of inheriting Lord Belmont's fortune, to which after Colonel Mandeville she is intitled, she seems incapable of tasting any good in life without her. Every[e] idea of happiness her gentle mind could form included Lady Julia's friendship; with her she wished to spend all her days; she was all to her tender Emily; without her she finds the world a desart.[101]

She is changed beyond conception by her grief, a grief which has not a moment's intermission: the almost dying paleness of her cheeks is a witness of the excess of her affliction; yet this very paleness has a thousand charms; her distress has something in it unspeakably lovely; adorned by sorrow, she puts me in mind of what Young describes woman in general;/

> – 'So properly the object of affliction,
> That Heaven is pleased[f] to make distress become her,
> And dresses her most amiably in tears.'[102]

122 *The History of Lady Julia Mandeville*

Tuesday Evening.

Bellville, I have been walking in a little wilderness of flowering shrubs once peculiarly happy in Lady Julia's favor: there is a rose which I saw planted by her hand; it still flourishes in youthful bloom, whilst she, the fairest flower Heaven ever formed, lies cropped by the cruel hand of Death.[a]

What force has the imagination over the senses! How[b] different is the whole face of nature in my eyes! The[c] once smiling scene has a melancholy gloom, which strikes a damp through my inmost soul: I look in vain for those vivid beauties which once charmed me; all beauty died with Lady Julia./

In this spot, where we have so often walked together, I give way to all the voluptuousness of sorrow; I recall those happy days which are never to return; a thousand tender ideas rush on my memory; I recollect those dear moments of confidence and friendship engraved for ever on my heart; I still hear the sweet accents of that voice, still behold that matchless form; I see her every moment before me, in all the playfulness of youth and innocence; I see her parents gazing on her as she passes, with that lively transport a parent only can know.

It was here her rising blushes first discovered to me the secret of her heart: it was here the loveliest of mankind first implored me to favor his passion for my sweet friend.

Pleased with the tender sorrow which possessed all my soul, I determined to indulge it to the utmost; and, revolving in my imagination the happy hours of chearful/ friendship to which that smiling scene had been witness, prolonged my walk till evening had, almost unperceived, spread its gloomy horrors round; till the varied tints of the flowers were lost in the deepening shades of night.

Awaking at once from the reverie in which I had been plunged, I found myself at a distance from the house, just entering the little wood so loved by my charming friend; the every moment encreasing[d] darkness gave an awful gloom to the trees; I stopped, I looked round, not a human form was in sight; I listened and heard not a sound but the trembling of some poplars in the wood; I called, but the echo of my own voice was the only answer I received; a dreary silence reigned around, a terror I never felt before seized me, my heart panted with timid apprehension; I breathed short, I started at every leaf that moved; my limbs were covered with a/ cold dew; I fancied I saw a thousand airy forms flit around me, I seemed to hear the shrieks of the dead and dying; there is no describing my horrors.

At the moment when my fears had almost deprived me of sense, I saw Colonel Mandeville approach; I concealed from him the terrors of my soul, lest they should add to the sorrow which consumed him: he addressed me in a faltering voice, conducted me to the house almost without speaking, and leading me into the saloon – Oh[e] Bellville! How[f] shall I describe what I felt on entering the room?

Volume II 123

Is not Death[a] of itself sufficiently dreadful, that we thus clothe it in additional terrors, by the horrid apparatus with which we suffer it to be attended? The room was hung with black, lighted up to show[b] the affecting objects it contained, and in the midst, in their coffins, the breathless bodies/ of the hapless lovers: on a couch near them, supported by Emily Howard, the wretched mother wringing her hands in all the agony of despair. Lord Belmont standing by the bodies, looking at them alternately, weeping over his child, and raising his desponding eyes to Heaven, beseeching the God of Mercy to relieve him from this load of misery, and to put a speedy period to that life which was now robbed of all its happiness.

I approached Lady Julia's coffin, I gazed eagerly on her angel countenance, serene as that of a sleeping infant; I kissed her lifeless lips, which still wore the smile of innocence and peace. Bellville, may my last end be like hers! May[c] I meet her in the regions of immortality! Never shall I forget her gentle virtues, or the delight I found in her friendship./

She was wrapped in a loose robe of white sattin:[d] her head covered with a veil of gause:[103e] the village maids, who laid her in the coffin, had adorned her with the freshest flowers; they stood at an awful[104] distance, weeping her hard fate and their own: they have entreated to watch around her this night, and to bear her to-morrow to the grave.

I had stood some time looking on the dear remains of Lady Julia, when Colonel Mandeville took my hand, and leading me to the coffin in which his son's were deposited; 'Lady Anne, said he, you[f] have forgot your once favored friend, your once gay, once lovely Harry Mandeville. Behold all that Death has left of the darling of a fond parent's heart! The graces of that form are lost, those lips have ceased to utter the generous sentiments of the noblest heart which ever beat; but never will his varied perfections be blotted from the mind of his father.'/

I approached the most lovely of men; the traces of sorrow were visible on his countenance; he died in the moment when he heard the happiness which had been vainly intended for him. My tears streamed afresh when I beheld him, when I remembered the sweet hours we had passed together, the gay scenes which hope had painted to our hearts; I wept over the friend I had so loved, I pressed his cold hand to my lips.

Bellville! I am now accustomed to horrors.

We have prevailed on the wretched parents to retire: Emily Howard and I, have entreated to watch our angel friends till midnight, and then leave them to the village maids, to whom Lady Julia's weeping attendants insist on being joined.

I dread the rising of to-morrow's sun; he was meant to light us to happiness./

124   *The History of Lady Julia Mandeville*

Thursday[105] Morning.

Bellville! this morning is come: this morning once so ardently expected: who shall ever dare to say, To-morrow I will be happy?[a]

At dawn of day we returned to the saloon, we bid a last adieu to the loved remains; my Lord and Colonel Mandeville had been before us: they were going to close the coffins, when Lady Belmont burst wildly into the room; she called eagerly for her Julia, for the idol of her agonizing soul: 'Let me once more behold my child, let me once more kiss those icy lips: O[b] Julia! this day first gave thee birth, this day fond hope set down for thy bridals, this day we resign thee to the grave!'

Overcome by the excess of her sorrow she fainted into the arms of her woman; we took that opportunity to convey her from/ this scene of terrors: her senses are not yet returned.

Thursday Evening.

What a day have I passed! may the idea of it be ever blotted from my mind!

Nine o'clock.

The sad procession begins; the whole village attend in tears; they press to perform the last melancholy duties; her servants crowd eagerly round; they weep, they beat their bosoms, they call on their angelic mistress, they kiss the pall that covers her breathless form. Borne by the youngest of the village maids – O[c] Bellville! never more shall I behold her! the loveliest of her sex, the friend on whom my heart doated – One[d] grave receives the hapless lovers –/

They move on – far other processions – but who shall resist the hand of heaven!

Emily Howard comes this way; she has left the wretched parents: there is a wildness in her air which chills my blood, she will behold her friend once more, she proposes to meet and join the procession; I embrace[e] the offer with transport – the transport of enthusiastic sorrow –

We have beheld the closing scene – Bellville, my heart is breaking – the pride of the world, the loveliest pair that ever breathed the vital air, are now cold and inanimate in the grave./

To Col. Bellville.

Sunday Morning.

I Am just come from chapel with Lady Belmont, who has been pouring out the sorrows of her soul to her Creator, with a fervor of devotion which a mind like hers alone can feel: when she approached the seat once filled by Lady Julia, the tears streamed involuntary down her cheeks; she wiped them away, she raised her eyes to Heaven, and falling on her knees, with a look of pious resignation,

Volume II 125

seemed to sacrifice her grief to her God, or at least to suspend the expression of it in his presence.

Next Sunday she goes to the parish church, where the angelic pair are interred; I dread her seeing the vault, yet think she cannot too soon visit every place which must renew the excess of her affliction; she/ will then, and not till then, find, by degrees, the violence of her sorrow subside, and give way to that pleasing melancholy, that tender regret, which, however strange it may appear, is one of the most charming sensations of the human heart.

Whether it be that the mind abhors nothing like a state of inaction, or from whatever cause I know not, but grief itself is more agreeable to us than indifference; nay, if not too exquisite, is in the highest degree delightful; of which the pleasure we take in tragedy,[106] or in talking of our dead friends, is a striking proof; we wish not to be cured of what we feel on these occasions; the tears we shed are charming, we even indulge in them; Bellville, does not the very word *indulge* shew the sensation to be pleasureable?[a]

I have just now a letter from my niece; she is in despair at this dreadful event; she sees the amiable, the venerable parents, whose happiness was the ardent wish of her/ soul, and from whom she had received every proof of esteem and friendship, reduced to the extremest misery, by the hand of him she loves: for ever excluded from Belmont, for ever to them an object of horror, she seems to herself guilty of their wretchedness, she seems to have struck the fatal blow.

Since Mr. Mandeville's death she has left Lady Mary, whose tears she fancied were redoubled at her sight.

Nor is she less wretched on Lord Melvin's account, she is distracted with her terrors for his life; which is however safe by Mr. Mandeville's generous care, who when expiring gave testimony to his innocence.

You will oblige me by begging of Lady Betty to take her at present under her protection: it ill suits the delicacy of her sex and birth to remain in London alone/ and unconnected: with your amiable mother, she cannot fail of being happy.

I had perswaded[b] Lady Belmont to walk in the garden, she went with me, leaning on my arm, when the door being opened the first object that struck her sight was the pavillion[c] raised for the marriage of her daughter, which none of us had thought of having removed.

She started, she returned hastily to her apartment, and throwing herself on a couch, gave a loose to all the anguish of her soul.

Bellville, every object she meets will remind her of the darling of her heart.

My Lord and Colonel Mandeville are together, they are projecting a tomb for their lovely children: a tomb worthy the ardour[d] of their own parental[e] affection; worthy to perpetuate the memory of their virtues,/ their love, and their wretched fate. How often shall I visit this tomb,[f] how often strow[g] it with the sweetest flowers!

126   *The History of Lady Julia Mandeville*

Sunday Afternoon.

As I passed this moment through the saloon, I went mechanically to the window from whence we used to contemplate the happy groups[a] of villagers. Bellville, how was I struck with the change! not one of the late joyous train appeared; all was a dismal scene of silent unsocial solitude: lost to the idea of pleasure, all revere, all partake, the sorrows of their godlike benefactors: with Lady Julia all joy has left the once charming shades of Belmont.

Lord Fondville is gone past with his bride, in all the splendor of exulting transport. Scarce can I forbear accusing Heaven;[b] the worthless live and prosper, the virtuous sink untimely to the grave./[c]

My Lord has ordered the pavillion[d] to be removed; he will build an obelisk on the spot where it stood, on the spot once dedicated to the happiness of his child.

A stranger has been to-day at the parish church, enquiring for the grave of Mr. Mandeville; his behaviour witnessed the most lively sorrow: it can be no other than Mr. Herbert. I have told this to my Lord, who will write and ask him to Belmont, that he may mix his tears with ours; whoever loved Mr. Mandeville will be here a most welcome guest.

Monday Morning.

I have perswaded[e] Lady Belmont to go out for an hour with me in my chariot this morning: we are to go a private road, where we are sure of not seeing a human being. Adieu!/[f]

To the Earl of BELMONT.

MOUNT MELVIN.
WEDNESDAY.

My LORD,

IF my regret for the late dreadful event, an event embittered by the circumstances your last letter communicated to me, could receive any encrease,[g] it certainly must from the generous behaviour of Mr. Mandeville, whose care for my unhappy son, when expiring, is a proof his blood was drawn from the same source as your Lordship's. Yes, he was indeed worthy the happiness you intended him, worthy the honored name of Mandeville.

Relieved, by the noble conduct of your lamented kinsman, from the fears I entertained for my son's life, my sorrow[h] for the/ miseries he has occasioned, is only the more severe: I feel with unutterable anguish that my ancient friend, the friend of my earliest youth, is childless by the crime of him who owes his being to me: the blow his hand unwillingly struck, has reached the heart of the incomparable Lady Julia; I think of her angelic perfections of the untimely fate which has robbed the world of its loveliest ornament, and almost wish never to have been a father.

Lady Rochdale and Louisa are in tears by me; for ever excluded from Belmont, they look on themselves as exiles, though at home. The horrors of mind under which my son labors are unutterable; he entreats to see Colonel Mandeville; to obtain his pardon for that involuntary crime, which has destroyed all the happiness of his life./

Will you, my friend, once more admit us? Allow[a] us one interview with yourself and Colonel Mandeville? I ask no more, nor will ever repeat the visit: I could not support the sight of Lady Belmont.

I am, My LORD,
YOUR LORDSHIP's most faithful,
though wretched friend,
ROCHDALE./

To the Earl of ROCHDALE.

BELMONT, WEDNESDAY.

My LORD,

Convinced Lord Melvin is more unfortunate than culpable, it would be cruel to treat him as a criminal: I feel a horror I cannot conquer at the idea of ever receiving the visit your Lordship has proposed; but, conscious of the injustice of indulging it, I sacrifice it to our antient[b] friendship, and only postpone, not refuse, the visit: I will struggle with the reluctance of my heart, to see the guiltless author of my misery, as soon as he is publicly exculpated from the crime he at present stands charged with:[c] Colonel Mandeville must appear as his accuser: wretched as his hand has made me, justice obliges me to bear witness to his innocence: Lady Anne Wilmot, who/ was present at Mr. Mandeville's[d] dying declaration, is ready to confirm my evidence: Lord Melvin therefore has nothing to fear. The trial once past, I will endeavor[e] to prevail on Colonel Mandeville and Lady Belmont, to make the same painful sacrifice to friendship, to which time and reason will, I hope, perfectly reconcile us; but your Lordship will, on a moment's reflexion, be convinced that, till this is past, it would be indecent in me to see Lord Melvin.

We are greatly obliged to Lady Rochdale and Lady Louisa; the time of whose visit their own politeness and sensibility will regulate; it is a severe addition to my wretchedness, that the family of my friend is so fatally involved in it.

Oh,[f] Lord Rochdale! you are a father, and can pity us: you can judge the anguish to which we must ever be a prey; never more shall we know a chearful hour;/ our lost child will be ever at our hearts: when I remember her filial sweetness, her angel virtues,[g] her matchless perfections – the only view we had in life

128   *The History of Lady Julia Mandeville*

was to see her happy: that is past, and all is now a dreary wild before us; time may blunt the keen edge of sorrow, and enable us to bear the load of life with patience; but never must we hope the return of peace.

The shortness of life, and the consideration how much of our own is past, are the only consolations we can receive: it cannot be long before we rejoin our beloved child: we have only to pray for that ardently expected[a] hour which will re-unite us to all we love.

Why will man lay schemes of lasting felicity? By an over-solicitude to continue my family and name, and secure the happiness of my child, I have defeated my own purpose, and fatally destroyed both./

Humbled in the dust,[107] I confess the hand of Heaven: the pride of birth, the grandeur of my house, had too great a share in my resolves!

Oh,[b] my friend! but I consider the hand which directed the blow, and submit to the will of my God.

I am, &c.

BELMONT./

To Colonel BELLVILLE.

BELMONT, Sunday Morning.

I AM desired by my Lord to ask you hither, and to beg you will bring my niece with you. Lady Belmont joins in the request; her nobleness of sentiment has conquered the reluctance she had to see her; she has even promised to endeavor[c] to bear the sight of Lord Melvin, but I fear this is more than is in her power; she fainted when the request was first made. Lady Mary is expected here this evening.

Bellville, you are coming to Belmont; once the smiling paradice[d] of friendship,[e] Alas! how changed from that once happy abode! Where are those blameless pleasures, that convivial joy, those sweet follies, which once gave such charms to this place? For ever gone,/ for ever changed to a gloomy sadness, for ever buried with Lady Julia.

Lady Belmont struggles nobly with her grief; she has consented to see her friends, to see all who will hear her talk of her child: a tender melancholy has taken place of those horrors, which it was impossible long to support and live.

Colonel Mandeville is to stay at Belmont; they are to indulge in all the voluptuousness of sorrow; they are to sit all day and talk of their matchless children, and count the hours till they follow them to the grave. They have invited all who will join in tears with them; the coach is gone to-day for Mr. and Mrs. Herbert.

Emily Howard and I bend our whole thoughts to find out means to soften their sorrows; I hope much from your conversation, and the endearing sensibility of your/ soul; it is not by resisting, but by soothing grief, that we must heal the wounded heart.

Volume II 129

There is one pleasure to which they can never be insensible, the pleasure of relieving the miseries of others: to divert their attention from the sad objects which now engross them, we must find out the retreats of wretchedness; we must point out distress which it is in their power to alleviate.

Oh,[a] Bellville! But in vain does the pride of human wisdom seek to explore the counsels of the Most High! Certain of the paternal care of our Creator, our part is submission to his will.

FINIS./

EDITORIAL NOTES

Volume I

1. *Julia*: Frances Brooke's fictional niece in her periodical *The Old Maid* is also called Julia. In choosing this name again for the female protagonist of her first novel, Brooke was following in the footsteps of Jean-Jacques Rousseau, whose *Julie ou La Nouvelle Héloïse*(1761) was translated the same year into English as *Eloisa; or a Series of Original Letters Collected and Published by J. J. Rousseau*. Brooke knew the French *roman* intimately: in 1760, she translated Marie Jeanne Riccoboni's *Lettres de Milady Juliette Catesby à Milady Henriette Campley*. Few French women novelists of the eighteenth century were as well connected to English booksellers as Riccoboni. David Hume and David Garrick, for example, were two great names among her British acquaintances with whom she corresponded regularly. See M. H. McMurren, *The Spread of Novels: Translation and Prose Fiction in the Eighteenth Century* (Princeton, NJ: Princeton University Press, 2010), p. 61.
2. *become*: to befit.
3. *independence*: Independence in this novel implies the type of economic security that makes servility redundant and therefore promises to keep corruption at bay. Thus, financial independence should help ensure an independence of mind.
4. *What a divine morning ... England*: The celebration of the countryside in Virgil's *Georgics* as well as Ovid's association of man with nature in *The Metamorphoses* shaped the imagination of fifteenth- and sixteenth-century Italian humanists and bore significantly on the eighteenth-century English landscape movement. See *The Oxford Companion to the Garden*, ed. P. Taylor (Oxford: Oxford University Press, 2006), p. 242.
5. *she permits ... her*: In romances, the male lover must obey courtship conventions and refrain from taking liberties without the lady's permission.
6. *wants*: lacks.
7. *female softness*: In *Paradise Lost* (1667), Milton established softness as the primeval character of the female sex through his contrasted descriptions of Adam and Eve: 'For contemplation hee and valorform'd / For softness shee and sweet attractive Grace', IV.297–8.
8. *sensibility*: Sensibility was a capacious idea in the eighteenth century: it denoted a physical capability of perception, the faculty of feeling, the manifestation of emotional response and most importantly the moral benevolence that resulted from the interplay of all these aspects. See G. J. Barker-Benfield, *The Culture of Sensibility: Sex and Society in Eighteenth-Century Britain* (Chicago, IL: Chicago University Press, 1992).

– 131 –

132 *Notes to pages 4–6*

9. *impressions*: In *An Essay Concerning Human Understanding* (1690), John Locke described the human mind as a *tabula rasa* upon which ideas left their imprints, or, what he called, 'impressions': 'the first Capacity of Human Intellect is that the Mind is fitted to receive the Impressions made on it'. See J. Locke, *The Works of John Locke*, 3 vols (London: J. Churchill and S. Manship, 1714), vol. 1, p. 39.

10. *tenderness*: Isaac Barrow (1633–1670), an extremely influential theologian whose sermons were emulated by many clergymen, preached that '"tenderness" was the quality essential for the reception of "impressions"'. See G. J. Barker-Benfield, *The Culture of Sensibility: Sex and Society in Eighteenth-Century Britain* (Chicago, IL: Chicago University Press, 1992), p. 68.

11. *raillery*: teasing, mockery.

12. *700l. a year*: According to the digitalized calculator of the National Archives of the British government, this sum corresponds to approximately £52,353.00 in 2005. See http://nationalarchives.gov.uk/currency [accessed 23 May 2012].

13. *twice as many thousands*: This means that Julia Mandeville's fortune amounts to circa £14,000 a year; however, the *Critical Review* writes that she has at her disposal £16,000 a year. *Critical Review or, Annals of Literature. By Society of Gentlemen* (London: Printed for A. Hamilton, in Falcon Court, Fleet Street, 1763), pp. 41–5, on p. 41.

14. *relation*: relative.

15. *celestial*: Petrarch depicts Laura in Sonnet 90 as 'un spirito celeste, un vivo sole', a celestial spirit, a living sun (13).

16. *poisoned cup*: Shakespeare, *Hamlet* (1603), V.ii.245: 'It is the poisoned cup'. The association of love with poison occurs in Virgil's *Aeneid*, where Cupid infuses love by means of his arrows, which are described as being mysteriously poisoned and infected.

17. *sovereign*: George III succeeded to the throne after his grandfather's sudden death in 1760, which is two years before the fictional time of *Julia Mandeville*. He ruled until 1811, when his mental illness forced parliament to issue the Regency Act, upon which his son the Prince of Wales acted as Prince Regent until his father's death. By designating George III as an 'accomplished sovereign', Brooke may be referring to his extensive study of science.

18. *conquest*: The Norman Conquest of England in 1066, a focal point in English history that brought about significant changes.

19. *simplicity of a cottage*: The eighteenth century saw the rise of the cottage's rustic simplicity as an emblem of moral purity. See K. Sayer, *Country Cottages: A Cultural History* (Manchester: Manchester University Press, 2000). Lady Belmont seems to unite the good breeding of court society with the purity and informality associated with the rural.

20. *admirable order*: Alexander Pope's praise of Lord Cobham's estate at Stowe had become the foundation for a non-invasive improvement of landscape that respected the particularities of nature. Pope's advice was 'Consult the Genius of the Place in all / That tells the waters or to rise or fall' (*Epistle to Burlington*, l. 57–8).

21. *fox chace*: hunting chase.

22. *French education*: In the opening letter of her periodical the *Old Maid* (1755–6), Brooke had spoken in favor of French education: 'A French woman of distinction would be more ashamed of wanting a taste for the Belles Lettres, than of being ill dressed; and it is owing to the neglect of adorning their minds that our travelling English ladies are at Paris the objects of unspeakable contempt, and are honored with the appellation of handsome savages'. *The Old Maid, By Mary Singleton, Spinster* (London: A Millar, 1764), pp. 18–19.

Notes to pages 7–9 133

23. *Inigo Jones*: Inigo Jones (1573–1652), a renowned architect who studied landscape painting in Italy and implanted Italian Renaissance architecture in England. He was also the stage designer for Ben Jonson's masques. His bust stands in the 'Temple of British Worthies' at Stowe, Buckinghamshire, a semi-circular edifice with sixteen niches, each containing the bust of an eminent Briton.

24. *avenue of the tallest trees*: The first avenues of trees were planted to mark a way through the forest for riding. However, during the seventeenth century and into the eighteenth century, the avenue was intended 'to extend the garden's formal design'. See G. S. Thomas, *Trees in the Landscape*, 2nd edn (London: Jonathan Cape, 1997), p. 26.

25. *patriarchal government*: Samuel Richardson linked the moral characteristics of the estate owner to the aesthetic quality of the estate in the *History of Sir Charles Grandison* (1753): 'The garden and lawns [...] seem to be as boundless as the mind of the owner, and as free and open as his countenance'. See S. Richardson, *The History of Sir Charles Grandison*, 7 vols, 3rd edn (London: A. Millar, 1754), vol. 7, p. 23.

26. 'that ... ever': Milton, *Comus* (1634): 'And the sweet peace that goodness bosoms ever', l. 368.

27. *Acton-Grange*: a township in Runcorn parish, Cheshire.

28. *golden age*: In Greek mythology, the golden age stands for a primeval time of simplicity, innocence and bounty. In Latin poetry, Virgil and Ovid are the most prominent figures who write about the golden age. In Virgil's poetry, in particular, the paradisiacal features of the golden age find expression in idyllic agriculture.

29. *Flora*: Roman goddess of flowers, fertility and spring.

30. *On a spacious lawn ...mean*: This excerpt was included in the *Lady's Magazine* in 1781 as a specimen of rural description under the heading 'The Rural Dance'.

31. *lustring*: a glossy silk cloth originally used for women's apparel; from Italian 'lustrino', 'lustro' for lustre.

32. *amaranthus*: In Greek, 'amaranth' means everlasting, ever fair, ever young. In Milton's *Paradise Lost*, amaranths grow next to the Tree of Life and adorn the angels' crowns: 'With solemn adoration down they cast / Their crowns inwove with amaranth and gold', III.351–2.

33. *Venus*: Roman goddess of love and erotic desire and Cupid's mother.

34. *Hebe*: Greek goddess of youth; she is known in literature as the goddess with the rosy cheeks.

35. *swift and downy pinions*: In his poem 'The Complaint; or Night Thoughts, on Life, Death and Immortality' (1743), Edward Young describes sleep as a realm of repose and escape: 'Swift on his downy pinions flies from woe', 1.4.

36. *highest degree criminal*: Criminal as in adulterous; at the time, the legal term for adultery was 'criminal conversation'.

37. *blush*: Since in sentimental novels blushing usually signals female modesty, it associates Henry Mandeville with both sensibility and femininity.

38. *journey to Rome*: The Grand Tour comprised a journey through the most eminent sites of European civilization and provided the final polish to a child's education. It was a markedly male enterprise. Joseph Addison addressed the practice in a tongue-in-cheek manner in the *Spectator*, 1 (1711), where he describes how the thirst for knowledge carried him not only to all European countries, but also to Cairo, from where he returned satisfied only after taking the measure of a pyramid. Brooke may have this piece in mind, because the young man in the *Spectator* embarks on his journey upon his father's death,

134   *Notes to pages 9–12*

while the same event calls Brooke's George Mordaunt back to England. *See also* Volume II, note 77.

39. *Cecisbeo*: Another word for the 'cavaliere servente', literally 'serving knight', a man chosen by a lady and often her husband to accompany the wife to social events and provide amusement. More often than not the relationship was of sexual nature. By the time Brooke wrote *Julia Mandeville*, suspicion had arisen about the educational value of the Grand Tour to the extent that it was considered to import rather vice than virtue. Brooke's introduction of the figure of the 'cecisbeo' may be voicing this suspicion. See A. Müller, *Framing Childhood in Eighteenth-century English Periodicals and Prints, 1689–1789* (Aldershot: Ashgate, 2009), p. 82.

40. *health seemed impaired*: Sentimental heroes and heroines undergo such love-induced illnesses. In Madame de La Fayette's *La Princess de Clèves* (1678), which served as a template for subsequent novels and romances, Monsieur and Madame de Clèves succumb to sickness and die of a broken heart.

41. *Enrico*: Italian for Henry.

42. 'How ... lovely': Milton, *Paradise Lost*, IV.846–8: 'Abashed the Devil stood, / And felt how awful goodness is, and saw / Virtue in her own shape how lovely; saw and pined'.

43. *Signor Enrico*: Italian for Mister Henry.

44. *a guardian angel ... precipice*: Edward Young, 'The Complaint; or Night Thoughts, on Life, Death and Immortality' (VI.1150–1): 'But wherefore infamy! – for want of faith / Down the steep of precipice of wrong he slides'.

45. *melancholy*: Within the discourse of sensibility, melancholy testified to an acute nervous system and a propensity to strong feelings.

46. *downcast eyes*: Henry Mandeville's body language resembles that of Richardson's Pamela: 'Look at Pamela's blushing face, and downcast eye.' See S. Richardson, *Pamela, or Virtue Rewarded* (London: T. Kinnersly, 1811), p. 335.

47. *closet*: A personal office or semiprivate dressing room increasingly used in the eighteenth century to receive close friends and acquaintances. It could hold paper, pencils, books and clothing. A woman's closet appears as a place of erotic encounters in a hilarious scene in Susanna Centlivre's comedy *The Busie Body* (1709).

48. *miniatures*: Richardson's Clarissa bequeaths two miniatures in her will: one to her cousin William Hourden and one to Charles Hickman. Brooke anticipates the emergence of the miniature by late-eighteenth century as 'the natural accessory to romantic mourning ... through which one might enter the idealizing space of the memory'. See T. Castle, 'The Spectralization of the Other in the *Mysteries of Udolpho*', in F. Nussbaum and L. Brown (eds), *The New Eighteenth Century: Theory, Politics, English Literature* (New York: Methuen, 1987), pp. 231–53, on p. 310.

49. *letters of recommendation*: a letter of introduction that secures the reception and protection of the letter holder.

50. *bathing with tears*: Richardson made ample use of similar scenes of emotional distress, for example in *Clarissa*, when Mrs Norton sees Clarissa's corpse, 'She bathed the face with her tears' (vol. 8, letter 29).

51. *carrying her off by force*: By contemplating abduction, Henry aligns himself with the rake. Richardson exploited this motif in his novels: Mr B abducts Pamela, Clarissa is abducted by Lovelace, and in *Sir Charles Grandison*, Harriet Byron falls victim to Sir Hargrave Pollexfen.

52. *libertine*: a person of loose morals and promiscuous behaviour.

Notes to pages 12–15

53. *hopeless a flame*: Alexander Pope, *Eloisa to Abelard* (1717), ll. 261–2: 'Ah hopeless, lasting flames like those that burn / To light the dead and the unfruitful urn'.
54. *Coquette*: a flirtatious woman.
55. *yield the palm*: submit.
56. *Col.*: abbreviation for Colonel.
57. *Antinous*: a young man that Emperor Hadrian brought to Rome from one of his provinces in what is today's north-west Turkey. The emperor held him as his most beloved companion and was so devastated by the youth's premature death that he sought to compensate for this loss by proclaiming Antinous a god.
58. *aquiline*: a nose with a pronounced bridge also called a Roman nose.
59. *You with envy, I with love*: John Gay, Fable XLV, 'The Poet and the Rose' (1727), ll. 29–30: 'One common fate we both must prove / you die with envy I with love'.
60. *tawdry*: showy without elegance or grace.
61. *coxcomb*: fop.
62. *outside*: appearance.
63. *placable*: easily calmed and forgiving.
64. *Gentle … violet*: Shakespeare, *Cymbelline* (1611), IV.ii.171–2: 'In these two princely boys! They are as gentle as Zephyrs blowing below the violet'.
65. *a little Pindaric*: After Abraham Cowley's *Pindarique Odes* (1656), which attempted to imitate the style of the ancient Greek poet Pindar. The term had come to signify irregular, incoherent and rambling style. In Brooke's lifetime, Thomas Gray wrote the best-known English Pindaric Odes, *The Progress of Poesy* and *The Bard* (1757).
66. *he makes the fine arts … purpose*: According to the Horatian maxim, poetry should instruct and delight (*aut prodesse, aut delectare*); Sir Philip Sidney wrote similarly in *Defence of Poesy* (1583): 'to delight and teach; and delight, to move men to take that goodness in hand, which without delight, they would fly as from a stranger, and teach to make them know that goodness whereunto they are moved'.
67. *hounds*: Dogs used for hunting. Brooke seems to have shared the growing dislike of this leisured activity. Eight years later, in *The Expedition of Humphrey Clinker* (1771), Tobias Smollet offered two examples of manhood, preferring the benevolent Charles Dennison over his fox-hunting brother.
68. *five and twenty years younger*: With Henry being twenty-three years old and twenty-five years younger than his father, Colonel Mandeville must therefore be about forty-eight.
69. *the late war*: the Seven Years War, 1756–63.
70. *Il divino Enrico*: Italian for the divine Henry.
71. *Penseroso*: Milton's poem *Il Penseroso* (1645) ponders pensive melancholy as opposed to its companion piece *Il Allegro* that celebrates a pleasure-seeking attitude.
72. *Entre nous*: French for between you and me.
73. *old adage*: a common saying or observation.
74. *e'en*: poetic contraction: even.
75. *cit*: abbreviation for 'cittadino', Italian for townsman.
76. *livery stable*: This hints at Mr Westbrooke's wealth coming from trade rather than landed property.
77. *Mademoiselle la Fille*: French for Miss, the daughter.
78. *brown*: of dark complexion.
79. *so unimportant a task … child*: The figure of the mother who favours studies over her daughter's education became prominent in Amelia Opie's *Adeline Mowbray, or The Mother and Daughter* (1805).

136   *Notes to pages 15–20*

80. *Faux Pas*: French for misstep; a misstep with visible consequences means a sexual indiscretion that led to a pregnancy.

81. *Change alley*: This is the area where London brokers transacted in the eighteenth century: 'Until the foundation of the Stock Exchange in 1773, the coffee-houses of ''Change Alley were the center for speculation'. See F. Braudel, *The Wheels of Commerce: Civilization and Capitalism, 15th–17th Century* (Berkley and Los Angeles, CA: University of California Press, 1992), p. 107.

82. *Methinks*: It seems to me.

83. *air*: a tune, a melodious song.

84. *l'amorose*: Italian for love, being in love.

85. *cabinet*: A cabinet was the most exported piece of furniture in the eighteenth century. It usually had 'two doors enclosing a set of small drawers and a small center cupboard'. The best quality cabinets came from Japan. See M. Berg, *Luxury and Pleasure in Eighteenth-Century Britain* (New York: Oxford University Press, 2005), p. 51.

86. *Adio*: Italian for farewell.

87. 'celestial rosy red': Milton, *Paradise Lost*, VIII. 619: 'celestial rosy red, love's proper hue'.

88. *hermitage*: Gilpin describes the hermitage at Stowe in his *Dialogue* as a place of similar aesthetic pleasure: 'Yon old Hermitage situated in the midst of this delightful Wilderness, has an exceeding good effect: it is of the romantic Kind.' See W. Gilpin, *A Dialogue upon the Gardens of the Right Honourable the Lord Viscount Cobham, at Stow in Buckinghamshire* (London: J. and J. Rivington, 1748), p. 6.

89. *tremblingly alive all o'er*: Alexander Pope, *Epistle on Man*, I.197.

90. *whispering Zephyrs*: ibid., *Epistle on Man*, I.204.

91. *Caro*: Italian for dear.

92. *domestic tenderness*: Brooke may be drawing on Marcia's description of her father, Cato, in Joseph Addison's *Cato* (1713), V.iv: 'Compassionate and gentle to his friends. / Fill'd with domestic tenderness, the best, the kindest father'

93. 'the milk-maid singing blithe': Milton, *L'Allegro* (1645), l.65–6: 'And the milkmaid singeth blithe / And the Mower whets his scythe.'

94. 'brightens the eyes': Possibly a reference to Psalm 13:3: 'Consider and hear me, O LORD my God: lighten mine eyes, lest I sleep the *sleep of* death'

95. *Happiness loves the vale*: Influenced by Johnson's *Rasselas* (1759), where a Utopian community is situated in an enclosed place named the 'Happy Valley'.

96. 'Health ... the labourer bears': Alexander Pope, *Moral Essays* (1731–5), IV.169–72:

   'Yet hence the Poor are cloath'd, the Hungry fed;
   Health to himself, and to his infants bread,
   The Labourer bears: What is hard Heart denies,
   His charitable Vanity supplies.'

97. *Gothic*: Gothic has several historical and ideological connotations, ranging from an attribute pertaining to Goth's language and Germanic culture to a characteristic of Middle Ages, the so-called 'dark ages', mostly used disparagingly in the early eighteenth-century. Lady Anne Wilmot may be drawing on the latter to drive home the ladies' lack of knowledge and refinement.

98. *La Lingua D'Amore*: Italian for the language of love.

99. *Mirtillo! Anima mia*: Italian for Mirtillo, my soul; from Battista Guarini's *Il Pastor Fido* (1590), III.iv.1, a tragi-comedy in five acts. A note following the preface of *Virginia* (1756), announces that the author (i.e. Brooke) will 'speedily' be publishing 'A Poetical

Notes to pages 20–3 137

Translation with Notes of *Il Pastor Fido, and Other Poems* from the original Italian of Signor Battista Guarini'.

100. *Ho vergogna, Signora*: Italian for I am ashamed, Madam.

101. *Penchant*: French for inclination.

102. *politesse*: French for politeness.

103. *Je suis votre*: French for I am yours.

104. *harpy*: Literally in ancient Greek the word meant 'that which snatches'. A harpy is a winged mythological creature that repeatedly stole food from Phineus, the King of Thrace.

105. *independent country gentlemen*: The figure of the independent country gentlemen will continue to inspire respect, as it does for example in Maria Edgeworth's *Vivian*, where the eponymous hero declares 'I think the life of an independent country gentleman the most respectable of others.' See *Tales and Novels* (London: Baldwin and Craddock, 1832), vol. 8, p. 38.

106. *Leviathans*: A Biblical figure mentioned in Job 41:1. Many paintings of the Middle Ages depict Leviathan as an all-devouring sea-monster and embodiment of Satan.

107. *Al fresco*: Italian for in the open air.

108. *romanesque*: The Oxford English Dictionary uses this sentence by Brooke to illustrate the meaning of the word as 'of the nature of or reminiscent of romance'.

109. *sentimental*: Lady Bradshaigh's correspondence with Samuel Richardson provides a description of what the word meant in the 1750s: 'What, in your opinion, is the meaning of the word sentimental, so much in vogue among the polite ... Everything clever and agreeable is comprehended in that word. I am frequently astonished to hear such a one is a sentimental man; we were a sentimental party; I have been taking a sentimental walk.' *The Correspondence of Samuel Richardson*, ed. A. L. Barbauld (London: R. Philips, 1804), pp. 282–3.

110. *Caro Sposo*: Italian for dear husband.

111. *levees*: A reception of visitors on rising from bed; a morning assembly held by a prince or person of distinction (*OED*).

112. 'Talk not ... way': Lady Anne borrows these words with little alteration form Nathaniel Lee's *Theodosius, or, The Force of Love* (1680), II.i:

'No more of this, no more; for I disdain
All pomp when thou art by; far be the noise
Of kings and courts from us, whose gentle souls
Our kinder stars have steer'd another way!'

113. *Adonis from the carr of Venus*: In Greek mythology, Adonis is the god of beauty and desire. Shakespeare wrote the poem *Venus and Adonis* (1592–3) drawing on Ovid's *Metamorphoses*. In Shakespeare's poem, Venus lusts after Adonis, but he shows more interest in hunting, where he loses his life after being kissed by Venus. Venus's chariot, a two-wheeled cart was traditionally depicted as being pulled by a group of sparrows or doves. *See also* Volume I, note 185.

114. *minuet*: a dance of French origin for two.

115. *Campagna*: Italian for the country.

116. *Elyzium*: Greek mythology refers to the island of Elysion as the 'Island of the Blessed', where the gods sent their chosen mortals after death to live a happy afterlife. Later, poets like Virgil, located Elysium in the underworld, as the dwelling of the dead that were found to have led a righteous life.

138   *Notes to pages 23–6*

117. *L'Amore*: Italian for love.
118. *Zephyrs*: The sculptures of Zephyr, the Greek God of the west wind, at Château de Versailles.
119. *la belle Angloise*: French for 'the beautiful Englishwoman'.
120. *Environs*: French for vicinity.
121. *Arriere-ban*: In France, men that qualified for military service were called the 'ban'. The arriere-ban was made up of the sub-vassals that a vassal could summon in the event of military conflict.
122. *Posse Comitatus*: Latin for Power of the County. The Posse Comitatus was raised by the Sheriff of the County to suppress a riot and called upon every able-bodied free man. The practice has its roots in the feudal system, when law enforcement was conducted by the king and his representatives.
123. 'brings down the natives upon us': unidentified.
124. *fan*: A woman's fan is a much admired accessory by the fop of the Restoration comedy. For example, in Colley Cibber's *Love's Last Shift* (1696), the coxcomb Sir Novelty Fashion is too clumsy to pick up Narcissa's fan.
125. *whisper*: In Cibber's *Love's Last Shift* (I.i), Young Worthy parodies the rules of gallantry addressing a group of ladies: 'Your pardon, ladies; I'll whisper with you all, one after another.'
126. *supernumerary*: exceeding what is due and necessary.
127. *South Sea bubble*: The South Sea bubble describes the stock-market crash that occurred in 1720 in England. It is deemed to be the first financial scandal, in which members of all social strata made and lost their fortunes. Its name came from the South Sea Company, which was granted a monopoly in trade with South America for giving a loan of £7 million to the government to finance the war with France. Thanks to what was thought of as the most lucrative monopoly in the world, the stocks in the South Sea Company were traded at unadjusted highly inflated prices until the directors of the company realized that their personal shares did not correspond to the actual value of the company and started selling their stocks hoping that no one would notice their withdrawal. This was a false hope that resulted in a crash with national and international ramifications. See H. Paul, *The South Sea Bubble: A Revision of Gambling Mania Theory* (New York and Oxon: Routledge, 2009). 'The Secret History of the South Sea Scheme' appeared among the writings of the philosopher John Toland, and, although not written by him, it was published in a collection of his works in 1726.
128. *enjouement*: French for gaiety.
129. *post chaise*: A horse-drawn, usually four-wheeled carriage used for carrying mail and passengers.
130. *amours*: French for love matters.
131. *undesigned*: unintentional.
132. *gratitude*: Brooke links gratitude to masculine love, while John Gregory in his *Father's Legacy to his Daughters* (1774) makes it the quintessence of female love: 'What is commonly called love among you, is rather gratitude and a partiality to the man who prefers you to the rest of your sex; and such a man you often marry with little of either personal esteem or affection.' See J. Gregory, *A Father's Legacy to His Daughters*, new edition (London: Millar, Law and Cater, 1789), p. 91.
133. *Toute ensemble*: French for altogether, overall.
134. *Degagée*: French for effortless.
135. *queen of Sweden*: Christina, Queen of Sweden (1626–89).

Notes to pages 26–9 139

136. *Mademoiselle le Fevre*: Anne Le Fèvre Dacier (1654–1720), renowned for her French translations of the classics.
137. 'with such an understanding, are not you ashamed to be handsome': unidentified. According to Mary Hays, who included Ann Dacier in her six-volume *Female Biography or Memoirs of Illustrious and Celebrated Women of All Ages and Countries* (1803), Christina, Queen of Sweden, wrote: 'By what secret charm have you known how to make accord the muses with the graces?' See M. Hays, *Female Biography; or, Memoirs of Illustrious and Celebrated Women of All Ages and Countries*, 6 vols (London: Richard Phillips, 1803).
138. *à Trio*: a set of three.
139. *O Dio*: Italian for O God.
140. *Arabians*: one of the oldest breeds of horse that originated on the Arabian Peninsula.
141. 'That bow might from the bidding of the gods command me': Shakespeare, *Antony and Cleopatra* (1623), III.ix.56: 'Thy beck might from the bidding of the Gods / Command me'.
142. *meer*: mere.
143. *Belle Esprit*: an intelligent and cultivated person.
144. *Methodist*: Methodist women displayed agency in their roles as preachers and teachers of Sunday schools. See G. J. Barker-Benfield, *The Culture of Sensibility: Sex and Society in Eighteenth-Century Britain* (Chicago, IL: Chicago University Press, 1992), p. 271.
145. *Fiat*: Latin for let it be done; decree or command.
146. *sapphic*: The Sapphic stanza owes its name to the Ancient Greek poetess Sappho, who lived in the seventh century BC.
147. *Orpheus*: a musician and poet in Greek mythology and religion. He was celebrated for his ability to charm living things and even stones with his music.
148. *Amphion*: the son of Zeus and of the nymph Antiope. He was given a golden lyre by Hermes, which he played so wonderfully that humans, animals and stones would follow him when he sang to them.
149. she fainted, sunk, and dyed away: Robert Vansittart 'The Power of Poetry': 'She sigh'd, she fainted, sunk and died away'. Vansittart's poetry appeared in Dodsley's journal *The Museum* (1746–1747).
150. *Oh! Ciel!*: French for Oh! Heavens!
151. *Caro*: Italian for dear.
152. 'Je suis votre amie tres fidelle': French for I am your very faithful friend.
153. 'Mean time ... fulfil': Mark Akenside, 'An Ode to the Country Gentlemen of England' (1758).
154. 'whom age and long experience render wise': from Alexander Pope's translation of Ovid's 'Vertumnus and Pomona'.
155. *chearful*: cheerful.
156. *sylvan*: a deity or spirit of the wood.
157. *Zephyr*: Greek god of the west wind, which is supposed to be fructifying and a messenger of the spring.
158. *à quarrée*: here French for a group of four people.
159. *syren*: siren.
160. 'The streams, the groves, the rocks remain / But Damon still I seek in vain': Brooke seems to be quoting with little alteration from John Dalton's adaptation (1738) of Milton's *Comus* (1634): 'The Hills, the Groves, the Streams remain / But Damon there I seek in vain.'
161. *Tete à Tete*: between two people.

140   *Notes to pages 29–40*

162. *en confidence*: From French 'être en/ dans confidence' for to share confidential information.

163. 'soft as the fleeces of descending snows': Alexander Pope, *Iliad*, III.283–4: 'But when he speaks what elocution flows!/ Soft as the fleeces of descending snows'.

164. *The preservation ... two*: There are three elements to the British constitution, the Monarch, the parliament elected by landowners and the judicature or law courts.

165. *When the house ... slaves*: According to Michael W. McCahill, the 'harmonious relationship between the Commons and the Lords that endured during George III's reign enhanced parliament's effectiveness'. See M. W. McCahill, *The House of Lords in the Age of George III, 1760–1811* (Oxford: Wiley Blackwell, 2009), p. 317.

166. *queen Anne's wars*: They were fought between England and France in North America for control of the continent.

167. *Lady Mary*: Brooke gives to this unmarried woman of authority the name she adopted for the fictional author of her periodical *The Old Maid*, Mary Singleton.

168. *Bellissima*: Italian for most beautiful.

169. *unequal marriages*: In Brooke's *Old Maid*, Mary Singleton is vehemently against unequal marriages: 'Marriage, where the disproportion of rank and fortune is very great, especially if the disadvantage is on the woman's side, seldom turns out happy.' See F. Brooke, *The Old Maid* (London: A. Millar, 1764), p. 53.

170. *saloon*: In comparison to the drawing-room which was smaller and less adorned, the saloon was more elaborately furnished in order to entertain a larger number of people. See C. Christie, *The British Country House in the Eighteenth Century* (Manchester: Manchester University Press, 2000), p. 246.

171. *frighted*: frightened.

172. *shellwork*: From the seventeenth century, shells became prominent in the decoration of the interior of garden buildings such as grottoes. *The Oxford Companion to the Garden*, ed. P. Taylor (Oxford: Oxford University Press, 2006), p. 440.

173. *Les Amies*: French for the friends.

174. *Lucretia's dagger–Rosamonda's bowl*: Alexander Pope, *Epistle to a Lady: Of the Characters of Women* (1735), l. 92. The incident of Lucretia's rape by the son of the last Roman king Lucius Tarquinius Superbus and her suicide led to riots that prompted prominent Roman families to establish the Roman Republic. Rosamund Clifford was the beloved of king Henry II of England (1133–89) and supposedly poisoned by his wife Eleanor of Aquitaine.

175. 'of wilful woman laboring for her purpose': Nicholas Rowe, *The Fair Penitent* (1703).

176. 'Now awful beauty puts on all its arms': Alexander Pope, *The Rape of the Lock* (1712), I.139–40: 'Now awful beauty puts on all its arms / The fair each moment rises in her charms.'

177. *Caro*: Italian for dear.

178. *Votre*: French for yours.

179. *rhapsody of tender nonsense*: Possibly a reference to John Dryden's preface to *Notes and Observations on The Empress of Morocco* (1674), where he calls Elkanah Settle's play a 'rhapsody of nonsense.'

180. 'He came, he saw, he conquered': Julius Caesar is reported to have said 'I came, I saw and I conquered' upon his swift conquest of the city of Zile in modern day Turkey.

181. *coronet*: a crown denoting a dignity inferior to that of the sovereign worn by the nobility and varying in rank.

182. *una Carrozza*: Italian for carriage.

Notes to pages 41–6 141

183. 'spring from the ground like feather'd Mercury': Shakespeare, *King Henry IV* (1597) Part I, IV.i.106: 'Rise from the ground like feather'd Mercury'

184. *Adonis*: According to the myth of Aphrodite and Adonis, Aphrodite was so in love with Adonis from the first moment she caught sight of the infant that she shut him up in a chest to prevent other gods from seeing his beauty. *See also* Volume I, note 113.

185. *great theatre of human life*: It was a common idea to compare the world to the stage and life to a theatre play. Two famous examples are Boissard's 'THEATRVM VITAE HUMANE', whose first plate reads 'Human life is a Theatre of All Miseries', and Shakespeare's reference in *As You Like It* (1623), II.vii.136: 'Thou sees we are not all alone unhappy: / this wide and universal theatre / Presents more woeful pageants than the scene / Wherein we play in.'

186. *se'nnight*: a week.

187. *in town*: in London.

188. *fettered by systems*: In the *Social Contract* (1762), Rousseau starts out with the poignant phrase: 'Man was born free and everywhere he is in chains.' J.-J. Rousseau, *The Social Contract*, ed. C. Betts (Oxford: Oxford University Press, 2008), p. 45.

189. *native freedom*: The father of Henry Mandeville holds on to a Rousseauian view of innate human freedom.

190. *Full of ... strength of mind*: In *Emile or on Education* (1762), Rousseau propagates a liberal education that prepares children to think for themselves. Among others, he addresses teachers asking ironically: 'About what do you want him to think when you think about everything for him?' See J.-J. Rousseau, *Emile or on Education*, ed. Allan Bloom (New York: Basic Books, 1979), p. 118.

191. *the seeds of virtue are innate*: Francis Hutcheson, professor of moral philosophy at the University of Glasgow (1729–46) and leader of the Scottish Enlightenment, maintained that virtue sprung from natural and disinterested feelings of benevolence. He articulated his theory in his influential *Inquiry into the Original of our Ideas of Beauty and Virtue* (1725). Hutcheson's theory went against Thomas Hobbes's and David Hume's thesis that distinctions between right and wrong, vice and virtue, were rooted in calculations of pain and pleasure.

192. *Confucius*: a political, religious figure and educator, who lived from 551 to 479 BC and founded the Ru School of Chinese thought, whose two main maxims were 'controlling one's selfish desires' and 'restablishing the ethical codes of conduct'.

193. *light*: A word that describes discernment and knowledge as in enlightenment. For example, Francis Bacon's Bensalemites in *New Atlantis* (1627) regard light as the goal of all endeavour: 'But thus you see we maintain a trade, not for gold, silver, or jewels; nor for silks; nor for spices; nor any other commodity of a matter; but only for God's first creature, which was *Light*; to have *light* (I say) of the growth of all parts of the world.' See *Three Early Modern Utopias: Utopia, New Atlantis, and the Isle of Pines*, ed. S. Bruce (Oxford: Oxford University Press, 2008), p. 168.

194. 'All ... they': Brooke identifies this as Abraham Cowley's verse, but they appear in John Norris's *Miscellanies: Consisting of Poems, Essays, Discourses and Letters Occasionally* (1687).

195. *dumb creation*: the animals; creatures incapable of speech.

196. *which ... inaction*: Samuel Johnson writes in *The History of Rasselas, Prince of Abissinia* (1759) that 'none are happy but by the anticipation of change' and that 'variety is ... necessary to content.' S. Johnson, *The Yale Edition of the Works of Samuel Johnson: The*

142   *Notes to pages 47–61*

History of Rasselas, Prince of Abissinia, ed. G. J. Kolb (New London and London: Yale University Press, 1990), p. 164.

197. 'O, can you ...stray'd': These are supposedly lines from a poem that Belville dedicated to Anne Wilmot.

198. *lock up in your bureau*: Molière, *Le Misanthrope* (1666), I. ii.374. The overly frank Alceste tells Oronte to put his poorly written sonnet in his closet: 'Candidly, you had better put it in your closet.'

199. *summumbonum*: Latin for the highest good.

200. *seraphic*: In the Bible, Seraphims are living creatures with six pairs of wings hovering above the throne of God in adoration. In Anne Wilmot's use, the adjective can mean ecstatically divine.

201. *billet-doux*: French for love-letter.

202. *in Amico*: Italian for as a friend.

203. The whispering ... rill: see Alexander Pope, *Essay on Man*, l. 204.

204. 'not obvious, not obtrusive': See Milton, *Paradise Lost*, VIII.504.

205. *Suivante*: French for attendant.

206. *antediluvians*: people who lived before the Biblical flood. The antediluvian period spans from Genesis to the deluge that God predicted to Noah.

207. *fix*: to set your heart upon, to settle.

208. *insects of an hour*: Cicero in the first book of his *Tusculan Disputations* (45 BC), drawing on Aristotle, compares human life with that of a species of insects that do not outlive the day they are born.

209. *Penchant*: French for inclination.

210. *Carissimo*: Italian for dearest.

211. *Mall*: A fashionable promenade bordered by trees in St James's park in London. Originally, it was an alley where the game of mall, a precursor to croquet, was played.

212. *the royal poet*: King David who allegedly authored many of the psalms. See Psalm 150:4–5: 'Praise him with tambourine and dance; praise him with strings and pipe! / Praise him upon the loud cymbals: praise him upon the high sounding cymbals.'

213. *the book of sports*: James I wrote the Book of Sports in 1618, where he declared that diversions such as May-games and dances could be performed on Sundays. It became a point of contention between Puritans and more moderate Protestants. In 1633, Charles I reissued the Book of Sports.

214. *Charles II*: In 1676, Charles II issued under Puritan influence a very strict law for the observance of Sunday was passed.

215. *Love ... human heart*: See Edward Young, *The Complaint, Night 8* (1742), ll. 595–6: 'The love of pleasure is man's eldest-born / Born in his cradle, living to his tomb.'

216. *Henry the great*: King Henry IV reigned in France from 1589–1610. He was involved in the religious wars between Huguenots and Catholics and displayed unusual concern for his subjects and groundbreaking religious tolerance.

217. *colonies*: The Seven Years' War involved the greatest European states and revolved around their conflicting interests in the colonies. A Peace Treaty between France, Britain, Spain and Portugal was signed in Paris on 10 February 1763, about four months prior to the publication of *Julia Mandeville*.

218. *happy event*: Probably the birth of George Augustus Frederick on 12 August 1762, the future George IV. He reigned from the death of his father, George III, on 29 January 1820 until 26 June 1830.

219. *magnifique*: French for magnificent.

Notes to pages 61–80 143

220. *Gusto*: Italian for taste.
221. *Handel*: George Friedrich Handel (1685–1759), German-British composer.
222. 'had in her sober livery all things clad': See Milton, *Paradise Lost*, IV.598–9: 'Now came still evening on, and Twilight gray / Had in her sober livery all things clad.'
223. *vermilion*: orange reddish pigment.
224. 'By ... friendship': See James Thomson, *Agamemnon* (1738), II.ii.110.
225. *pity ... love*: In his *Treatise of Human Nature* (1739–40), David Hume writes 'There is always a mixture of love or tenderness with pity.' See D. Hume, *A Treatise of Human Nature* (London: T. and J. Allman, 1817), p. 65.
226. *grave*: serious.
227. *Certainement*: French for certainly.

Volume II

1. *meerly*: merely.
2. *Pride ... detestable*: Henry Mandeville seems to align himself with Christian moralists, who considered pride to be a cardinal sin. However, in the late eighteenth century, David Hume's and Adam Smith's distinction between pride that led to both positive and negative actions 'became the mantra among the enlightened'. See P. Knox-Shaw, *Jane Austen and the Enlightenment* (Cambridge: Cambridge University Press, 2004), p. 71.
3. *derangé*: French for out of sorts.
4. *mine*: Under the law of coverture, a woman's property passes on to her husband: 'What was her personal property before marriage, such as money in hand, money at the bank, jewels, household goods, clothes, etc., becomes absolutely her husband's, and he may assign or dispose of them at his pleasure whether he and his wife live together or not.' B. Leigh-Smith [Bodichon], *A Brief Summary in Plain Language of the Most Important Laws Concerning Women, Together with a Few Observations Thereon* (London: J. Chapman, 1854), pp. 3–11.
5. *politician*: In the eighteenth century, the word meant a theorist, while someone involved in politics was called a statesman.
6. *Mon cher ami*: French my dear friend.
7. *lolling*: swinging.
8. *settee*: A seat (for indoors) holding two or more persons, with a back and (usually) arms
9. *Chinese summer-house*: In 1738, the first Chinese house to decorate an English garden was built at Stowe, the family estate of Richard Temple, first Viscount Cobham. It was a small, one-room hut, standing on stilts in a pond.
10. *minister*: The Earl of Bute was Prime Minister from 26 May 1762 to 8 April 1763.
11. *natural history*: the discipline engaged with more or less anything connected with the natural world. The French philosopher, George Buffon wrote a thirty-six-volume study of the animal and mineral world titled *Histoire naturelle, générale et particulière* (1749–88).
12. *microscope*: The invention of the microscope is closely connected with the development of optics. Generally, it is accepted that the Dutch Johannes and Zacharia Jansen, father and son both spectacle makers, produced the first modern microscope composed of two lenses held together in a tube in 1590. Later, Henry Baker popularized microscopy in his *Microscope Made Easy* (1743).
13. *strolling play*: a play performed by strolling actors.

144   *Notes to pages 81–4*

14. *shell-flowers, cuts paper*: Making flowers from shells, paper, wax and feather was a popular handicraft in the late eighteenth century that continued well into the Victorian period.
15. 'Love's a gentle generous passion': a popular song at the time.
16. 'I'll not wed Paris, Romeo is my husband': Brooke is quoting from Garrick's version of the death scene (V.iii.118) in *Romeo and Juliet* performed at Drury Lane in 1748. In Shakespeare's play, Juliet's words differ: 'I will not marry yet; and when I do, I swear / It shall be Romeo, whom you know I hate / Rather than Paris'. See *Romeo and Juliet* (1597), III.v.124–6.
17. *Buona Notte*: Italian for good night.
18. *harvest home*: Harvest was one of the two annual feasts organized by the farmers, the other one being sheep shearing. Harvest home was celebrated at the beginning of autumn and sheep shearing in the spring, but neither was set on a particular day.
19. *tabor*: the earlier name of the drum; in later use (especially since the introduction of the name drum in the sixteenth century); a small kind of drum, used chiefly as an accompaniment to the pipe or trumpet (*OED*).
20. *he-wretches*: men.
21. *toute au contraire*: French for quite the contrary.
22. *romantic*: The term appeared in English in the seventeenth century and has its roots in the French *romaunt*. It consisted of a range of Renaissance tales, from ballad to epic, which represented fictitious places, enchanted worlds and extreme passion and feelings. See A. Day, *Romanticism* (New York: Routledge, 1996), pp. 79–84.
23. *worm of discontent*: The well-known Puritan preacher, Jeremiah Burroughs compared discontent to a worm in his *Rare Jewel of Christian Contentment* (1649), writing that 'Discontent is like a worm that eats the meat out of the nut.'
24. *battle of Almanza*: An important battle fought on 25 April 1707 as part of the War for Spanish Succession (1701–14), in which Britain and its allies, Portugal and the Netherlands, were defeated by the Franco-Spanish forces. Almansa is a Spanish town in the community of Castile-La Mancha.
25. *city marriage*: a marriage into a family whose money came from trade.
26. *Queen Mary's court*: Mary II reigned with her Protestant husband William of Orange during the time following the Glorious Revolution from 1689 until her death in 1694.
27. *Churchill*: John Churchill, Duke of Marlborough, was the husband of Sarah Jennings, Queen Anne's closest friend and advisor. John Churchill later became Queen Anne's general and leader of the Allied forces during the War of the Spanish Succession.
28. *cits*: abbreviation for citizens; usually applied, rather contemptuously, to a townsman or 'cockney' as distinguished from a countryman, or to a tradesman or shopkeeper as distinguished from a gentleman (*OED*). See also Volume I, note 75.
29. *pique*: a feeling of animosity.
30. *Hill*: John Hill, cousin of Sarah Jennings, later Duchess of Marlborough, commanded a brigade in the battle of Almansa. He was also appointed commander-in-chief of the expedition against Quebec in 1711.
31. *peace*: The treaty of Paris, signed on 10 February 1763, about five months prior to the publication of *The History of Julia Mandeville*, ended the Seven Years War, during which Great Britain had captured Canada from the French. Britain restored Guadeloupe, Martinique, Saint Lucia, Gorée to France and in return France ceded, among other territories, Canada.
32. *Sugar-islands*: the sugar plantations on the colonies, especially those of the West Indies, the islands in and around the Caribbean.

Notes to pages 86–97 145

33. *five hundred pounds*: The heroine of Brooke's last novel, *The Excursion*, is assisted out of her debts by an anonymous benefactor, who offers her £100.
34. *West-Indian*: probably a West Indian planter.
35. *dared ... my wife*: Married women's vulnerability to the predatory advances of men who pose as their husbands' promoters is a central topic in Henry Fielding's *Amelia* (1751).
36. *the proud man's contumely*: Shakespeare, *Hamlet*, III.i.72: 'The oppressor's wrong, the proud man's contumely'.
37. *'Which ... takes'*: Shakespeare, *Hamlet*, III.i.75: 'That patient merit of the unworthy takes.'
38. *mean time*: meantime.
39. *hopes of youth*: Henry Mandeville's disenchanted view of his own desires comes close to the opening lines of Samuel Johnson's *Rasselas* (1759): 'Ye who listen with credulity to the whispers of fancy, and pursue with eagerness the phantoms of hope; who expect that age will perform the promises of youth, and that the deficiencies of the present day will be supplied by the morrow, attend to the history of Rasselas, Prince of Abyssinia.'
40. *Celadon and Urania*: Frances Brooke refers here to Celadon and Astrée, the protagonist lovers of Honoré d'Urfé pastoral romance *L'Astrée* (1607–27). Urania is the Muse of Astronomy and also a shepherdess in Mary Wroth's *The Countess of Mountgomery's Urania* (1621), which was strongly influenced by *L'Astrée*.
41. *apropos*: French for in regard to.
42. *tub to the whale*: The comparison appears in Swift's *A Tale of a Tub* (1704). I could not identify the French author Brooke has in mind.
43. *Grosvenor-street*: A fashionable part of London and Colonel Belville's residence, from where later in the novel he will send a letter to Lady Anne.
44. *Une avanture*: French for an adventure.
45. *Thelemites*: The term described a pleasure-seeking attitude in *Gargantua et Pantagruel* (1532), the work of the French monk and writer François Rabelais, where he describes the Abbey of Thélème, a utopian place whose one and only maxim was 'Do what thou wilt'. Its most well-known followers in Brooke's time were the members of the Hellfire Club founded by Sir Francis Dashwood (1708–81).
46. *pulled the string*: A string is connected with the rod, so that by pulling the string the rod is rotated and the bell rings.
47. *rencounter*: unexpected, unplanned meeting.
48. *carving ... trees*: Virgil, *Eclogues*, X.ii.53–4: 'it is better to suffer and carve my love on young trees, they will grow; thou too my love will grow.' See also Abraham Cowley's *The Tree* (1647), II.3–4: 'I cut my love into its gentle Bark, / and in three day behold 'tis dead.'
49. *winter*: In the winter, London with its attractions, particularly in the form of assemblies that offered dancing, card games and conversation, became the mainstay of the social season, whereas the countryside represented a recreational retreat for the summer.
50. *machine style*: In his *Discourse on the Method* (1637), the French philosopher René Descartes (1596–1650) compared the human body to a machine created according to a certain order and purpose. The nerves receive impulses which they transmit to the brain and convert into thoughts and ideas, thus making the body a thinking machine. A more recent publication was Julien Offray de la Mettrie's purely materialistic work *L'Homme Machine* (1747).
51. *Laws of Attraction*: Isaac Newton (1643–1727) laid out in his *Philosophiae Naturalis Principia Mathematica* (1678) the theory of gravity, which put an end to the view that the celestial realm required a different science from the sublunar, a view that had domi-

146 *Notes to pages 97–102*

nated since Aristotle. Newton argued that the force that keeps the planets in their orbits is of the same kind as terrestrial gravity.

52. *threescore*: three times twenty (*OED*).

53. *heroics*: sentimental behaviour modelled upon romance lovers.

54. *constancy*: Constancy, a particularly female virtue, was idealized in pastoral romances. Mary Wroth's *The Countess of Mountgomery's Urania* (1621) explores this theme; however, her shepherdess Urania expresses a similar scepticism to Lady Anne's when she calls for a rational and moderate appreciation of constancy: "Tis pity ... that ever fruitless thing Constancy was ever taught you as a vertue, since for virtues sake you will love it, as having true possession of your soule, but understand, this virtue hath limits to hold it in, being a virtue but thus that it is a vice in them that break it, but those with whom it is broken, are by the breach free to leave or choose againe where most staidness may be found.' M. Wroth, *The Countess of Montgomery's Urania*, ed. J. A. Roberts (Binghamton: State University of New York, 1995), p. 470.

55. *scruple*: a small weight of unit or measurement, apothecaries' weight (*OED*).

56. *nosegay*: a small bouquet of flowers or herbs, especially ones having a sweet smell; a floral motif in pastoral poetry, see John Gay's *Poem, The Shepherd's Week* (1714): 'My Shepherd gathered none nosegays but what are the growth of our own fields.'

57. *chagrin*: French for worry and melancholy.

58. *ennui*: The feeling of mental weariness and dissatisfaction produced by want of occupation, or by lack of interest in present surroundings or employments (*OED*).

59. *ortolans*: A migratory bunting, which breeds in parts of southern and eastern Europe, Scandinavia, and western central Asia. It has mainly brown plumage with a yellow throat and a grey or (in the male) olive-green head, and was formerly widely regarded as a delicacy (*OED*).

60. *heart of a tygress*: Shakespeare, *3 Henry VI*, I.iv.137: 'O tiger's heart wrapp'd in a woman's hide!'

61. *'Will ... Ally Croaker?'*: a song performed in George Colman's *The Jealous Wife* (1761).

62. *billet*: a note, usually of romantic content.

63. *inamorato*: Italian for someone in love.

64. *Graces*: In Sandro Botticelli's painting *Spring* (1482), the three Graces, companions of Venus, are portrayed dancing a roundelay.

65. *Paris*: The son of the king of Troy, Paris was abandoned on Mount Ida due to a prophecy that he would bring about the fall of Troy. Also on Mount Ida, Paris was to decide which of the three goddesses, Athena, Aphrodite and Hera was the most beautiful.

66. *Hebe*: the goddess of youth in Greek mythology, daughter of Zeus and Hera

67. *event*: Peter III of Russia was deposed and succeeded by his wife Catherine on 9 July, 1762. Only few days later, on 17 July, Peter III was murdered, presumably in a conspiracy led by his wife, whose coronation took place on 12 September 1762.

68. *Bolingbroke*: Henry St John, first Viscount of Bolingbroke (1678–1751), leader of the Tories in the reign of Queen Anne, prominent in the Jacobite rebellion of 1715 that sought to overthrow George I.

69. *Atterbury*: Francis Atterbury (1663–1732), politician and bishop, who also sided with the Tories and supported the Jacobite rebellion. His *Sermons and Discourses on Several Subjects and Occasions*, published in two volumes in 1723, were praised for their rhetorical vigour.

70. *Addison*: Joseph Addison (1672–1719), man of letters and essayist. He contributed frequently to Richard Steele's periodical the *Tatler* (1709–11) and, after the *Tatler* was

Notes to pages 102–12 147

dropped, published the *Spectator* (1711–12). In his writings, Addison allied himself with the Whigs, promoting a shift of moral authority 'from traditional institutions (the Monarchy and the Church) to a new model of civil society with its own authorities'. See L. E. Klein, 'Joseph Addison's Whiggism', in D. Womersley (ed.), *Cultures of Whiggism: New Essays on English Literature and Culture in the Long Eighteenth Century* (Newark, DE: University of Delaware Press, 2005), pp. 108–26, on p. 110.

71. *petticoat-politics*: women's political beliefs and alliances.

72. *female-machine*: Indebted to Descartes's comparison of the body with a machine that follows the natural laws of extension and motion.

73. *la bella Julia*: Italian for the beautiful Julia.

74. *Cæsars*: Gaius Julius Caesar (100 BC–44 BC), Roman general and politician. Under his leadership, the Roman Republic grew into an empire.

75. *Catalines*: Born to one of the oldest patrician families of Rome, Catiline (108 BC–62 BC) contested the aristocratic power of the Senate through two conspiracies, known as the Catilinarians.

76. *tour of Europe*: Also called the Grand Tour was considered an important element in the education of the young men of aristocratic and gentry families. It generally included Paris and Rome and increasingly Germany, Switzerland, Spain and Portugal. See also Volume I, note 38.

77. *houshold*: household.

78. *Lady Julia rose this morning with the sun*: A possible reference to Romeo's comparison of Juliet with the sun: 'It is the east, and Juliet is the sun', *Romeo and Juliet*, II.ii.3.

79. *Cestus*: A belt or girdle for the waist; particularly that worn by a bride in ancient times (*OED*). Venus, the Goddess of Love, wore a girdle that represented anything that could arouse amorous feelings in the beholder. Juno borrowed this girdle in order to secure Jupiter's love.

80. *se'nnight*: one week.

81. *masquerade*: The second decade of the eighteenth century saw the masquerade, a ball of masks, established as a 'fashionable commercial entertainment'. See T. Castle, *Masquerade and Civilization: The Carnivalesque in Eighteenth-Century English Culture and Fiction* (Stanford, CA: Stanford University Press, 1986), p. 9.

82. *temple to Love and Friendship*: Frances Brooke may have been inspired by the Temple of Friendship built at Stowe in 1737.

83. *cor mio! son confuso*: Italian for my heart! I am confused.

84. *capricioso*: Italian for whimsical, unpredictable.

85. *stomacher*: An ornamental covering for the chest (often adorned with jewels) worn by women under the lacing of the bodice (*OED*).

86. *sleeve-knots*: a knot of ribbon worn on the sleeve.

87. *Princess of the blood of France*: unidentified.

88. *native beauty of virtue*: Francis Hutcheson (1694–1746), author of *Inquiry into the Origins of our Ideas of Beauty and Virtue, in Two Treatises* (1725), was the most influential proponent of innate ideas. He opposed Thomas Hobbes and David Hume, who rooted ideas such as virtue and vice solely in the experience of hedonic pleasure and pain. Hutcheson argued that, due to an innate moral sense, humans pursue virtue, because compliance with our innate moral sense instinctively leads to pleasure.

89. *charmante*: French for charming.

90. *minion of fortune*: someone favoured by circumstances or luck.

91. *caro Enrico*: Italian for dear Henry.

148   *Notes to pages 113–28*

92. *the pen drops from my hand*: Brooke emulates the 'writing to the moment' that Richardson had successfully introduced in *Pamela*, a technique that offered 'an intimate access to the ebb and flow of consciousness, unhindered by the distancing and flattening effects of retrospection'. See T. Keymer and P. Sabor (ed.), *Pamela in the Marketplace: Literary Controversy and Print Culture in Eighteenth-Century Britain and Ireland* (Cambridge: Cambridge University Press, 2005), p. 21.

93. *sympathized*: Brooke seems to be influenced by Adam Smith's definition of sympathy in *Theory of Moral Sentiments* (1759): 'By the imagination we place ourselves in his situation, we conceive ourselves enduring all the same torments, we enter as it were into his body, and become in some measure the same person with him.' A. Smith, *The Theory of Moral Sentiments*, ed. D. D. Raphael and A. L. Macfie (London: Oxford University Press, 1976), p. 9.

94. *sacrificer's knife*: In the Book of Genesis, God asked of Abraham as a token of unconditional obedience to sacrifice his only son, Isaac (Genesis 22:5 and 22:8).

95. *distracted:* distraught.

96. *How vain are the designs of man*: Lady Anne's desperation echoes Samuel Johnson's poem *The Vanity of Human Wishes* (1749).

97. *a clod of senseless clay*: Alexander Pope's translation of *The Iliad*, XXII.563: 'a senseless corpse! inanimated clay'.

98. *cup of sorrow*: Samuel Johnson, *Rambler 203*: 'No man past the middle point of life, can sit down to feast upon the pleasures of youth, without finding the banquet embittered by the cup of sorrow.'

99. *corse*: corpse.

100. *The bridal couch is the bed of death*: As in Shakespeare's *Romeo and Juliet*, affliction becomes particularly unbearable by the intrusion of death in the midst of bridal preparations and the reversal of joy to grief:

'All things that we ordained festival,
Turn from their office to black funeral
Our instruments to melancholy bells,
Our wedding cheer to a sad burial feast,
Our solemn hymns to sullen dirges change
Our bridal flowers serve for a buried corse,
And all things change them to the contrary.' (*Romeo and Juliet*, IV.v.84–90)

101. *desart*: desert.

102. 'So properly ... tears': From Edward Young's play *The Revenge* (1721).

103. *gause*: gauze, a thin transparent fabric initially made of silk.

104. *awful*: here respectful.

105. *Thursday*: Brooke's choice of Thursday as the day of Henry Mandeville's death, Julia's birthday and the young couple's wedding day now turned into the day of their funeral could have been influenced by the dialogue between Richardson's Pamela and Mr B. In this conversation, Pamela insists on being wedded on a Thursday, since this is the day when the most important events of her life have taken place.

106. *tragedy:* See David Hume's pronouncements on the pleasure of tragedy in his essay 'Of Tragedy', where he writes: 'It seems an unaccountable pleasure, which the spectators of a well wrote tragedy receive from sorrow, terror, anxiety, and other passions, which are in themselves disagreeable and uneasy.' D. Hume, *Essays and Treatises on Several Subjects*, 2 vols (London: A. Millar, 1767), vol. 1, p. 243.

107. *Humbled in dust*: Job describes himself as being humbled by God in similar terms: 'Therefore I despise myself and repent in dust and ashes,' Job 42:6.

TEXTUAL VARIANTS

Volume I

3a encrease] increase *1763c; 1765; 1769; 1773; 1782; 1788*
3b for.] for; *1763a*
3c nature! The] nature! the *1763c; 1765; 1769; 1773; 1782; 1788*
3d England.] England! *1763c; 1765; 1769; 1773; 1782; 1788*
4a she] She *1769; 1773; 1782; 1788*
4b endevour] endeavor *1769; 1773; 1782; 1788*
4c woman kind] woman-kind *1763c; 1769; 1773; 1782; 1788*; womankind *1764; 1765*
4d softness. Her] softness, her *1763a*
4e promises;] promises: *1763c; 1769; 1773; 1782; 1788*
4f pain;] pain: *1763c; 1769; 1773; 1782; 1788*
4g 700 l.] seven hundred pounds *1763c; 1769; 1773; 1782; 1788*; 700 *l. 1764; 1765*
4h long very] long, very *1763c; 1764; 1765; 1769; 1773; 1782; 1788*
4i mine)] mine!) *1763c; 1765; 1769; 1773; 1782; 1788*
5a musick] music *1763c; 1769; 1773; 1782; 1788*
5b studyed] studied *1763c; 1769; 1773; 1782; 1788*
5c domestic] domestick *1763a*
5d happy: impartial] happy. Impartial *1763c; 1769; 1773; 1782; 1788*
5e inferior: by] inferior. By *1763c; 1769; 1773; 1782; 1788*
5f her: encouraged] her. Encouraged *1763c; 1769; 1773; 1782; 1788*
5g best,] best *1763c; 1769; 1773; 1782; 1788*
5h domestic] domestick *1763a*
6a constraint:] constraint. *1763c; 1765; 1769; 1773; 1782; 1788*
6b dishonour] dishonor *1763c; 1769; 1773; 1782; 1788*
6c English woman] Englishwoman *1765; 1769; 1773; 1782*
6d marryed] married *1763c; 1769; 1773; 1782; 1788*
6e 3000 l.] three thousand pounds *1763c; 1769; 1773; 1782; 1788*
6f 'squire] squire *1763c; 1769; 1773; 1782; 1788*

150   *The History of Lady Julia Mandeville*

6g   fox chace] fox-chace *1763c*; *1765*; *1769*; *1773*; *1782*; *1788*

6h   Coquet] coquette *1763c*; *1769*; *1773*; *1782*; *1788*

6i   domestic] domestick *1763a*

6j   We read, we walk, we ride, we converse] we read, we ride, we converse *1763c*; *1769*; *1773*; *1782*; *1788*. Probably omitted to keep the symmetry of the subsequent trio 'we play, we dance, we sing'. we read, we dance, we ride, we converse *1765*.

6k   musick] music *1763a*; *1765*;*1769*; *1773*; *1782*; *1788*

6l   favourite] favorite *1763c*; *1769*; *1773*; *1782*; *1788*

7a   domestic] domestick *1763a*

7b   honoured] honored *1763c*; *1769*; *1773*; *1782*; *1788*

7c   slowly rising] slowly-rising *1763c*; *1765*; *1769*; *1773*; *1782*; *1788*

7d   hill] still *1763a*

7e   cascade which] cascade, which *1763c*; *1765*; *1769*; *1773*; *1782*; *1788*

7f   romantic] romantick *1763a*

7g   diversified] diverify'd *1763a*

7h   Every] every *1763c*; *1765*; *1769*; *1773*; *1782*; *1788*

7i   Omitted in *1763a*.

7j   rustic] rustick *1763a*

8a   pipe: Round] pipe; round *1763a*; pipe. Round *1763c*; *1769*; *1773*; *1782*; *1788*

8b   lustring] lutestring *1763c*; *1764*; *1765*; *1769*; *1773*; *1782*; *1788*

8c   night gown] night-gown *1763c*; *1769*; *1773*; *1782*; *1788*

8d   bosom:] bosom. *1763c*; *1769*; *1773*; *1782*; *1788*

8e   once. – Paint] once – paint *1763a*

8f   Hebe; – however] Hebe. – However *1763a*

8g   partie] party *1763c*; *1765*; *1769*; *1773*; *1782*; *1788*

8h   interesting; none] interesting. None *1763c*; *1769*; *1773*; *1782*; *1788*

8i   Omitted in *1763a*.

9a   accomplishments. As] accomplishments: as *1763a*

9b   well-educated] well educated *1763a*

9c   sentiment. Whilst] sentiment Whilst *1763a*

9d   friendship, unless] friendship unless *1763a*

10a   showed] shewed *1763c*; *1764*; *1765*; *1769*; *1773*; *1782*; *1788*

10b   shew'd] shewd *1763a*

10c   its] it's *1763a*

10d   colours] colors *1763c*; *1769*; *1773*; *1782*; *1788*

10e   pitied] pityed *1763a*

10f   saw, and pitied, my] saw and pitied my *1763c*; *1769*; *1773*; *1782*; *1788*

10g   disappoint.] disasappoint; *1763a*

10h   past] passed *1763c*; *1769*; *1773*; *1782*; *1788*

Textual Variants   151

10i affection:] affection. *1763c; 1765; 1769; 1773; 1782; 1788*

10j welfare. When] welfare: when *1763a*

10k countess:] countess. *1763a*

10l Rome:] Rome; *1763a; 1765*; Rome. *1763c; 1769; 1773; 1782; 1788*

11a witness, till] witness till *1769; 1782*

11b faltered, I trembled,] faltered; I trembled; *1763c; 1765; 1769; 1773; 1782; 1788*

11c husband, be assured] husband, be assured, *1763c; 1765; 1769; 1773; 1782; 1788*; husband be assured *1763a*

11d encreases] increases *1763c; 1769; 1773; 1782; 1788*

11e you: may] you. May *1763c; 1769; 1773; 1782; 1788*

12a heart. The] heart: the *1763a*

12b wrote] written *1763c; 1769; 1773; 1782; 1788*

12c name:] name. *1763c; 1769; 1773; 1782; 1788*

12d cure.] cure: *1763a*

12e New paragraph in *1763c, 1765, 1769, 1773, 1782, 1788.*

13a which time, absence,] which, time absence, *1763a*

13b esteem.] esteem *1763c; 1765; 1769; 1773; 1782; 1788*

13c blessing?] blessing! *1763a*

13d Omitted in *1763a.*

13e reformation:] reformation! *1763c; 1769; 1773; 1782; 1788*

13f Sunday?] Sunday! *1763c; 1769; 1773; 1782; 1788*

13g attentive;] attentive! *1763c; 1769; 1773; 1782; 1788*

13h countenance open] countenance open *1773*

13i creature,] creature! *1763c; 1764; 1765; 1769; 1773; 1782; 1788*

13j Some... outside.] 'Some... outside.' *1763c; 1773; 1782; 1788*; 'Some... outside!' *1769*

14a Pindaric.] Pindaric? *1763c*; Pindaric! *1769; 1773; 1782; 1788*

14b endeavour] endeavor *1763c; 1789; 1773; 1782; 1788*

14c extreamly] extremely *1763c; 1764; 1765; 1769; 1773; 1782; 1788*

14d thinking: the Col.] thinking! The Col. *1763c; 1769; 1773; 1782; 1788*

15a endeavour] endeavor *1763c; 1789; 1773; 1782; 1788*

15b that,] that! *1763c; 1769; 1773; 1782; 1788*

15c melancholy] melancholy *1763a*

15d livery stable] livery-stable *1763c; 1782; 1788*

15e certain rank] *certain rank 1763c; 1769; 1773; 1782; 1788*

15f entrusted] intrusted *1763c; 1769; 1773; 1782; 1788*

15g Change alley] 'Change-alley *1763c*; Change-Alley *1764; 1765*; Change-alley *1769; 1773; 1782; 1788*

15h 80,000*l.*] eighty thousand pounds *1763c; 1769; 1773; 1782; 1788*

16a no,] No, *1763c; 1764; 1765; 1769; 1773; 1782; 1788*

152   *The History of Lady Julia Mandeville*

16b   Omitted in *1763a*.
16c   together] together, *1763c*; *1765*; *1769*; *1773*; *1782*; *1788*
16d   farm house] farm-house *1763c*; *1764*; *1765*; *1769*; *1773*; *1782*; *1788*
16e   wood bines] wood-bines *1763a*; *1764*; *1765*; woodbines *1763c*; *1769*; *1773*; *1782*; *1788*
16f   form. We] form: We *1763a*
16g   sweetly varied] sweetly-varied *1763c*; *1765*; *1769*; *1773*; *1782*; *1788*
16h   arbours] arbors *1763c*; *1769*; *1773*; *1782*; *1788*
16i   hands. Lady] hands: Lady *1763a*
17a   day: Her] day: her *1763c*; *1769*; *1773*; *1782*; *1788*
17b   day:] day. *1763c*; *1769*; *1773*; *1782*; *1788*
17c   place I am told] place, I am told, *1763c*; *1764*; *1765*; *1769*; *1773*; *1782*; *1788*
17d   those particularly] those who are particularly *1763c*; *1764*; *1765*; *1769*; *1773*; *1782*; *1788*
17e   Omitted in *1763a*.
17f   Lord,] Lord! *1763c*; *1765*; *1769*; *1773*; *1782*; *1788*
17g   tremblingly alive all o'er] 'tremblingly alive all o'er' *1763c*; *1765*; *1769*; *1773*; *1782*; *1788*
17h   moderation;] moderation: – *1763c*; *1765*; *1769*; *1773*; *1782*; *1788*
17i   company–] company! – *1763c*; *1765*; *1769*; *1773*; *1782*; *1788*
17j   die] dye *1763c*; *1782*; *1788*
17k   times] times, *1763c*; *1764*; *1765*; *1769*; *1773*; *1782*; *1788*
17l   Really my dear, says I, I ... suppose] 'Really my dear,' says I, 'I ... suppose–' *1763c*; *1769*; *1773*; *1782*; *1788*
17m   carryed] carried *1763c*; *1764*; *1765*; *1769*; *1773*; *1782*; *1788*
18a   Omitted in *1763a*.
18b   labour] labor *1763c*; *1769*; *1773*; *1782*; *1788*
18c   dutchess] Dutchess *1763a*; duchess *1763c*; *1773*; *1782*; *1788*
18d   envyed] envied *1763c*; *1769*; *1773*; *1782*; *1788*
19a   tho'] though *1763c*; *1764*; *1765*; *1769*; *1773*; *1782*; *1788*
19b   Happiness] happiness *1763a*;*1763c*; *1764*; *1765*; *1769*; *1773*; *1782*; *1788*
19c   royalty] Royalty *1763c*; *1765*; *1769*; *1773*; *1782*; *1788*
19d   heaven] Heaven *1763c*; *1764*; *1765*; *1769*; *1773*; *1782*; *1788*
19e   supreme being] Supreme Being *1763c*; *1769*; *1773*; *1782*; *1788*
19f   estate:] estate. *1763c*; *1764*; *1765*; *1769*; *1773*; *1782*; *1788*
20a   labourer] laborer *1763c*; *1769*; *1773*; *1782*; *1788*
20b   heaven] Heaven *1763c*; *1764*; *1765*; *1769*; *1773*; *1782*; *1788*
20c   Creator] creator *1763a*
20d   Omitted in *1763a*.

Textual Variants 153

20e Ho vergogna Signora,] 'Ho vergogna, Signora,' *1763c; 1765; 1769; 1773; 1782; 1788*

20f upon] Upon *1763c; 1764; 1765; 1769; 1773; 1782; 1788*

20g he] He *1763c; 1765; 1769; 1773; 1782; 1788*

20h Cittadina] cittadina *1763c; 1765; 1769; 1773; 1782; 1788*

21a Wilmot.] Wilmot? *1763c; 1764; 1765; 1769; 1773; 1782; 1788*

21b Omitted in *1763a.*

21c my] My *1763c; 1769; 1773; 1782; 1788*

21d Obedient] obedient *1763c; 1769; 1773; 1782; 1788*

21e repay] re-pay *1763c; 1769; 1773; 1782; 1788*

22a the bank of friendship] 'the bank of friendship' *1763c; 1769; 1773; 1782; 1788*

22b dear] Dear *1763c; 1769; 1773; 1782; 1788* These editions start a new line here.

22c chant] chaunt *1765; 1769; 1773; 1782*

22d gently breathing] gently, breathing *1763c;* gently-breathing *1764; 1769; 1773; 1782; 1788*

22e western] Western *1763c; 1765; 1769; 1773; 1782; 1788*

22f well absolutely] well, absolutely, *1763c; 1765; 1769; 1773; 1782; 1788;* well, absolutely *1764*

22g tho'] though *1763c; 1764; 1765; 1769; 1773; 1782; 1788*

22h 'squires] squires *1763c; 1769; 1773; 1782; 1788*

22i steered] steer'd *1763c; 1769; 1773; 1782; 1788*

22j long tailed] long-tailed *1763c; 1765; 1769; 1773; 1782; 1788*

22k Arabians – by] Arabians. – By *1763c; 1769; 1773; 1782; 1788*

22l himself]himself! *1763c; 1769; 1773; 1782; 1788*

22m creature] creature! *1763c; 1769; 1773; 1782; 1788*

23a O] Oh! *1763c; 1765; 1769; 1773; 1782; 1788*

23b blight-coloured] light-colored *1763a;* light coloured *1763*

23c well-scented] wellscented *1763a;* well scented *1764*

23d ladyship] Ladyship *1763c; 1765; 1769; 1773; 1782; 1788*

23e retirement] tetirement *1763c*

23f tho'] though *1763c; 1764; 1765; 1769; 1773; 1782; 1788*

23g Well ... there.] 'Well ... there.' *1763c; 1765; 1769; 1773; 1782; 1788*

23h Why ... solitude.] 'Why ... solitude.' *1763c; 1769; 1773; 1782; 1788*

23i O ... well.] 'Oh ... well.' *1763c; 1769; 1773; 1782; 1788;* Oh *1765*

23j And ... attractions.] 'And ... attractions.' *1763c; 1769; 1773; 1782; 1788*

23k Attractions ...Rome–] 'Attractions ...Rome–' *1763c; 1769; 1773; 1782; 1788*

23l But ... absence?] 'But ... absence?' *1763c; 1769; 1773; 1782; 1788*

23m In ... Angloise.] 'In ... Angloise!' *1763c; 1769; 1773; 1782; 1788*

154   *The History of Lady Julia Mandeville*

23n   And Miremont?] 'And Miremont?' *1763c*; *1769*; *1773*; *1782*; *1788*

23o   Inconsolable ... operas.] 'Inconsolable ... operas.' *1763c*; *1769*; *1773*; *1782*; *1788*

23p   Is ... company.] 'Is ... company.' *1763c*; *1769*; *1773*; *1782*; *1788*

23q   Any body one knows?] 'Any body one knows?' *1763c*; *1769*; *1773*; *1782*; *1788*

23r   I rather think not.] 'I rather think not.' *1763c*; *1769*; *1773*; *1782*; *1788*

23s   What the good company of the Environs, the Arriere ban, the Posse Comitatus?] 'What! the good company of the Environs, the Arriere ban, the Posse Comitatus?' *1763c*; *1769*; *1773*; *1782*; *1788*; What, *1764*; What! *1765*

23t   Even so: my lord 'brings down the natives upon us,' but, to do the creatures justice, one shall seldom see tamer savages.]'Even so: my lord brings down the natives upon us, but, to do the creatures justice, one shall seldom see tamer savages.' *1763c*; *1769*; *1773*; *1782*; *1788*

23u   wainscoat] wainscot *1763c*; *1769*; *1773*; *1782*; *1788*

24a   Fondville (he would not have you omit Viscount for the world)] Fondville, he would not have you omit Viscount for the world, *1763a*

24b   onesself] one's self *1763c*; *1769*; *1773*; *1782*; *1788*; one self *1765*

24c   enjouement] enjoüement *1763c*; *1769*; *1773*; *1782*; *1788*

24d   Adio!] Adio? *1763a*

24e   body: really] body. Really *1763c*; *1769*; *1773*; *1782*; *1788*

24f   Adieu] adieu *1763c*; *1769*; *1773*; *1782*; *1788*

24g   June 13th.] June 13. *1763c*; *1769*; *1773*; *1782*; *1788*

25a   wrote] written *1763c*; *1769*; *1773*; *1782*; *1788*

25b   enclose] inclose *1763c*; *1769*; *1773*; *1782*; *1788*

25c   conceal.] conceal: *1763a*

25d   The entire letter is inserted within quotation marks in the editions from *1763c*, *1769*, *1773*, *1782* and *1788*.

25e   tho'] though *1763c*; *1769*; *1773*; *1782*; *1788*

25f   tho'] though *1763c*; *1769*; *1773*; *1782*; *1788*

26a   esteem; determined] esteem. Determined *1763c*; *1769*; *1773*; *1782*; *1788*

26b   Omitted in *1763a*.

26c   women,] women – *1763c*; *1769*; *1773*; *1782*; *1788*

27a   wrote] written *1763c*; *1769*; *1773*; *1782*; *1788*

27b   a dull] adull *1763a*

27c   married] marryed *1763a*

27d   endeavoured] endeavored *1769*; *1773*

27e   But] but *1763c*; *1769*; *1773*; *1782*; *1788*

27f   June 20th.] June 20 *1763c*; *1769*; *1773*; *1782*; *1788*

Textual Variants 155

28a country.] country? *1763c; 1764; 1765; 1769; 1773; 1782; 1788*
28b other:] other. *1763c; 1769; 1773; 1782; 1788*
28c same:] same. *1763a*
28d encreased] increased *1763c; 1769; 1773; 1782; 1788*
28e flourishing.] flourishing; *1763a*
28f most] the most *1763c; 1788*
29a enlivens] enliven *1763a*
29b a pretty man about town,] 'a pretty man about town,' *1763c; 1769; 1773; 1782; 1788*
29c Hermitage] hermitage *1763c; 1764; 1765; 1769; 1773; 1782; 1788*
29d Bellville.] Belville! *1763c; 1764; 1765; 1769; 1773; 1782; 1788*
29e Your's] Yours *1763c; 1764; 1765; 1769; 1773; 1782; 1788*
29f Omitted in *1763a.*
30a O] Oh! *1763c; 1765; 1769; 1773; 1782; 1788*
30b loveliness:] loveliness. *1763c; 1769; 1773; 1782; 1788*
30c Belmont.] Belmont! *1763c; 1769; 1773; 1782; 1788*
30d The letter is inserted within quotation marks in the following editions: *1763c, 1769, 1773, 1782, 1788.*
30e heaven grant that moment to be far distant!] Heaven grant that moment to be far distant! *1763c; 1764; 1765; 1769; 1773; 1782; 1788*
30f when the house of lords can make a house of commons, liberty and prerogative will cease to be more than names, and both prince and people become slaves.] when the House of Lords can make a House of Commons, Liberty and Prerogative will cease to be more than names, and both Prince and People become slaves. *1763c; 1765; 1769; 1773; 1782; 1788*
30g tho'] though *1763c; 1769; 1773; 1782; 1788*
30h unbiased] unbyassed *1763a*
30i tho'] though *1763c; 1769; 1773; 1782; 1788*
30j ballance] balance *1763c; 1765; 1769; 1773; 1782; 1788.* The present editions consistently uses 'balance'.
30k tho'] though *1763c; 1769; 1773; 1782; 1788*
31a neighbours] neighbors *1769; 1773*
31b parliament] Parliament *1763c; 1765; 1769; 1773; 1782; 1788*
31c queen] Queen *1763c; 1765; 1769; 1773; 1782; 1788*
31d 500*l*] five hundred pounds *1763c; 1769; 1773; 1782; 1788*
31e tho'] though *1763c; 1769; 1773; 1782; 1788*
31f 2000*l.*] two thousand pounds *1763c; 1769; 1773; 1782; 1788*
31g 14000*l.*] fourteen thousand pounds *1763c; 1769; 1773; 1782; 1788*
31h prince] Prince *1763c; 1764; 1765; 1769; 1773; 1782; 1788*
31i tho'] though *1763c; 1769; 1773; 1782; 1788*

156   *The History of Lady Julia Mandeville*

31j   prince] Prince *1763c*; *1764*; *1765*; *1769*; *1773*; *1782*; *1788*
31k   enlighten'd] enlightened *1763c*; *1765*; *1769*; *1773*; *1782*; *1788*
32a   shew'd] shewed *1763c*; *1769*; *1773*; *1782*; *1788*
32b   100*l.*] an hundred pounds *1763c*; *1769*; *1773*; *1782*; *1788*
32c   characteristick] characteristic *1763c*; *1765*; *1769*; *1773*; *1782*; *1788*
32d   Adieu. Your affectionate BELMONT.] Adieu, Your affectionate BEL-MONT. *1769*; *1773*; Your affectionate BELMONT. Omitted in *1763a*.
32e   what] What *1763c*; *1765*; *1769*; *1773*; *1782*; *1788*
32f   mention'd] mentioned *1763c*; *1765*; *1769*; *1773*; *1782*; *1788*
32g   me; her] me. Her *1763c*; *1769*; *1773*; *1782*; *1788*
32h   excus'd] excused *1763c*; *1765*; *1769*; *1773*; *1782*; *1788*
32i   it's] its *1763c*; *1782*; *1788*
32j   Omitted in *1763a*.
33a   advanc'd] advanced *1763c*; *1765*; *1769*; *1773*; *1782*; *1788*
33b   confus'd] confused *1763c*; *1765*; *1769*; *1773*; *1782*; *1788*
33c   disorder'd] disordered *1763c*; *1765*; *1769*; *1773*; *1782*; *1788*
33d   stop'd] stopt *1763c*;*1765*; *1769*; *1773*; *1782*; *1788*
33e   cit:] cit! *1763a*
33f   thro'] through *1763c*; *1769*; *1773*; *1782*; *1788*
33g   happen'd]*1763c*; *1765*; *1769*; *1773*; *1782*; *1788*
33h   disdain'd] disdained *1763c*; *1769*; *1773*; *1782*; *1788*
33i   falshood] falsehood *1763c*; *1769*; *1773*; *1782*; *1788*
33j   walk'd] walked *1763c*; *1769*; *1773*; *1782*; *1788*
33k   stay'd] staid *1763c*; *1769*; *1773*; *1782*; *1788*
33l   ask'd] asked *1763c*; *1769*; *1773*; *1782*; *1788*
33m   past] passed *1763c*; *1769*; *1773*; *1782*; *1788*
33n   charms. We] charms: we *1763a*
34a   talked] talk'd *1763a*
34b   assumed] assum'd *1763a*
34c   seem'd] seemed *1763c*; *1765*; *1769*; *1773*; *1782*; *1788*
34d   O! Conscience! Conscience!] Oh! conscience! conscience! *1763c*; *1769*; *1773*; *1782*; *1788*; Oh! Conscience! Conscience! *1765*
34e   soul. That] soul: that *1763c*; *1769*; *1773*; *1782*; *1788*
34f   The entire passage from 'she cannot see me ...she is' stands within quotation marks in *1763c, 1769, 1773, 1782, 1788*.
34g   child–hood] childhood *1763c*; *1769*; *1773*; *1782*; *1788*
35a   chair:] chair. *1763c*; *1769*; *1773*; *1782*; *1788*
35b   chit chat] chit-chat *1763c*; *1769*; *1773*; *1782*; *1788*
35c   a Trio] *à trio* *1763c*; *1769*; *1773*; *1782*; *1788*; à Trio *1765*
35d   humor] humour *1763c; 1782*; *1788*
35e   Adio.] Adio! *1763c*; *1764*; *1765*; *1769*; *1773*; *1782*; *1788*

Textual Variants

35f   Omitted in *1763a*.

35g   My] my *1763a*

36a   neighborhood] neighbourhood *1763c*; *1764*; *1765*; *1769*; *1773*; *1782*; *1788*

36b   O Mordaunt!] Oh! Mordaunt! *1763c*; *1765*; *1769*; *1773*; *1782*; *1788*

36c   show] shew *1763c*; *1765*; *1769*; *1773*; *1782*; *1788*

36d   to bed] to-bed *1764*; *1765*; *1769*; *1773*

36e   Omitted in *1763a*.

36f   showing] shewing *1763c*; *1765*; *1769*; *1773*; *1782*; *1788*

36g   partiality] Penchant *1763a*

36h   meerly] merely *1763c*; *1764*; *1765*; *1769*; *1773*; *1782*; *1788*

37a   O heavens!] Oh! Heavens! *1763c*; *1769*; *1773*; *1782*; *1788*; Oh! heavens! *1765*

37b   to-night] to night *1763c*

37c   perplext] perplexed *1763c*; *1769*; *1773*; *1782*; *1788*

37d   letter.] letter! *1763c*; *1769*; *1773*; *1782*; *1788*

37e   drest] dressed *1763c*; *1769*; *1773*; *1782*; *1788*

37f   Adio! Caro! Votre] *Adio, caro! Votre, 1763c*; *1769*; *1773*; *1782*; *1788*

37g   Omitted in *1763a*.

38a   But Oh, how changed! But oh! how changed; *1763c*; *1769*; *1773*; *1782*; *1788*

38b   heroicks] heroic *1763c*; *1769*; *1773*; *1782*; *1788*

38c   poor Harry!] poor Harry, *1763a*

38d   lovesick] love-sick *1763c*; *1788*

38e   suspended:] suspended. *1763c*; *1769*; *1773*; *1782*; *1788*

38f   that it was impossible any body should think of dancing minuets after them;] 'that it was impossible any body should think of dancing minuets after them;' *1763c*; *1769*; *1773*; *1782*; *1788*

38g   sentiment] sentiments *1764*; *1765*; *1769*; *1773*

38h   endeavor'd] endeavoured *1763c*; *1788* endeavored *1769*; *1773*; *1782*

39a   O, Heavens! Fondville, said I, you are an inhuman creature; you have absolutely forgot your partner:] 'Oh, Heavens! Fondville,' said I, 'you are an inhuman creature; you have absolutely forgot your partner.' *1763c*; *1769*; *1773*; *1782*; *1788*

39b   then] Then *1763c*; *1769*; *1773*; *1782*; *1788*

39c   entreat] intreat *1763c*; *1769*; *1773*; *1782*; *1788*

39d   I knew her rage for title, tinsel, and 'people of a certain rank;'] 'I knew her rage for title, tinsel, and people of a certain rank,' *1763a*

40a   exchange-broker] exchange broker *1763a*

40b   coronet;] coronet. *1763c*; *1769*; *1773*; *1782*; *1788*

40c   the amiable ignorant] The amiable ignorant! *1763c*; *1782*; *1788*

158 *The History of Lady Julia Mandeville*

40d   neighborhood] neighbourhood *1763c; 1764; 1765; 1769; 1773; 1782; 1788*

40e   endeavoring] endeavouring *1764; 1765*

40f   praise-worthy] praise worthy *1763a; 1765*

40g   June 23d.] July 23d. *1763a;* June 23. *1763c; 1769; 1773; 1782; 1788*

41a   my] My *1763c; 1769; 1773; 1782; 1788*

41b   to-night] tonight *1763a*

41c   to-morrow] tomorrow *1763a*

41d   hearts?] hearts! *1763a*

41e   Farewel!] Farewell! *1763c; 1764; 1765; 1769; 1773; 1782; 1788.* Omitted in *1763a.*

41f   Omitted in *1763a.*

41g   feather'd] feathered *1763c; 1773; 1782; 1788*

41h   charm'd] charmed *1763c; 1769; 1773; 1782; 1788*

41i   coloring] colouring *1764; 1765*

42a   Tho'] Though *1763c; 1769; 1773; 1782; 1788*

42b   Prince] prince *1763a*

42c   Prince] prince *1763a*

42d   endeavouring] endeavoring *1763c; 1769; 1773; 1782; 1788*

42e   it's] its *1763c; 1769; 1773; 1782; 1788*

42f   Farewel.] Farewell. *1763c*

42g   Omitted in *1763a.*

42h   house. That] house: that *1763c; 1769; 1773; 1782; 1788*

43a   500*l.*] five hundred pounds *1763c; 1769; 1773; 1782; 1788*

43b   sentiments:] sentiments *1763a*

43c   endeavour] endeavor *1763c; 1769; 1773; 1782; 1788*

43d   pass'd] passed *1763c; 1764; 1765; 1769; 1773; 1782; 1788*

43e   Oh] O *1763a*

43f   I know] I know, *1763c; 1764; 1765; 1769; 1773; 1782; 1788*

44a   instance,] instance *1763c; 1769; 1773; 1782; 1788*

44b   Tomorrow] To-morrow *1763c; 1769; 1773; 1782; 1788*

44c   se'nnight] sevennight *1763c; 1764; 1765; 1769; 1773; 1782; 1788*

44d   expectations: my] expectations. My *1763c; 1769; 1773; 1782; 1788*

44e   crampt] cramped *1763c; 1769; 1773; 1782; 1788*

44f   destroy'd] destroyed *1763c; 1769; 1773; 1782; 1788*

45a   shoots] shoot *1763c; 1764; 1765; 1769; 1773; 1782; 1788*

45b   virtue does not consist in never erring, which is impossible, but in recovering as fast as we can from our errors.] 'virtue does not consist in never erring, which is impossible, but in recovering as fast as we can from our errors.' *1763c; 1769; 1773; 1782; 1788*

Textual Variants 159

45c But why do I doubt you!] But why do I doubt you? *1763c; 1765; 1769; 1773; 1782; 1788*

45d with-hold] withhold *1763c; 1769; 1773; 1782; 1788*

46a arbour] arbor *1763c; 1769; 1773; 1782; 1788*

46b well-being] well being *1763c; 1764; 1765; 1788*

46c honours] honors *1763c; 1769; 1763; 1782; 1788*

46d ever-new] ever new *1763a*

47a Omitted in *1763a.*

47b heaven! earth!] heaven and earth! *1763c; 1769; 1773; 1782; 1788*

47c four-and-twenty] four-and-twenty! *1763c*

47d papers.] papers *1763c; 1769; 1773; 1782; 1788*

47e sudden?] sudden! *1763c; 1788*

47f intolerably.–] intolerably – *1763c; 1765; 1769; 1773; 1782; 1788*

47g stray'd.'] stray'd?' *1763c; 1764; 1765; 1769; 1773; 1782; 1788*

48a Adieu!] Adieu. *1763a*

48b Omitted in *1763a.*

48c 30,000*l.*] thirty thousand pounds *1763c; 1769; 1773; 1782; 1788*

48d 50,000*l.*] fifty thousand pounds *1763c; 1769; 1773; 1782; 1788*

48e veins: we] veins. We *1763c; 1769; 1773; 1782; 1788*

48f Fondville's valet] Fondville's valet! *1763c; 1769; 1773; 1782; 1788*

48g possible] possible? *1763c; 1769; 1773; 1782; 1788*

48h letter.] letter! *1763c; 1769; 1773; 1782; 1788*

48i This letter and Lord Belmont's response are inserted within quotation marks in *1763c, 1769, 1773, 1782, 1788.*

48j Yet] yet *1763c; 1769; 1773; 1782; 1788*

48k family! –] family – *1763c; 1769; 1773; 1782; 1788*

49a favourably] favorably *1765*

49b Lordship's] Lordships *1763a*

50a But, O Mordaunt!] But oh! Mordaunt! *1763c; 1769; 1773; 1782; 1788;* But, Oh! Mordaunt *1765*

50b shall I be the happiest?] shall I be the happiest! *1763a;* shall I be the happier? *1763c; 1769; 1773; 1782; 1788*

50c felicity:] felicity. *1763c; 1769; 1773; 1782; 1788*

50d enjoyments] enjoyment *1763c*

50e species: yes] species. Yes *1763c; 1769; 1773; 1782; 1788*

50f his] this *1763c; 1773; 1782; 1788*

50g desire: Good heaven,] desire. Good Heaven! *1763c; 1769; 1773; 1782; 1788*

50h perfection!] perfection?

50i Adieu! H. Mandeville] Omitted in *1763a.*

50j How] how *1763c; 1769; 1773; 1782; 1788*

50k	One] one *1763c; 1769; 1773; 1782; 1788*
51a	Oh! for a cooling breeze!] O for a cooling breeze! *1763a*
51b	her;] her! *1763a*
51c	Omitted in *1763a*.
51d	TUESDAY] TUESDAY, *1765*; Tuesday, *1763c; 1769; 1773; 1782; 1788*
51e	tyger] tiger *1763c; 1764; 1765; 1769; 1773; 1782; 1788*
51f	object:] object. *1763c; 1769; 1773; 1782; 1788*
52a	'Yes, the] Yes, 'the *1763a*
52b	favourable] favorable *1763c; 1769; 1773; 1782; 1788*
52c	perswasions] persuasions *1763c; 1769; 1773; 1782; 1788*
52d	O,] Oh! *1763c; 1765; 1769; 1773; 1782; 1788*
52e	wrote] written *1763c; 1765; 1769; 1773; 1782; 1788*
52f	him; the] him? The *1763c; 1764; 1765; 1769; 1773; 1782; 1788*
52g	cruel; they] cruel? They *1763c; 1769; 1773; 1782; 1788*
52h	Ever yours, A. Wilmot] Omitted in *1763a*.
53a	try'd] tried *1763c; 1765; 1769; 1773; 1782; 1788*
53b	O heavens!] Oh! Heavens! *1765*
53c	blush'd] blushed *1763c; 1764; 1765; 1769; 1773; 1782; 1788*
53d	confirm'd] confirmed *1763c; 1764; 1765; 1769; 1773; 1782; 1788*
53e	Morning.] night *1763c; 1769; 1773; 1782; 1788*
53f	pass'd] passed *1763c; 1764; 1765; 1769; 1773; 1782; 1788*
54a	she] She *1763c; 1769; 1773; 1782; 1788*
54b	What] what *1763c; 1769; 1773; 1782; 1788*
54c	O] Oh! *1763c; 1769; 1773; 1782; 1788*
54d	Dr. H.] Dr. H— *1763c; 1764; 1765; 1769; 1773; 1782; 1788*
54e	musick] music *1763c; 1765; 1769; 1773; 1782; 1788*
54f	mall] Mall *1763c; 1769; 1773; 1782; 1788*
54g	royal poet] Royal Poet *1763c; 1769; 1773; 1782; 1788*
54h	to praise him in the cymbals and dances.] 'to praise him in the cymbals and dances.' *1763c; 1769; 1773; 1782; 1788*
55a	Charles the 1st] Charles the First *1763c; 1764; 1765; 1769; 1773; 1782; 1788*
55b	Charles the 2d] Charles the Second *1763c; 1764; 1765; 1769; 1773; 1782; 1788*
55c	Omitted in *1763a*.
55d	engag'd] engaged *1763c; 1764; 1765; 1769; 1773; 1782; 1788*
55e	dy'd] died *1763c; 1769; 1773; 1782; 1788*
55f	arbour] arbor *1763c; 1769; 1773; 1782; 1788*
55g	letter. When] letter: when *1763a*
55h	flushed] flush'd *1763a*
55i	eyes!] eyes. *1763c; 1769; 1773; 1782; 1788*

Textual Variants

55j   dar'd] dared *1763c; 1764; 1769; 1773; 1782; 1788*

55k   look'd] looked *1763c; 1764; 1769; 1773; 1782; 1788*

55l   stab'd] stabbed *1763c; 1764; 1765; 1769; 1773; 1782; 1788*

55m The] the *1763a*

56a   intirely] entirely *1763c; 1769; 1773; 1782; 1788*

56b   would] wou'd *1763a*; could *1763c; 1769; 1773; 1782; 1788*

56c   supreme] Supreme *1763c; 1769; 1773; 1782; 1788*

56d   O Mordaunt!] Oh! Mordaunt *1763c; 1769; 1773; 1782; 1788*

57a   O Mordaunt!] Oh! Mordaunt, *1763c; 1769; 1773; 1782; 1788*; Oh! Mordaunt! *1765*

57b   Can] can *1763c; 1769; 1773; 1782; 1788*

57c   O Mordaunt!] Oh! Mordaunt, *1763c; 1765; 1769; 1773; 1782; 1788*

57d   beg'd] begged *1763c; 1769; 1773; 1782; 1788*

57e   'Hate you, Mr. Mandeville, O heaven!'] 'Hate you, Mr. Mandeville! O Heaven!' *1763c; 1764; 1769; 1773; 1782; 1788*; Oh! Heaven! *1765*

58a   endeavouring] endeavoring *1764; 1765*

58b   countess!] countess. *1763a*

58c   O Mordaunt!] Oh! Mordaunt! *1763c; 1769; 1773; 1782; 1788*

58d   angels] angels! *1763c; 1769; 1773; 1782; 1788*

58e   Adieu.] Adieu! *1763c*

58f   Omitted in *1763a.*

58g   Aug. 6th.] August 6. *1763c; 1769; 1773; 1782; 1788*

58h   wide extended] wide-extended *1763c; 1764; 1765; 1769; 1773; 1782; 1788*

59a   great] Great *1763c; 1765; 1769; 1773; 1782; 1788*

59b   prerogative] prerogatives *1763c*

59c   constitution: let] constitution. Let *1763c; 1769; 1773; 1782; 1788*

59d   Omitted in *1763c, 1764, 1765, 1769, 1773, 1782,1788.*

59e   August 11th.] August 11 *1763c*; Aug. 11th *1765; 1769; 1773; 1782; 1788*

60a   endeavored] endeavoured *1764; 1765*

60b   soul.] soul: *1763a*

60c   O, Emily! Do I indeed hate him!] Oh! Emily! Do I indeed hate him? *1763c; 1782; 1788* Oh! Emily! Do I indeed hate him! *1765; 1769; 1773*

60d   mankind?] mankind! *1763c; 1782; 1788*

60e   Is he not worthy all my tenderness?] is he not worthy all my tenderness? *1763c; 1765; 1769; 1773; 1782; 1788*

60f   How] how *1763c; 1769; 1773; 1782; 1788*

60g   O, my Emily,] Oh! my Emily, *1763c; 1765; 1769; 1773; 1782; 1788*

60h   'My congratulations, says he, would] "My congratulations', says he, 'would *1763c; 1769; 1773; 1782; 1788*

162 *The History of Lady Julia Mandeville*

61a   bosom'.] bosom'. *1763c; 1769; 1773; 1782; 1788*

61b   this was a favor, for these kind of people were only gentlemen by the courtesy of England.] 'this was a favor, for these kind of people were only gentlemen by the courtesy of England.' *1763c; 1769; 1773; 1782; 1788*

61c   sunbeams: the] sun-beams. The *1763c; 1764; 1765; 1769; 1773; 1782; 1788*

61d   Tables] tables *1763c; 1769; 1773; 1782; 1788*

61e   How I pity him! His] How I pity him, his *1763a*; how I pity him *1763c; 1782; 1788*

61f   A. Wilmot. Added in *1763c, 1769, 1773, 1782, 1788.*

61g   August 17th:] August 17. *1763c; 1769; 1773; 1782; 1788*

61h   absence;] absence? *1763a*

61i   give?] give: *1763a*

61j   tenderness!] tenderness? *1763a*

62a   entreated] intreated *1763c; 1769; 1773; 1782; 1788*

62b   How shall I hide my concern?] How shall I hide my concern! *1763a*; how shall I hide my concern? *1763c; 1769; 1773; 1782; 1788*

62c   O Emily!] Oh! Emily! *1763c; 1765; 1769; 1773; 1782; 1788*

62d   The editions from *1763c, 1769, 1773, 1782* and *1788* omit this dash.

62e   confidente] confidante *1763c; 1769; 1773; 1782; 1788*

62f   14,000*l*,] fourteen thousand pounds *1763c; 1769; 1773; 1782; 1788*

62g   endeavour] endeavor *1763a; 1769*

63a   determinations,] determination, *1763c; 1769; 1773; 1782; 1788*

63b   Omitted in *1763a.*

63c   not obvious, not obtrusive,] 'not obvious, not obtrusive' *1763c; 1769; 1773; 1782; 1788*

63d   O Mordaunt!] Oh! Mordaunt! *1763c; 1765; 1769; 1773; 1782; 1788*

63e   Omitted in *1763a.*

64a   its] in *1763c; 1769; 1773; 1782; 1788*

64b   mellowed] mellow'd *1763c; 1769; 1773; 1782; 1788*

64c   years. There] years: there *1763a*

64d   Relaxation] relaxation *1763c; 1769; 1773; 1782; 1788*

65a   endeavour] endeavor *1763c; 1769; 1773; 1782; 1788*

65b   childless] childish *1763a; 1763c*

65c   Omitted in *1763a.*

66a   desolation: his] desolation. His *1763c; 1769; 1773; 1782; 1788*

66b   tho'] though *1763c; 1765; 1769; 1773; 1782; 1788*

66c   I am, my Lord, &c.] I am, my Lord, Your Lordship's &c. *1763c; 1769; 1773; 1782; 1788*

66d   past] passed *1763c; 1769; 1773; 1782; 1788*

Textual Variants 163

67a   Ought I at present to wish more?] Ought I at present to wish more! *1763a*

67b   alone: shall] alone. Shall *1763c*; *1769*; *1773*; *1782*; *1788*

67c   OH,] OH! *1763c*; *1769*; *1773*; *1782*; *1788*

67d   but] But *1763c*; *1769*; *1773*; *1782*; *1788*

67e   The closing quotation mark is missing in this edition. The entire conversation between Lady Anne and Lady Belmont is inserted within quotation marks in the editions from *1763c, 1769, 1773, 1782* and *1788*.

67f   a-kin] a kin *1763a*; *1763c*

68a   O heavens!] Oh, Heavens! *1765*

68b   Have] have *1763c*; *1769*; *1773*; *1782*; *1788*

68c   If fellows will follow one, how is it to be avoided?] if fellows will follow one, how is it to be avoided! *1763a*

68d   3000*l.*] three thousand pounds *1763c*; *1769*; *1773*; *1782*; *1788*

68e   carryed] carried *1763c*; *1769*; *1773*; *1782*; *1788*

68f   Have] have *1763c*; *1769*; *1773*; *1782*; *1788*

68g   confest] confessed *1763c*; *1769*; *1773*; *1782*; *1788*

68h   Have] have *1763c*; *1769*; *1773*; *1782*; *1788*

68i   really] Really *1763c*; *1769*; *1773*; *1782*; *1788*

68j   resolution] reputation *1763c*; *1769*; *1773*; *1782*; *1788*

69a   characteristicks] characteristics *1763c*; *1769*; *1773*; *1782*; *1788*

69b   past] passed *1763c*; *1769*; *1773*; *1782*; *1788*

69c   enchantment] inchantment *1763c*; *1773*; *1782*; *1788*

69d   open: must] open. Must *1763c*; *1769*; *1773*; *1782*; *1788*

69e   suited] suitable *1763c*; *1764*; *1769*; *1773*; *1782*; *1788*

69f   happy:] happy. *1763c*; *1769*; *1773*; *1782*; *1788*

70a   Adieu! for the present! it] Adieu, for the present! It *1763c*; *1769*; *1773*; *1782*; *1788*

70b   one's] ones *1763a*

70c   sacrifised] sacrificed *1763c*; *1764*; *1769*; *1773*; *1782*; *1788*

70d   Lady Julia?] Lady Julia! *1763c*; *1788*

70e   Omitted in *1763c*; *1764*; *1765*; *1769*; *1773*; *1782*; *1788*

70f   Omitted in *1763a*.

70g   Oh, Lady Anne!] O Lady Anne! *1763a*; Oh! Lady Anne! *1763c*; *1764*; *1765*; *1769*; *1773*; *1782*; *1788*

70h   endeavouring] endeavoring *1763a*; *1763c*; *1769*; *1773*; *1782*; *1788*

70i   a] A *1763c*; *1769*; *1773*; *1782*; *1788*

70j   you] You *1763a*

70k   Omitted in *1763a*.

70l   *The* End *of the* First Volume.] END OF VOL. I. *1763c*; *1769*; *1773*; *1782*; *1788*

164   *The History of Lady Julia Mandeville*

Volume II

71a   How inconsistent is a heart in love!] how inconsistent is a heart in love! *1763c; 1769; 1773; 1782; 1788*

71b   but I wish he wrote less often:] But I wish he wrote less often: *1763a*

71c   Have not I an equal right to expect, Emily!] Have not I an equal right to expect, Emily? *1763c; 1769; 1773; 1782; 1788*

71d   How do all men sink on the comparison!] How do all men sink on the comparison? *1763a*; how do all men sink on the comparison! *1763c; 1769; 1773; 1782; 1788*

72a   parents?] parents! *1763a*; parent? *1763c; 1788*

72b   Emily!] Emily. *1763c; 1773; 1782; 1788*

72c   Omitted in *1763a*.

72d   intirely] entirely *1763c; 1769; 1773; 1782; 1788*

72e   says] said *1763c; 1769; 1773; 1782; 1788*

72f   favours.] favors *1763c; 1769; 1773; 1782; 1788*

72g   Why] why *1763c; 1769; 1773; 1782; 1788*

72h   Where is my chaise?] where is my chaise? *1763c; 1769; 1773; 1782; 1788*

73a   The dialogue between Henry Mandeville and Lord T– is inserted within quotation marks in the following editions *1763c, 1769, 1773, 1782, 1788.*

73b   Omitted in *1763a*.

73c   coquet] coquette *1763c; 1764; 1765; 1769; 1773; 1782; 1788*

73d   stile] style *1763c; 1788*

73e   O,] Oh *1763c; 1769; 1773; 1782; 1788*

74a   confidente] confidante *1763c; 1769; 1773; 1782; 1788*

74b   statu-quo] *statu quo 1763c; 1769; 1773; 1782; 1788*

74c   ruin?] ruin! *1763c; 1765; 1769; 1773; 1782; 1788*

75a   and receiving the utmost she could hope then, at the present.] and receiving at the present the utmost she could then hope for. *1763c; 1765; 1769; 1773; 1782; 1788*

75b   enclosed] inclosed *1763c; 1769; 1773; 1782; 1788*

75c   endeavour] endeavor *1763c; 1769; 1773; 1782; 1788*

75d   lives.] lives! *1763c; 1769; 1773; 1782; 1788*

75e   Omitted in *1763a*.

75f   prest] pressed *1763c; 1769; 1773; 1782; 1788*

76a   People] people *1763c; 1769; 1773; 1782; 1788*

76b   It] it *1763c; 1769; 1773; 1782; 1788*

76c   The editions from *1763c, 1769, 1773, 1782* and *1788* insert Lord T–'s indirect speech in quotation marks: 'He was sorry for me ... independence.'

Textual Variants

76d this] his *1763c; 1765; 1769; 1773; 1782; 1788*

76e intirely] entirely *1763c; 1765; 1769; 1773; 1782; 1788*

76f accepted. That] accepted – that *1763c; 1769; 1773; 1782; 1788*

76g characters; that] characters – that *1763c; 1769; 1773; 1782; 1788*

76h earth. That] earth – that *1763c; 1769; 1773; 1782; 1788*

76i The editions from *1763c, 1769, 1773, 1782* and *1788* insert Henry Mandeville's indirect speech in quotation marks: 'I was much obliged ... blessing'.

77a apply? Lord T –] apply? – Lord T – *1763c; 1769; 1773; 1782; 1788*

77b Lady Anne's letter follows in quotation marks in the editions from *1763c, 1769, 1773, 1782* and *1788.*

77c Sure] sure *1763c; 1769; 1773; 1782; 1788*

77d So] so *1763c; 1769; 1773; 1782; 1788*

77e Lord Fondville's letter is inserted in quotation marks in the editions from *1763c, 1769, 1773, 1782* and *1788.*

77f intirely] entirely *1763c; 1769; 1773; 1782; 1788*

77g No] no *1763c; 1769; 1773; 1782; 1788*

78a Lord Belmont's letter to Fondville is inserted in quotation marks in the editions from *1763c, 1769, 1773, 1782* and *1788.*

78b endeavoured] endeavored *1763c; 1769; 1773; 1782; 1788*

78c endeavour] endeavor *1763c; 1769; 1773; 1782; 1788*

79a How] how *1763c; 1769; 1773; 1782; 1788*

79b mind! That] mind? that *1763c; 1769; 1773; 1782; 1788*

79c happiness!] happiness? *1763a; 1763c; 1769; 1773; 1782; 1788*

79d hours?] hours! *1763a*

79e Omitted in *1763a.*

79f wretched. I] wretched, I *1773; 1782; 1788*; wretched; I *1763c; 1788*

79g Julia] Julia! *1763c; 1769; 1773; 1782; 1788*

79h O Mordaunt] O Mordaunt! *1763a*

79i Can] can *1763c; 1769; 1773; 1782; 1788*

80a wrote] written *1763c; 1769; 1773; 1782; 1788*

80b Great] great *1763c; 1769; 1773; 1782; 1788*

80c it?] it *1763a*

80d mischief.] mischief: *1763c; 1769; 1773; 1782; 1788*

80e perswading] persuading *1763c; 1769; 1773; 1782; 1788*

80f sacrifise] sacrifice *1763c; 1769; 1773; 1782; 1788*

80g ones] one's *1763c; 1769; 1773; 1782; 1788*

80h kinds] kind *1763a*

80i Never] never *1763c; 1769; 1773; 1782; 1788*

81a harvest home] harvest-home *1763a; 1763c; 1769; 1773; 1782; 1788*

81b various coloured] various-coloured *1763c*

166   *The History of Lady Julia Mandeville*

81c   encrease] increase *1763c, 1769, 1773, 1782, 1788*
81d   Lord Belmont and Lady Anne's dialogue stands in quotation marks in
       1763c, 1769, 1773, 1782, 1788
82a   spirit?] spirit! *1763a*
82b   livery;] livery! *1763c;1764; 1765; 1769; 1773; 1782; 1788*
82c   footman;] footman! *1763c; 1769; 1773; 1782; 1788*
82d   if he knew me, the heart of the host was all I should care for; and that I
       should relish the homely meat of chearful friendship, as well as the splen-
       did profusion of luxury and pride.] 'if he knew me, the heart of the host
       was all I should care for; and that I should relish the homely meat of
       chearful friendship, as well as the splendid profusion of luxury and pride.'
       1763c; 1769; 1773; 1782; 1788
84a   meer] mere *1763c; 1788*
84b   endeavour,] endeavor *1763c; 1769; 1773; 1782; 1788*
84c   But] but *1763c; 1769; 1773; 1782; 1788*
84d   two or three] 2 or 3 *1763a*
84e   acquisition?] acquisition! *1763c; 1773; 1782; 1788*
85a   A Wilmot.] A. Wilmot. *1763c; 1769; 1773; 1782; 1788*; omitted in
       1763a.
85b   Mr. Herbert's account follows in quotation marks in the editions from
       1763c, 1765, 1769, 1773, 1782 and *1788.*
85c   every where,] every-where, *1782*
86a   compleated] completed *1782; 1788*
86b   As a means] In order to *1763c; 1765; 1769; 1773; 1782; 1788*
86c   public; ashamed] public. Ashamed *1763c; 1765; 1769; 1773; 1782;*
       1788
86d   a town,] town, *1763c; 1765; 1769; 1773; 1782; 1788*
87a   encreased] increased *1763c; 1769; 1773; 1782; 1788*
87b   blest] blessed *1763c; 1769; 1773; 1782; 1788*
87c   agree] agreed *1763c; 1765; 1769; 1773; 1782; 1788*
87d   Hark you, Herbert, this blockhead thinks a parson a gentleman; and
       wonders/ at my treating, as I please, a fellow who eats my bread.] 'Hark
       you, Herbert, this blockhead thinks a parson a gentleman; and wonders/
       at my treating, as I please, a fellow who eats my bread.' *1763c; 1769;*
       1773; 1782; 1788
88a   Mr. Herbert's response stands in quotation marks in the editions from
       1763c, 1769, 1773, 1782, 1788.
88b   embarassed] embarrassed *1763c; 1764; 1765; 1769; 1773; 1782; 1788*
88c   encreased] increased *1763c; 1764; 1765; 1769; 1773; 1782; 1788*

Textual Variants

88d Resign the living, said she, and trust to that Heaven whose goodness is over all his creatures.] 'Resign the living, said she, and trust to that Heaven whose goodness is over all his creatures.' *1763c; 1769; 1773; 1782; 1788*

88e honor] honour *1765*

88f Oh] Oh! *1763c; 1765; 1769; 1773; 1782; 1788*

88g its] his *1763c; 1765; 1769; 1773; 1782; 1788*

89a Mordaunt!]Mordaunt, *1763c; 1769; 1773; 1782; 1788*

89b This letter is in quotation marks in *1763c, 1769, 1773, 1782, 1788.*

89c Esteem did I say? Where did I learn this coldness of expression? Let me own,] esteem did I say? where did I learn this coldness of expression? let me own, *1763c; 1769; 1773; 1782; 1788*

89d hope;] hope – *1763c; 1769; 1773; 1782; 1788*; hope: *1765*

89e from] *of 1763c; 1769; 1773; 1782; 1788*

89f from] *from 1763c; 1769; 1773; 1782; 1788*

89g O] Oh! *1765*

89h How] how *1763c; 1769; 1773; 1782; 1788*

89i Her love, her most ardent love] 'Her love, her/ most ardent love' *1763c; 1765; 1769; 1773; 1782; 1788*

89j How] how *1763c; 1769; 1773; 1782; 1788*

89k No,] no, *1763c; 1769; 1773; 1782; 1788*

90a Omitted in *1763a.*

90b Urania.] Urania! – *1763c; 1769; 1773; 1782; 1788*

90c honorable] honourable *1763c; 1773; 1782; 1788*

90d apropos] *à propos 1763c; 1769; 1773; 1782; 1788*; à propos *1764; 1765*

90e a wise writer, to divert the fury of criticism from his works, should throw it now and then an indiscretion in his conduct to play with, as seamen do a tub to the whale.] 'a wise writer, to divert the fury of criticism from his works, should throw it now and then an indiscretion in his conduct to play with, as seamen do a tub to the whale.' *1763c; 1769; 1773; 1782; 1788*

90f musick,] music, *1763c; 1769; 1773; 1782; 1788*

91a past] passed *1763c; 1769; 1773; 1782; 1788*

91b air.] air! *1763c; 1769; 1773; 1782; 1788*

91c his] her *1763c*

92a Good Heaven! Lady Anne Wilmot! Is it possible!] 'Good Heaven! Lady Anne Wilmot! Is it possible!' *1763c; 1769; 1773; 1782; 1788*

92b endeavouring] endeavoring *1763c; 1769; 1773; 1782; 1788*

93a encreased] increased *1763c; 1769; 1773; 1782; 1788*

93 Omitted in *1763a.*

93b past] passed *1763c; 1765; 1769; 1773; 1782; 1788*

93c O] Oh! *1763c; 1765; 1769; 1773; 1782; 1788*

168   *The History of Lady Julia Mandeville*

93d   William's;] William *1763c*
94a   How] how *1763c*; *1769*; *1773*; *1782*; *1788*
94b   Could] could *1763c*; *1769*; *1773*; *1782*; *1788*
94c   Once] once *1763c*; *1769*; *1773*; *1782*; *1788*
94d   This letter stands within quotations marks in the following editions *1763c*, *1769*, *1773*, *1782*, *1788*.
94e   tender] great *1763c*; *1764*; *1765*; *1769*; *1773*; *1782*; *1788*
94f   her: to] her. To *1763c*; *1765*; *1769*; *1773*; *1782*; *1788*
94g   intreated] entreated *1763c*; *1764*; *1765*; *1769*; *1773*; *1782*; *1788*
94h   honorable] honourable *1763c*; *1765*; *1788*
94i   encreased] increased *1763c*; *1769*; *1773*; *1782*; *1788*
95a   well-dissembled] well dissembled *1763a*
95b   manner: convinced] manner. Convinced *1763c*; *1769*; *1773*; *1782*; *1788*
96a   a life,] my life *1763c*; *1769*; *1773*; *1782*; *1788*
96b   O] Oh *1763c*; *1769*; *1773*; *1782*; *1788*; Oh! *1765*
96c   How] how *1763c*; *1769*; *1773*; *1782*; *1788*
96d   How] how *1763c*; *1769*; *1773*; *1782*; *1788*
96e   Omitted in *1763a*.
97a   of you] youof *1763a*
98a   He] he *1763c*; *1769*; *1773*; *1782*; *1788*
98b   fortune.] fortune! *1763c*; *1769*; *1773*; *1782*; *1788*
98c   O] Oh! *1763c*; *1765*; *1769*; *1773*; *1782*; *1788*
98d   intirely] entirely *1763c*; *1769*; *1773*; *1782*; *1788*
98e   wrote] written *1763c*; *1769*; *1773*; *1782*; *1788*
98f   to-morrow] To-morrow *1765*
98g   thought,] thought! *1763c*; *1782*; *1788*
98h   entreated] intreated *1773*; *1782*; *1788*
98i   My] my *1763c*; *1769*; *1773*; *1782*; *1788*
99a   happy] sorry *1765*
99b   Can] can *1763c*; *1769*; *1773*; *1782*; *1788*
100a   past] passed *1763c*; *1769*; *1773*; *1782*; *1788*
100b   Sudley-Farm] Sudley Farm *1763a*
100c   Are] are *1763c*; *1769*; *1773*; *1782*; *1788*
100d   Or] or *1763c*; *1769*; *1773*; *1782*; *1788*
100e   love?] love. *1763c*; *1773*; *1782*; *1788*
100f   it] it it *1769*
100g   tygress] tigress *1763c*; *1765*; *1769*; *1773*; *1782*; *1788*
100h   How] how *1763c*; *1769*; *1773*; *1782*; *1788*
100i   A billet. Some despairing inamorato: Indeed?]a billet! some despairing inamorato indeed! *1769*; *1773*; *1782*; *1788*; some despairing inamorato indeed? *1763c*

Textual Variants 169

100j tidi didum] tidi-didum *1763c; 1769; 1773; 1782; 1788*

100k this; that] this: 'That *1763c; 1769; 1773; 1782; 1788*. The passage from here to 'consent' is in quotations marks in the editions from *1769, 1773, 1782, 1788.*

100l honour] honor *1763a; 1763c; 1764; 1765; 1769; 1773; 1782; 1788*

101a 'Almost prevailed on.'] 'Almost prevailed on!' *1763c; 1765; 1769; 1773; 1782; 1788*

101b Really these are pretty airs.] Really these are pretty airs! *1763c; 1769; 1773; 1782; 1788*

101c Miss Hastings,] Miss Hastings! *1763c; 1764; 1769; 1773; 1782; 1788*

101d equal.] equal! *1763c; 1764; 1769; 1773; 1782; 1788*

101e teizing] teazing *1763c; 1764; 1765; 1769; 1773; 1782; 1788*

101f to] too *1763c*

101g niece?] niece! *1763c; 1788*

101h honor] honour *1763c; 1782; 1788*

101i Or suppose, Madam, said I, the three Goddesses on mount Ida, with Harry Mandeville for our Paris?] 'Or 'suppose, Madam,' said I, 'the three Goddesses on mount Ida, with Harry Mandeville for our Paris?' *1763c; 1769; 1773; 1782; 1788*

101j Omitted in *1763a.*

102a shall] shal *1763c*

102b wish!] wish. *1763c; 1769; 1773; 1782; 1788*

102c Omitted in *1763a*

102d hath] has *1763c; 1769; 1773; 1782; 1788*

102e honored] honoured *1763c; 1788*

102f Tory!] Tory? *1763a*; tory! *1763c; 1769; 1773; 1782; 1788*

102g petticoat-politics] petticoat politics *1763a*

102h Lord,] Lord! *1763c; 1769; 1773; 1782; 1788*

103a Yes,] Yes: *1763c; 1769; 1773; 1782; 1788*

103b Should] should *1763c; 1769; 1773; 1782; 1788*

103c There] there *1763c; 1769; 1773; 1782; 1788*

103d She] she *1763c; 1769; 1773; 1782; 1788*

103e In] in *1763c; 1769; 1773; 1782; 1788*

103f How] how *1763c; 1769; 1773; 1782; 1788*

103g My] my *1763c; 1769; 1773; 1782; 1788*

103h enclosed] inclosed *1763c; 1769; 1773; 1782; 1788*

103i The correspondence between Lord Belmont and J. Mandeville is inserted in quotation marks in the following editions: *1763c, 1769, 1773, 1782, 1788.*

103j 1752] 1751 *1763c; 1769; 1773; 1782; 1788*

103k Col.] Colonel *1763c; 1769; 1773; 1782; 1788*

170 *The History of Lady Julia Mandeville*

103l   favour] favor *1763c*; *1765*; *1769*; *1773*; *1782*; *1788*
103m   flaw,] flaw *1763c*; *1765*; *1769*; *1773*; *1782*; *1788*
103n   blest] blessed *1763c*; *1769*; *1773*; *1782*; *1788*
103o   agreeable] agreable *1769*
104a   court-dependence] court dependence *1763a*
104b   of mind] of the mind *1763c*; *1773*; *1782*; *1788*
104c   any] an *1763c*; *1769*; *1773*; *1782*; *1788*
105a   controll] control *1763c*; *1773*; *1782*; *1788*
105b   ones] one's *1763c*; *1769*; *1773*; *1782*; *1788*
106a   children.] children! *1782*; *1788*
106b   Obedient] obedient *1763a*; *1763c*; *1769*; *1773*; *1782*; *1788*
106c   happiness: the] happiness. The *1763c*; *1769*; *1773*; *1782*; *1788*
106d   What] what *1763c*; *1769*; *1773*; *1782*; *1788*
106e   coquette: if] coquette. If *1763c*; *1769*; *1773*; *1782*; *1788*
106f   Or] or *1763c*; *1769*; *1773*; *1782*; *1788*
106g   'Dear madam, said I, if your Ladyship would lend one your Cestus.']
        'Dear madam,' said I, 'if your Ladyship would lend one your Cestus.'
        1763c; *1769*; *1773*; *1782*; *1788*
106h   Lady Belmont's answer follows in a new paragraph in *1763c, 1769, 1773,
        1782, 1788.*
107a   se'nnight] sevennight *1763c*; *1769*; *1773*; *1782*; *1788*
107b   pavillion] pavilion *1763c*; *1764*; *1765*; *1782*; *1788*
107c   Not] not *1763c*; *1769*; *1773*; *1782*; *1788*
107d   Something] something *1763c*; *1769*; *1773*; *1782*; *1788*
107e   affair] affair! *1763c*; *1769*; *1773*; *1782*; *1788*
107f   What] what *1763c*; *1769*; *1773*; *1782*; *1788*
108a   enclosed] inclosed *1763a*; *1769*; *1773*; *1782*; *1788*
108b   'I will'] I will *1763a*; 'I will.' *1763c*; *1769*; *1773*; *1782*; *1788*
108c   O heavens] Oh! Heavens! *1765*; O Heavens!
108d   forgot] forget *1763c*; *1769*; *1773*; *1782*; *1788*
108e   'An interesting event.'] 'An interesting event!' *1763c*; *1765*; *1769*; *1773*;
        1782; *1788*
109a   humor] humour *1763c*; *1765*; *1773*; *1782*; *1788*
109b   enclosed] inclosed *1769*; *1773*; *1782*; *1788*
109c   This letter follows in quotation marks in *1763c, 1769, 1773, 1782, 1788.*
109d   recomending] recommending *1763a*; *1763c*; *1769*; *1773*; *1782*; *1788*
109e   behavior] behaviour *1763c*; *1769*; *1773*; *1782*; *1788*
109f   persons] person *1763c*; *1765*; *1769*; *1773*; *1782*; *1788*
110a   endeavoured] endeavored *1763c*; *1769*; *1773*; *1782*; *1788*
110b   entreat] intreat *1763c*; *1773*; *1782*; *1788*
110c   pavillion] pavilion *1763c*; *1764*; *1765*; *1782*; *1788*

Textual Variants

110d We] we *1763a*

110e Farewel] Farewell *1763c; 1788*

110f Do not you doat on a masquerade, Bellville?] Do you not doat on a masquerade, Bellville? *1763c; 1765; 1769; 1773; 1782; 1788*

110g enchanting.] enchanting! *1763c; 1769; 1773; 1782; 1788*

110h Heavens … A. WILMOT] Omitted in *1763a.*

111a past] passed *1763c; 1769; 1773; 1782; 1788*

111b ardently expected] ardently-expected *1763c; 1764; 1769; 1773; 1782; 1788*

111c blood. My] blood: my *1763a*

111d Let] let *1763c; 1764; 1765; 1769; 1773; 1782; 1788*

111e May] may *1763c; 1769; 1773; 1782; 1788*

111f May] may *1763c; 1769; 1773; 1782; 1788*

111g Yes] yes *1763c; 1769; 1773; 1782; 1788*

111h marriage: over-awed] marriage. Over-awed *1763c; 1769; 1773; 1782; 1788*

111i First] first *1763c; 1769; 1773; 1782; 1788*

111j Heaven] Heaven? *1763c; 1764; 1769; 1773; 1782; 1788*

111k My] my *1763c; 1764; 1769; 1773; 1782; 1788*

111l Yes,] yes *1763c; 1769; 1773; 1782; 1788*

111m What] what *1763c; 1764; 1769; 1773; 1782; 1788*

111n distraction.] distraction – *1763a*; distraction! *1763c; 1765; 1769; 1773; 1782; 1788*

112a Harry's? Raised] Harry's; raised *1763c; 1765; 1769; 1773; 1782; 1788*

112b How] how *1763c; 1769; 1773; 1782; 1788*

112c Oh,] Oh! *1763c; 1769; 1773; 1782; 1788*

112d to-bed] to bed *1763c; 1788*

112e endeavor] endeavour *1765*

112f justice,] justice: *1763c; 1788*

113a despair] Despair *1763c; 1764; 1765; 1769; 1773; 1782; 1788*

113b Oh,] Oh! *1763c; 1765*

113c How is this scene of happiness changed!] How is this scene of happiness changed? *1763a*; how is this scene of happiness changed! *1763c; 1769; 1773; 1782; 1788*

113d ill-suited] ill suited *1763a; 1763c; 1769; 1773; 1782; 1788*

113e these] those *1763c; 1773; 1782; 1788*

113f letter] Letter *1763c; 1773; 1782; 1788*

113g Oh,] Oh! *1763c; 1765; 1769; 1773; 1782; 1788*

113h If he dies – But] If he dies, but *1763c*

113i sentence! – The] sentence! The *1763c; 1788*

113j He] he *1769; 1782*

172 *The History of Lady Julia Mandeville*

113k Oh,] Oh! *1769; 1782*
113l enclosed] inclosed *1763c; 1769; 1773; 1782; 1788*
114a This letter follows in quotation marks in the editions *1763c, 1769, 1773, 1782, 1788.*
114b arrival] arrival, *1763c; 1765; 1769; 1773; 1782; 1788*
114c will] I will *1763c; 1769; 1773; 1782; 1788*
115a behavior] behaviour *1763c; 1769; 1773; 1782; 1788*
115b 'How ill, said he, has] 'How ill,' said he, 'has *1763c; 1769; 1773; 1782; 1788*
115c Who shall tell this to Lady Julia, yet how conceal it from her?] Who shall tell this to Lady Julia? yet how conceal it from her? *1763c; 1769; 1773; 1782; 1788;* Who shall tell this to Lady Julia? Yet how conceal it from her? *1764; 1765*
116a bedside] bed-side *1763c; 1782*
116b 'Lady Anne, said she, does he live?'] 'Lady Anne,' said she, 'does he live?' *1763c; 1769; 1773; 1782; 1788*
116c Oh,] Oh! *1763c; 1769; 1773; 1782; 1788*
116d I wept with her. She saw my tears,] I wept with her: she saw my tears, *1763a*
116e parents] Parents *1764*
116f May] may *1763c; 1769; 1773; 1782; 1788*
116g suffer.] suffer! *1763c; 1769; 1773; 1782; 1788*
116h Friendship] friendship *1763c; 1773; 1782; 1788*
116i Oh,] Oh! *1763c; 1765; 1769; 1773; 1782; 1788*
116j Yes] yes *1763c; 1765; 1769; 1773; 1782; 1788*
116k But] but *1763c; 1765; 1769; 1773; 1782; 1788*
117a beings] Beings *1764*
117b Why] why *1763c; 1769; 1773; 1782; 1788*
117c But whither am I wandering?] But whither am I wandering; *1763c; 1788*
117d How] how *1763c; 1769; 1773; 1782; 1788*
117e She will live;] she will live! *1763c; 1769; 1773; 1782; 1788*
117f prayers. –] prayers. *1763c; 1769; 1773; 1782; 1788*
117g She] she *1763c; 1769; 1773; 1782; 1788*
118a Can] can *1763c; 1769; 1773; 1782; 1788*
118b Shall] shall *1763c; 1769; 1773; 1782; 1788*
118c entreated] intreated *1763c; 1769; 1773; 1782; 1788*
118d past] passed *1763c; 1769; 1773; 1782; 1788*
119a Where] where *1763c; 1769; 1773; 1782; 1788*
120a her,] her? *1763c; 1765; 1769; 1773; 1782; 1788*
120b clay. Those] clay; those *1763a*
120c vermillion] vermilion *1763c; 1782; 1788*

120d	on] one *1763c*; *1788*
120e	Youth] youth *1763c*; *1769*; *1773*; *1782*; *1788*
120f	air. Alas!] air; alas! *1763c*; *1769*; *1773*; *1782*; *1788*
120g	us all to retire.] us to retire. *1763c*; *1769*; *1773*; *1782*; *1788*
120h	What] what *1763c*; *1769*; *1773*; *1782*; *1788*
120i	Oh, Bellville! but shall presumptuous man dare to arraign the ways of Heaven!] Oh! Belville – But shall presumptuous man dare to arraign the ways of Heaven! *1765*; Oh! Belville! – But shall presumptuous man dare to arraign the ways of Heaven? *1763c*; *1769*; *1773*; *1782*; *1788*
120j	encrease] increase *1763c*; *1769*; *1773*; *1782*; *1788*
121a	endeavoring] endeavouring *1763c*; *1782*; *1788*
121b	emotions abate] emotion abates *1763c*; *1782*; *1788*; emotions abates *1765*; *1769*; *1773*
121c	encrease] increase *1763c*; *1769*; *1773*; *1782*; *1788*
121d	if] if, *1763c*; *1769*; *1773*; *1782*; *1788*
121e	her. Every] her; every *1763a*
121f	pleased] pleas'd *1763c*
122a	Death] death *1763c*; *1769*; *1773*; *1782*; *1788*
122b	How] how *1763c*; *1769*; *1773*; *1782*; *1788*
122c	The] the *1763c*; *1769*; *1773*; *1782*; *1788*
122d	encreasing] increasing *1763c*; *1769*; *1773*; *1782*; *1788*
122e	Oh] Oh! *1763c*; *1765*; *1769*; *1773*; *1782*; *1788*
122f	How] how *1763c*; *1769*; *1773*; *1782*; *1788*
123a	Death] death *1763c*; *1769*; *1773*; *1782*; *1788*
123b	show] shew *1763c*; *1769*; *1773*; *1782*; *1788*
123c	May] may *1763c*; *1769*; *1773*; *1782*; *1788*
123d	sattin:] satten *1764*; *1765*; *1769*
123e	gause] gauze *1763c*; *1769*; *1773*; *1782*; *1788*
123f	'Lady Anne, said he, you] 'Lady Anne,' said he, 'you *1763c*; *1769*; *1773*; *1782*; *1788*
124a	To-morrow I will be happy?] 'tomorrow I will be happy?' *1763c*; *1769*; *1773*; *1782*; *1788*
124b	O] Oh! *1763c*; *1769*; *1773*; *1782*; *1788*
124c	O] oh! *1763c*; Oh! 1765
124d	One] one *1763c*
124e	embrace] embraced *1763c*; *1765*; *1769*; *1773*; *1782*; *1788*
125a	pleasureable] pleasurable *1763c*; *1764*; *1765*; *1769*; *1773*; *1782*; *1788*
125b	perswaded] persuaded *1763c*; *1769*; *1773*; *1782*; *1788*
125c	pavillion] pavilion *1763c*; *1764*; *1765*; *1773*; *1782*; *1788*
125d	ardour] ardor *1763c*; *1769*; *1773*; *1782*; *1788*
125e	parental] paternal *1763c*; *1769*; *1773*; *1782*; *1788*

174 *The History of Lady Julia Mandeville*

125f   tomb,] tomb! *1763c; 1769; 1773; 1782; 1788*

125g   strow] strew *1763c; 1764; 1765; 1769; 1773; 1782; 1788*

126a   groups] group *1763c; 1782; 1788*; groupe *1769; 1773;*

126b   Heaven;] Heaven! *1763c; 1769; 1773; 1782; 1788*

126c   grave.] grave! *1763c; 1769; 1773; 1782; 1788*

126d   pavillion] pavilion *1763c; 1765; 1782; 1788*

126e   perswaded] persuaded *1763c; 1769; 1773; 1782; 1788*

126f   In *1763c, 1769, 1773, 1782* and *1788*, this letter is signed A. Wilmot.

126g   encrease] increase *1763c, 1769, 1773, 1782, 1788*

126h   sorrow] sorrows *1763a*

127a   Allow] allow *1763c; 1769; 1773; 1782; 1788*

127b   antient] ancient *1763c; 1782; 1788*

127c   with:] with. *1763c; 1769; 1773; 1782; 1788*

127d   Mr. Mandeville's] Mr. Madeville *1763c*

127e   endeavor] endeavour *1763c; 1764; 1765; 1782; 1788*

127f   Oh,] Oh! *1763c; 1765; 1769; 1773; 1782; 1788*

127g   angel virtues] angel-virtues *1763c; 1782; 1788*

128a   ardently expected] ardently-expected *1763c; 1782; 1788*

128b   Oh, my friend] Oh! my friend – *1763c; 1769; 1773; 1782; 1788*

128c   endeavor] endeavour *1763c; 1773; 1782; 1788*

128d   paradice] paradise *1763c; 1764; 1765; 1769; 1773; 1782; 1788*

128e   friendship,] friendship. *1763c; 1764; 1765; 1769; 1773; 1782; 1788*

129a   Oh,] Oh! *1763c; 1765; 1769; 1773; 1782; 1788*

SILENT CORRECTIONS

Volume I

p. 1, l. 8:   Thr SECOND EDITION.] THE SECOND EDITION.

p. 4, l. 36:   poisened] poisoned

p. 9, l. 11:   must] most

p. 12, l. 1:   faithfull] faithful

p. 13, l. 16:   sprightilness] sprightliness

p. 15, l. 30:   opressive] oppressive

p. 15, l. 34:   dont] don't (Emendation follows the editions from 1763c, 1764, 1765, 1769, 1773, 1782, 1788.)

p. 17, l. 38:   was.] was illnatured

p. 18, l. 33:   acquainance] acquaintance

p. 19, l. 7:   his] is

p. 20, l. 36:   he he] he (Emendation follows the editions from 1763c, 1764, 1765, 1769, 1773, 1782, 1788.)

p. 22, l. 33:   way.] way.' (Emendation follows the editions from 1763c, 1764, 1765, 1769, 1773, 1782, 1788.)

p. 26, l. 33:   the the] the

p. 26, l. 36:   Espirit] Esprit

p. 27, l. 7:   absoulutely] absolutely

p. 28, l. 11:   arouud] around

p. 28, l. 36:   theyare] they are

p. 34, l. 23:   life,] life.

p. 36, l. 4:   clok] clock

p. 39, l. 27:   as to cruelty of rejecting] as to the cruelty of rejecting (Emendation follows the editions from 1763c, 1769, 1773, 1782, 1788.)

p. 41, l. 6:   eveining] evening

p. 41, l. 11:   me yet:] me: yet (Emendation follows the editions from 1763c, 1769, 1773, 1782, 1788.)

p. 48, l. 21:   its] it is (Emendation follows the editions from 1763c, 1765, 1769, 1773, 1782, 1788.)

p. 49, l. 16:   ncessary] necessary

176   *The History of Lady Julia Mandeville*

p. 49, l. 36:   my] may
p. 51, l. 6:   adition] addition
p. 51, l. 16:   ones] one's (Emendation follows the editions from 1763c, 1769, 1773, 1782, 1788.)
p. 51, l. 17:   ones] one's (Emendation follows the editions from 1763c, 1769, 1773, 1782, 1788.)
p. 53, l. 1:   ones] one's (Emendation follows the editions from 1763c, 1765, 1769, 1773, 1782, 1788.)
p. 56, l. 9:   stoped] stopped (Emendation follows the editions from 1763c, 1764, 1765, 1769, 1773, 1782, 1788.)
p. 59, l. 12:   are are] are
p. 59, l. 25:   aprobation] approbation
p. 63, l. 28:   sweets] sweet
p. 63, l. 33   to night] to-night (Emendation follows the editions from 1763c, 1764, 1765, 1769, 1773, 1782, 1788.)
p. 64, l. 9:   generl] general
p. 65, l. 9:   many] may
p. 65, l. 28:   properly] improperly (Emendation follows the editions from 1763a, 1763c, 1764, 1765, 1769, 1773, 1782, 1788.)
p. 65, l. 31:   childless] childless,
p. 66, l. 11:   Yestrday] Yesterday
p. 68, l. 12:   unconected] unconnected (Emendation follows the editions from 1765, 1769, 1773, 1782, 1788.)
p. 68, l. 12:   (The editions from 1763a, 1763b, 1764 and 1765 continue after this dash with Lady Anne's response without a line break. The emendation follows the editions from 1763c, 1769, 1773, 1782 and 1788, which start a new paragraph.)
p. 69, l. 4:   known] unknown

Volume II

p. 73, l. 35:   The second edition does not distinguish between Lady Anne's speech to Lady Julia and her commentary, but continues in the same line. The emendation follows the editions from 1763c, 1769, 1773, 1782 and 1788 for reason of clarity.
p. 77, l. 21:   disapprove] disapproves
p. 79, l. 39:   but all conspires to do unto me:] but all conspires to undo me:
p. 80, l. 18:   buterflies] butterflies
p. 82, l. 4:   expelled my estate] expelled from my estate
p. 82, l. 5:   delared] declared (Emendation follows the editions from 1763a, 1763c, 1769, 1773, 1782, 1788.)

Silent Corrections

p. 89, l. 10: I I] I (Emendation follows the editions from 1763a, 1763c, 1769, 1773, 1782, 1788.)
p. 90, l. 28: it] in (Emendation follows the editions from 1763c, 1773, 1782, 1788.)
p. 95, l. 24: can conceive I what] can conceive what
p. 95, l. 37: solem] solemn
p. 96, l. 41: makes it] makes us (Emendation follows 1763c and 1788.)
p. 98, l. 18: trasport] transport
p. 109, l. 4: thir] their
p. 110, l. 4: abborrence] abhorrence
p. 110, l. 6: mortal] moral
p. 110, l. 9: conversanion] conversation
p. 111, l. 4: soul,] soul.
p. 111, l. 34: of of] of
p. 112, l. 8: to to-night] to-night
p. 116, l. 15: betweeen] between
p. 117, l. 36: and tears] and with tears (Emendation follows the editions from 1763c, 1773, 1782, 1788.)
p. 18, l. 25: tenderterness] tenderness
p. 118, l. 32: enteated] entreated (Emendation follows the editions from 1763a, 1764, 1765); enteated] intreated 1763c; 1769; 1773; 1782; 1788

APPENDIX A: CONTEMPORARY REVIEWS

From the *Critical Review or, Annals of Literature* (London: A. Hamilton, 1763), vol. 16, pp. 41–5.

This history, like those of Grandison, &c. is carried on in a series of letters, each of which, without any introduction, sufficiently points out its author. Lady Julia, one of the most amiable young creatures that ever nature formed, is the daughter of the earl of Belmont, and heiress to 16,000l. a year. She lives at her father's noble seat in the country, under the eye of her parents, the most worthy couple in England, and is sometimes visited by a young gentleman, a relation of her own, one Mr. Mandeville, who has all the accomplishments both external and internal that nature and education can give him, but his father is still alive, and his fortune just sufficient to support him as a gentleman. [...]

Such, or something like it, is the outline of this performance; but whatever opinion the reader may have of the design, he will find it an original in point of execution, especially colouring. Several episodes, tending to promote the main subjects, are introduced with great judgment. The character of Lord T. a man of sense and experience, but swayed by interest, and the fashion of despising obscure merit, is drawn with exquisite judgment. We cannot, however, on the whole, help thinking, that that of Lady Anne Wilmot is by far the greatest ornament of the work, and is supported in her letters with a spirit and propriety that is not excelled, if equalled, by any author in this species of writing. [...]

If we were disposed to find fault with this agreeable performance it would be for the author's introducing politics at all; though we cannot disown it is done with great propriety, and her wheeling us too much about in easy chair, on the carpet of description. In the main, however, she is as sentimental as Rousseau, and as interesting as Richardson, without the caprice of the one, or the tediousness of the other. We cannot recommend the catastrophe.

180 *The History of Lady Julia Mandeville*

From the *Monthly Review or Literary Journal* (London: R. Griffiths, 1763), vol. 29, pp. 159–60.

This performance is distinguished from the common production of the novel tribe, by ease and elegance of style, variety and truth of character, delicacy and purity of sentiment. The plan is simple and natural, the incidents are interesting and important, the catastrophe highly affecting, and exemplary. A tender love-tale is the basis of the work, which is carried on in a series of letters, less tedious, because less laboured, than those of the celebrated Richardson: of whose writings, this most agreeable history seems, however, in some respects, to be an imitation. If we have any fault with to find it, it is that which some have objected to Clarissa; the heart-rending, tragic *event*; scarce to be supported by a Reader of any feeling.

The unhappy fate of the amiable Harry Mandeville, and his lovely Julia, with the unutterable distress of their worthy parents, is, indeed, most dreadful. We really could not support the perusal, without giving, way to those tender emotions which the ingenious unknown Writer so well knows to inspire; and from which we were gladly relieved by the reflection, that the story is fictitious. The moral, however, is excellent; and we doubt not, but the exemplary fate of the rash and infatuated Mandeville, will preach more powerfully against the horrid practice of duelling, than all the dispassionate reasoning in the world: not excepting, perhaps, even the masterly arguments contained in Rousseau's Eloisa.

From *The London Magazine for Gentleman's Monthly Intelligencer* (London: R. Baldwin, 1763), vol. 32, pp 374–8, 433–6.

This piece, lately published in two volumes 12 mo, consists of a series of letters from Henry Mandeville, Esq; to George Mordaunt, Esq; his friend, and from lady Anne Wilmot, to her admirer, col. Belville, with a few intermediate ones from lord Belmont, &c. &.c relating the following incidents.

Mr. Henry Mandeville, indebted to the best of fathers for every accomplishment education could bestow, and to nature for an excellent heart and a fine person, is a guest at the seat of lord Belmont, a worthy nobleman and his near relation, where he conceives a violent passion for lady Julia, that nobleman's daughter, and only child, which, for some time, he miscalls friendship. The characters of that young lady and the rest of the family are thus drawn: [...]

The circumstance of Mr. Mandeville may be gathered from the following quotation. [...]

Awed by the inferiority of his fortune, he long struggles to conceal his ardent passion; but lord Belmont and his lady leaving the young ladies in his charge, upon a sudden call to London, gave him such, frequent opportunities of con-

Appendix A 181

versing with, and discovering still new charms in the object of his wishes, that he forms a resolution of leaving Belmont and all its delights, rather than be ungrateful to his lordship, or cruelly involve the young lady in his misery. To this resolve he is still more and more prompted by the goodness of lord Belmont, who, by a letter, proposes to him the being a candidate for a borough, the then member being in a state of health that rendered his life uncertain, [...]

The dreadful condition of the surviving parents and friends of these ill-fated lovers is not to be expressed in other words than those of the author, therefore we shall draw a veil over their sorrows, and conclude this article by observing that the interesting and engaging volumes we have thus loosely epitomized, are replete with refined and exalted sentiments, abound in just and spirited reflections and animated descriptions: The characters are well drawn, and the interwoven adventures extremely entertaining – In short, nothing but the horrid catastrophe, could abate of that high satisfaction, the perusal must convey to every generous and delicate mind.

La Gazette Littéraire de l'Europe (Paris: Imprimerie de la Gazette de France, 1764), pp. 331–4 (my translation). It reviewed the third edition of the novel.

This novel, like those of Richardson, is a collection of letters which the characters write to each other. As these performers all have different dispositions and each of them takes a different view on things, the result is a sort of drama, in which the hero and the heroine of this piece, as well as their respective confidantes, announce what had happened, providing the exposition, intrigue and the denouement.

The History of Julia Mandeville is perhaps the best novel from this genre that has appeared in England since *Clarissa* and *Grandison*. We find truth and interest in it; and the works of all genres, even those of history, owe their success to the art of awakening interest; for stronger reasons, this is even more applicable to novels, which are imagined stories.

Elie Fréron (ed.), *L'Année Littéraire* (Amsterdam: C. J. Panckoucke, 1764), vol. 5, pp. 172–202 (my translation).

This work surely deserves to succeed, yet one should beware of comparing it to *Clarissa* or *Grandison*. It would be like comparing a beautiful Scene to a beautiful Tragedy in five Acts. *Julia Mandeville* excites the strongest emotions at the very end of the second volume: one's heart is moved, touched, torn; one is penetrated by the horrifying truth that, in this world, virtue seems destined to suffer all adversities ... Those Readers who have little taste for tear-shedding, will find that, in general, the first volume and the first half of the second lack action. But,

182 *The History of Lady Julia Mandeville*

Sir, what happy details! What truth above all in the manners! What purity of sentiments! The translator is worthy of the model; his style is lively, noble & full of the interest that breathes through the original.

From Anna Laetitia Barbauld (ed.), *British Novelists*, 50 vols (London: Rivington, 1810), vol. 27, pp. 1–212.

The two novels by which she [Frances Brooke] is best known are *Emily Montague* and *Julia Mandeville*. The latter is a simple, well connected story, told with elegance and strong effect. It is a forcible appeal to the feelings against the savage practice of duelling. Emily Montague is less interesting in the story, which serves as a thread to connect a great deal of beautiful description of the manners and scenery of Canada, which country the author had visited. Mrs. Brooke was perhaps the first female novel-writer who attained a perfect purity and polish of style.

APPENDIX B: FROM FRANCES BROOKE'S WEEKLY PERIODICAL THE *OLD MAID* (1755–1756) AND FICTION

From the *Old Maid*, 1 (15 November 1755)

Amidst the present glut of essay papers it may appear an odd attempt in a woman to think of adding to the number; but as most of them like summer insects, just make their appearance and are gone; I see no reason why I may not buz among them a little; though it is possible I may join the short-liv'd generation, and this day month be as much forgot as if I had never existed. Be that as it may, in defiance of all criticism, I will write: everybody knows an English woman has a natural right to expose herself as much as she pleases, a right some of us seem lately to have made a pretty sufficient use of; and since I feel a violent inclination to show my prodigious wisdom to my contemporaries, I should think it giving up the privileges of the sex, to desist from my purposes; at the same time leaving my fellow subjects the same liberty of reading or not as they shall think meet.

From the *Old Maid*, 7 (27 November 1755)

My niece, Julia, has not only sentiments of her own with regard to marriage, very different from the generality of the world and such as I think a little imprudent; but is encouraged in this way of thinking by a friend she is extremely fond of; a very good girl, about her own age: one I approve upon the whole, but, from passing the greatest part of the time in the country, inclined to be romantic, a circumstance I am by no means pleased with: indeed, though I am an enemy to what is called a town education, yet I think young women, whose circumstances will admit of now and then a visit to London, may be too much confined to the country: living there, in simplicity, and a degree of ignorance, unacquainted with life, and the dangers to which our sex are exposed, they fancy the world like the shades of Arcadia; and too often fall a sacrifice to the first military swain who happens to be quartered in the nearest market town: if they have fortunes, they are run away within an honest way; and if not, the Lord have mercy upon them

– 183 –

184   *The History of Lady Julia Mandeville*

... Marriage, where the disproportion of rank and fortune is very great, especially if the disadvantage is on the woman's side, seldom turns out happy. There is so much delicacy required on the obliging side, to lessen the pain of receiving a benefit, and so much circumspection on the part of the obliged to prevent suspicion of interestedness, that it is next to impossible that their lives be passed agreeably. Equality is necessary to friendship; and without friendship marriage must be at the best insipid, but oftener a state of perfect misery.

From Frances Brooke's translation of Marie Jeanne Riccoboni's *Letters from Juliet Lady Catesby to Lady Henrietta Campley* (1760)

Letter III

Thursday, Lord Danby's.

I write to you from the most agreeable Place, perhaps, in Nature: From my Window I have a View of Woods, Waters, Meadows, the most beautiful landscape imaginable: Everything expresses Calmness and Tranquillity: This smiling Abode, is an Image of the Soft Peace, which reigns in the Soul of the Sage, who inhabits it. This amiable Dwelling carries one insensibly to reflect; to retire into one's Self; but one cannot at all Time relish this kind of Retreat; one may find in the Recesses of the Heart more importunate Pursuers than those from whom Solitude delivers us. Lord Danby received us perfectly well; could one imagine a Man like him would not think Retirement a Misfortune? It is rare, very rare, my Dear, that Persons born in a High Rank, educated in the Hurry of the World, in the toilsome Inactivity of a Court can find in themselves the Resources against Lassitude. The Remembrance of the past, often offers nothing to their View but a Chain of Follies and Weaknesses, which seen in cold Blood, appear in their true Colour. One must have all my Lord *Danby's* virtues, to find the Examination of one's own Heart a pleasing Employment.

From *The History Emily Montague* (1769)

Letter 80
To Miss RIVERS, Clarges Street

Silleri, Feb. 25.

THOSE who have heard no more of a Canadian winter than what regards the intenseness of its cold, must suppose it a very joyless season: 'tis, I assure you, quite otherwise; there are indeed some days here of the severity of which those who were never out of England can form no conception; but those days seldom exceed a dozen in a whole winter, nor do they come in succession; but at intermediate periods, as the winds set in from the North-West; which, coming some hundred leagues, from frozen lakes and rivers, over woods and mountains cov-

Appendix B 185

ered with snow, would be insupportable, were it not for the furs with which the country abounds, in such variety and plenty as to be within the reach of all its inhabitants.

Thus defended, the British belles set the winter of Canada at defiance; and the season of which you seem to entertain such terrible ideas, is that of the utmost chearfulness and festivity.

But what particularly pleases me is, there is no place where women are of such importance: not one of the sex, who has the least share of attractions, is without a levee of beaux interceding for the honor of attending her on some party, of which every day produces three or four.

I am just returned from one of the most agreable jaunts imagination can paint, to the island of Orleans, by the falls of Montmorenci; the latter is almost nine miles distant, across the great bason of Quebec; but as we are obliged to reach it in winter by the waving line, our direct road being intercepted by the inequalities of the ice, it is now perhaps a third more. You will possibly suppose a ride of this kind must want one of the greatest essentials to entertainment, that of variety, and imagine it only one dull whirl over an unvaried plain of snow: on the contrary, my dear, we pass hills and mountains of ice in the trifling space of these few miles. The bason of Quebec is formed by the conflux of the rivers St. Charles and Montmorenci with the great river St. Lawrence, the rapidity of whose flood tide, as these rivers are gradually seized by the frost, breaks up the ice, and drives it back in heaps, till it forms ridges of transparent rock to an height that is astonishing, and of a strength which bids defiance to the utmost rage of the most furiously rushing tide.

This circumstance makes this little journey more pleasing than you can possibly conceive: the serene blue sky above, the dazling brightness of the sun, and the colors from the refraction of its rays on the transparent part of these ridges of ice, the winding course these oblige you to make, the sudden disappearing of a train of fifteen or twenty carrioles, as these ridges intervene, which again discover themselves on your rising to the top of the frozen mount, the tremendous appearance both of the ascent and descent, which however are not attended with the least danger; all together give a grandeur and variety to the scene, which almost rise to enchantment.

From the Preface to the second edition of *The Excursion* (1785)

"I APPEAL TO THE PEOPLE," was the celebrated form in which a citizen of ancient Rome refused his acquiescence in any sentence of which he felt the injustice.

On giving a second edition of THE EXCURSION to the public, I find myself irresistibly impelled to use the same form of appeal from an illiberal spirit of prejudice, and perhaps of affectation, which has lately endeavoured not only to depreciate works of imagination in general, but to exclude from the road of literary fame, even by the flowery paths of romance, a sex which from quick sensibility, native delicacy of mind, facility of expression, and a style at once animated and natural, is perhaps, when possessed of real genius, most peculiarly qualified to excel in this species of moral painting.

It confers the highest honour on this branch of composition, as well as on this age and kingdom, that some of the brightest ornaments of literature among the other sex have not disdained the meed of inventive fancy; and that the novel, which in other times, and other countries, has been too often made the vehicle of depravity and licentiousness, has here displayed the standard of moral truth, and breathed the spirit of the purest virtue.

In naming Richardson as an illustrious example of my assertion, I silence the voice of prejudice itself ...

What is here said, with so much justice, by authorities more important than mine, of the moral tendency of Richardson's divine writings, is not less true in general of the more select novels of the present age; the writers of which, like him, have pursued the noble purpose of alluring the heart to virtue, and deterring it from vice, by well-drawn pictures, and striking examples, of both.

In this laudable pursuit, if the female sex have not been undistinguished, if they have unlocked the stores of imagination, and employed the well-wrought fable, to paint moral rectitude in the glowing colours lent by truth; far from acquiescing in the wild and inconsiderate censure of a late critic, it appears to be a circumstance which places our sex in the fairest point of view, and of which the most timid modesty may be allowed to boast.